MW01094058

LACANDÓN MAYA IN THE TWENTY-FIRST CENTURY

Maya Studies

UNIVERSITY PRESS OF FLORIDA

Florida A&M University, Tallahassee
Florida Atlantic University, Boca Raton
Florida Gulf Coast University, Ft. Myers
Florida International University, Miami
Florida State University, Tallahassee
New College of Florida, Sarasota
University of Central Florida, Orlando
University of Florida, Gainesville
University of North Florida, Jacksonville
University of South Florida, Tampa
University of West Florida, Pensacola

Lacandón Maya in the Twenty-First Century

Indigenous Knowledge and Conservation
in Mexico's Tropical Rainforest

James D. Nations

Foreword by Diane Z. Chase and Arlen F. Chase

UNIVERSITY PRESS OF FLORIDA

Gainesville/Tallahassee/Tampa/Boca Raton
Pensacola/Orlando/Miami/Jacksonville/Ft. Myers/Sarasota

28 27 26 25 24 23   6 5 4 3 2 1

Library of Congress Cataloging-in-Publication Data
Names: Nations, James D., author. | Chase, Diane Z., writer of foreword. |
    Chase, Arlen F. (Arlen Frank), 1953– writer of foreword.
Title: Lacandón Maya in the twenty-first century : indigenous knowledge
    and conservation in Mexico's tropical rainforest / James D. Nations ;
    foreword by Diane Z. Chase and Arlen F. Chase.
Other titles: indigenous knowledge and conservation in Mexico's tropical
    rainforest
Description: 1. | Gainesville : University Press of Florida, [2023] |
    Includes bibliographical references and index. | Summary: "This book
    tells the story of how Lacandón Maya families have adapted to the
    contemporary world while applying their ancestral knowledge to create an
    ecologically sustainable future in Mexico's largest remaining tropical
    rainforest"— Provided by publisher.
Identifiers: LCCN 2023012292 (print) | LCCN 2023012293 (ebook) | ISBN
    9780813069784 (hardback) | ISBN 9780813080246 (paperback) | ISBN
    9780813070568 (pdf) | ISBN 9780813072937 (ebook)
Subjects: LCSH: Lacandon Indians—Mexico—Social conditions. | Lacandon
    Indians—Social life and customs. | Lacandon Indians—History. | BISAC:
    SOCIAL SCIENCE / Anthropology / Cultural & Social | NATURE /
    Environmental Conservation & Protection
Classification: LCC F1221.L2 N38 2023 (print) | LCC F1221.L2 (ebook) |
    DDC 305.897/427—dc23/eng/20230331
LC record available at https://lccn.loc.gov/2023012292
LC ebook record available at https://lccn.loc.gov/2023012293

The University Press of Florida is the scholarly publishing agency for the State University System
of Florida, comprising Florida A&M University, Florida Atlantic University, Florida Gulf Coast
University, Florida International University, Florida State University, New College of Florida,
University of Central Florida, University of Florida, University of North Florida, University of
South Florida, and University of West Florida.

University Press of Florida
2046 NE Waldo Road
Suite 2100
Gainesville, FL 32609
http://upress.ufl.edu

For the rising generation of **Jach Winik**, and for Keagan, Sienna, Vaughn, Ellis James, Caris, Lucas Noel, Ruby, Vivian, George, Eve, Nora Ann, and the little ones yet to come.

Never stop going on adventures.

Contents

Figures

Foreword

Anthropologists don't always become professors who teach at universities. Some feel a different call to action. James D. Nations initially planned to be an academic professor. However, while pursuing his PhD studies on the Lacandón Maya, he became acutely aware of how they were being forced to adapt to a changing world that was encroaching both on their way of life and on the green forests in which they lived. Three years into his fieldwork, after successfully learning the language and building strong friendships with the people he had come to study, he decided there was something more important to do. He became instead an environmental conservationist, devoting the rest of his forty-year career to protecting cultural heritage and natural environments across the Americas. However, he continued to make return visits to the Lacandón whenever possible, painstakingly recording everything he learned—from vocabulary to stories.

This book contains key knowledge about the Lacandón Maya and is also a personal ethnographic account, documenting Nations' reflections on his experiences and making clear his affection and respect for the Lacandón Maya, the subject of his original anthropological study. It makes clear the impact of his long relationship with them and details the knowledge they shared through their stories. It is a fitting testimony to their way of life and the strong bond that Nations shared with them.

Nations's conservation efforts throughout the Western Hemisphere, much like his early dissertation work, were undertaken in person on-ground rather than from the safety of an office; they included walking through the forests and borderlands of countries that were in dispute and in danger of being ravaged by modernization. We met James Nations many years ago far from civilization on one of these journeys. He appeared one morning in our jungle camp at Caracol, Belize, having slept the night before in the bush in the southern part of the site some 3 kilometers away. He and Sharon Matola, the founding director of the Belize Zoo, had been examining the damage caused by the influx of Guatemalan settlers along the Belize border. Starting with a survey of newly settled communities on the Guatemalan side of the border, they had then followed roads and paths far to the south of our camp that eventually took them out of Guatemala and into Belize. These same paths and roads were also guiding illegal settlement, logging, and looting. In our four decades at Caracol, he and Sharon were the only nonlocal individuals to have made such an entrance into our camp from that direction. His appearance in our field kitchen that morning is just one example of his determined passion for conservation and his long-term willingness to endure those rigors of the unknown "bush" in support of a greater good—the preservation of both landscapes and cultural heritage.

We are pleased to add this book to the Maya Studies series published by the University Press of Florida. This very personal set of stories told to Nations by the living Lacandón and the details of the issues that they face make a compelling case for the importance of Indigenous knowledge and understanding of a changing landscape. It complements an earlier work published in the series by Joel Palka in 2005 titled *Unconquered Lacandon Maya: Ethnohistory and Archaeology of Indigenous Culture Change*; Nations' treatment of the Lacandón adds deep insight and a vitality to these people beyond that possible with archaeological data alone.

Diane Z. Chase and Arlen F. Chase
Series Editors

Preface

What we can construct, if we keep notes and survive, are hindsight
accounts of the connectedness of things that seem to have happened:
pieced-together patternings, after the fact.

Clifford Geertz[1]

This book presents stories I heard and lessons I learned from the Lacandón
Maya (**Jach Winik**), who live in the rainforest of eastern Chiapas, Mexico.
I make no claim to know what it's like to be Lacandón Maya, and I do not
pretend to speak for them. All I can claim is that I've known them for half a
century and that I've watched them adapt, survive, and thrive.

I moved to Mexico in the mid-1970s to spend a year—only one, I
thought—to do anthropological fieldwork with Lacandón Maya families.
The first task was to learn the Lacandón language, a task that took longer
than I expected. No surprise there: the Lacandón languages (there are actually two of them) are unrelated to English or Spanish or any other European language, and the only training aid available at the time was Roberto
Bruce's *Gramática del Lacandón*, in Spanish (Bruce 1968). Everything else
one had to do by listening, transcribing, and repeating.

I could measure my linguistic progress by the age of the Lacandones I
hung out with. I started out with five-year-olds, who laughed when I talked,
but kept talking to me anyway. In a forest settlement with no television—in
fact, no electricity at the time—I was the closest thing they had to a stand-
up comic.

By the third month in Chiapas, I was hiking the forest with Lacandón
teenagers, who would gently suggest corrections to my grammar ("I say it
this way") and would stop on the trail to teach me the names of plants and
animals. Back in the community, I did my best to engage the parents, who
tolerated me with grace and good humor.

Every time I heard a new word, I wrote it down on one of the index cards I carried in my shirt pocket. At night, I studied the words by the light of a kerosene lamp, and the next day I'd try to use them in a conversation.

By the end of five months, I could ask adults a question, but I frequently couldn't understand the answer. [Note to self: This is going to take longer than a year.] Fortunately, my research was funded through a Mexico–United States student exchange program, so I asked for and was granted a second year of study—at US$225 per month, a sum that made me a poor graduate student in the United States but a wealthy man by Lacandón standards. By the end of the second year, I could sit around the fire with Lacandón friends and take an active part in the jokes and conversation. During the third year, I could focus on serious research.

Most days were exhilarating—the people, the wildlife, the lakes, the forest—but it wasn't always easy. I managed to contract a good portion of the tropical diseases I'd read about: hepatitis, salmonella, shigellosis, round worms, amoebas, bott flies, various iterations of influenza known as "jungle crud," and a particularly nasty case of gangrene, the product of a spider bite on my hand. Basically, I got every disorder available to the neophyte anthropologist except malaria and snakebite, for which I am eternally grateful.

When I began traveling to the Lacandón settlement of Mensäbäk (Puerto Bello Metzabok), there were two ways to get there. I could pay a pilot in the highland town of San Cristóbal de Las Casas to fly me to the community's mud and grass airstrip in a single-engine Cessna at an exorbitant price, or I could travel by land, climbing onto a chicken and monkey bus that groaned down gravel roads for nine hours to the jungle jump-off town of Palenque, best known for the Classic Maya ruins of the same name. In Palenque, I'd transfer to another dilapidated bus that traveled down a mud-rut road through the sawmill town of Chancalá and past a dozen newly establishing colonist settlements until both the bus and the road exhausted themselves.

I'd jump off in the Tzeltal Maya community of Damasco, which lay due east over the mountains from the Lacandón families at Mensäbäk. At the time, Damasco was nothing more than a dozen makeshift houses with roofs of palm thatch or corrugated tin. Someone had built a small evangelical church with missionary dollars, but there was no school, and every family was a farm family, including the one that had hinged a fold-down board panel on the front of their house to create a community store. The open window exposed three unpainted wooden shelves stocked with cans of chilies, tiny bags of detergent, an assortment of junk foods, and flashlight batteries of questionable age and duration.

Damasco was the last grace note of "civilization" before entering a forest with no buses, no roads, no electricity, and no telephones. I'd climb down from the bus, and the *ayudante* would climb onto the metal rack on top of the bus and hand down my backpack and the cardboard box of rice, beans, and cooking oil I carried as gifts for the families I would stay with. Occasionally, I'd see Tzeltal Maya friends who were returning home to El Tumbo, a community that lay an hour's walk beyond Mensäbäk. I'd hike with them as far as Mensäbäk, three hours into the forest, and they'd continue for another hour beyond that. Sturdy people, the Tzeltales.

On one trip, I hiked the trail with Tomás Mendoza, the world's smallest and strongest Tzeltal (and a fine human being). Tomás never grew more than 127 centimeters (4 feet) tall, probably as a result of the genetic condition known as growth hormone deficiency. Affected individuals have properly proportioned torso and limbs, but are stunted in size overall. Tomás was clear-headed and good-humored and seemed to take it all in stride.

He was also one powerful individual. I was carrying what I thought was a heavy backpack, loaded with field notebooks, camera, tape recorder, and survival food. Tomás was carrying a 50-kilogram sack of white sugar on a bark fiber tumpline strapped across his forehead.

I was amazed that he could carry so much weight, hiking steadily through the milpas (agricultural fields) and pastures on the far side of Damasco, past the boundary line where the Lacandones' forest begins, up and down hills, the trail a shaded tunnel through the rainforest, mud everywhere.

Tomás walked the entire way and on past Mensäbäk to El Tumbo—a hard four hours—without ever sitting down. Not once.

At one point several hours into the trip, I collapsed into a pile by the side of the trail, shucked off my backpack and moaned, "I'm tired, I need a rest."

Tomás stopped on the trail and stood there, swiveling around, looking at the trees, taking an occasional swig of water from a bottle gourd hung over his shoulder.

"Don't you want to sit down?" I asked.

"No, I'll be fine," he said. "I'll just stand here. If I sit down I'll never be able to get up."

Once I made it to Mensäbäk, I was good for three weeks to a month. I'd hand the cardboard box of rice, chilies, cooking oil, and sugar to the family

I was staying with, and they would adopt me into their larder. I ate what the family ate: sometimes rice and tortillas, frequently beans and tortillas, occasionally a bit of meat—chicken or *tepesquintle*, a plentiful and tasty forest rodent—and always with lots of warm, hand-patted tortillas.

When the time came, I'd make the trip in the opposite direction, this time lightly loaded, having eaten the food and delivered all the "next-time-can-you-bring-me?" items the Lacandones always requested, and which I was happy to deliver.

After two years of work in Mexico, I still was barely dipping beneath the surface of what the Lacandones knew about the tropical forest. Lacandones have lived in the rainforest watershed of Guatemala and Mexico for centuries, and they know more about forest ecology than any Western scientist will ever learn. They're born into the tropical ecosystem, and their understanding of it begins when they're toddlers. I kept figuring out ways to stay in Mexico until, toward the end of my third year, one of my professors sent me a telegram (people still sent telegrams back then) to ask whether I was "coming home or going native?"

I had to think about it.

I had gone to Mexico with the goal of becoming a university professor, but my experiences with the Lacandones changed my plans. As I listened to the families talk about their lives in the forest, I also watched them worry about the future.

Chan K'in José Valenzuela stated it clearly one afternoon: "Look, you know that we've lived in this forest for a long time, and it's still alive. But now we see outsiders coming in to build roads and steal our trees. They burn the forest, and they plant grass and bring in cattle. We're afraid of cattle. We don't know what to do."

He looked at me with an expression that seemed to ask, "Is there any way that you can help us?"

Chan K'in José's dilemma made me sad and made me angry, and I began to abandon my plans for academia and consider instead how an outsider could help Indigenous people protect their land and environment.

The question morphed into a forty-year career in environmental conservation that allowed me to work with teams creating and protecting Indigenous territories, national parks, biosphere reserves, and wildlife refuges throughout South, Central, and North America, from Bolivia to Belize to Alaska. As a professional conservationist, I returned to the Selva Lacandona a dozen times, and when the legal opportunity appeared, I joined a team of Mexican professionals to support the Lacandones of Naja' and Mensäbäk as they legalized their communal lands (*ejidos*) as Áreas de Protección de Flora y Fauna, "Flora and Fauna Protection Areas" (CONANP 2006a, 2006b).

When I retired from paid work, I returned to the Lacandón communities to complete a grammar and dictionary of Northern Lacandón, the end product of all the index cards I had scratched out while following Lacandones down forest trails. As the manuscript took shape, I sat down with Lacandón women and men and verified each entry. Dozens of times, when I'd call out the name of a plant or animal, a Lacandón friend would repeat it, define it, and then say, "Let me tell you a story about that." And they would. And I wrote down the stories as well. The corrected words went into the dictionary, and the stories went into this book.

Lacandones will someday write their own stories from their own points of view, adding written history to their rich oral archive of fables, myths, and songs. In the meantime, I offer this description of some of the things I saw and learned from them between 1974 and today. I am thankful to the **Jach Winik** for allowing me to share them.

In the twenty-first century, Lacandón society is a vibrant fusion of tradition and change. Farming practices 500 years old, hairstyles from the eighteenth century, and carry bags made from pounded tree bark interweave with pickup trucks, social media, and television soap operas beamed from Mexico City. The continuum of human personalities ranges from the father of a lone family still hiding in the forest to young women seeking university degrees in natural history. Teenage boys stand in the bed of a pickup as it grinds up the only road in town, their long hair streaming behind them, blue jeans beneath their white cotton tunics like a hyphen between two worlds. One lone man in the community of Naja' still chants to the gods of the Lacandón pantheon, while a talented artist from the same community paints scenes of jaguars and religious ceremonies and travels to Mexico City to show his work in galleries.

Taken together, the diversity of personalities and the people's continuing respect for nature engender faith that Lacandón society will survive as long as the families honor their past and keep their rainforest alive.

Every year that travel has been possible, I've continued to visit the Selva Lacandona and the families I've kept up with for half a century. The five-year-olds I once rewarded with chewing gum and toothbrushes are now tribal elders, and at dinner I sit around the fire, bathed in lifelong friendship and community acceptance. Their grandchildren punch each other and ask, "Who's the white-haired guy with the weird accent?"

I feel like the fellow I once heard interviewed on National Public Radio. Asked what he would do if he had his life to live over, he said, "I wouldn't do anything differently. I would just be more awake."

Acknowledgments

A lifetime of thanks to my Lacandón friends for sharing stories about their history, lives, and rainforest. Thanks to the many friends and colleagues who helped me capture, understand, and write down these stories: Debra Schumann, Kippy and Ron Nigh, Daniel Komer, Genevieve "Nuk" Buot, Santiago Billy, Reginaldo Chayax Huex, Chip Morris, Steve Bartz, Jamie Kibben, José Hernández Nava, John E. Clark, Juan José Castillo Mont, Liza Grandia, Luisa Maffi, Mary E. Hartman, Claudia Torres de León, Sue Marcus, John Burstein, Mary Jill Brody, Ricardo Hernández Sánchez, John Cloud, Mimi and Bob Laughlin, Peter Hubbell, Donna Birdwell, David Bray, Sherry Klein, Ruth Jiménez, Ira R. Abrams, Solomon H. Katz, Ben J. Wallace, Alyse Laemmle, David and Judy Campbell, Ingrid Neubauer, Gertrude Duby Blom, Patricia López Sanchez, and the staff of Museo Na Bolom.

A thousand thanks to Carol Karasik for her astute and graceful editing skills, to Didier Boremanse for insight into Lacandón myths and fables, to Joel Palka for reviewing the chapters on archaeology and history, to Jon McGee for improving the chapters on religion, to Ronald B. Nigh for expert input on agroecology, and to John N. Williams for advice on forest history. Many thanks to Ignacio March Mifsut for keeping me up to date on research by Mexico's professional cadre of field researchers and conservationists.

I extend my thanks and admiration to Didier Boremanse, Roberto Bruce, Suzanne Cook, Jon McGee, and Alice Balsanelli for recording and preserving the crucial corpus of Lacandón Maya oral history. And like everyone who studies the Selva Lacandona, I owe a great debt to the late Jan de Vos for his decades of historical excavation in the archives of Chiapas, Mexico City, and Spain.

Special thanks to Sergio Montes Quintero, José "El Felix" Feliciano Dominguez Hernández, and José Hernández Nava of Mexico's Consejo

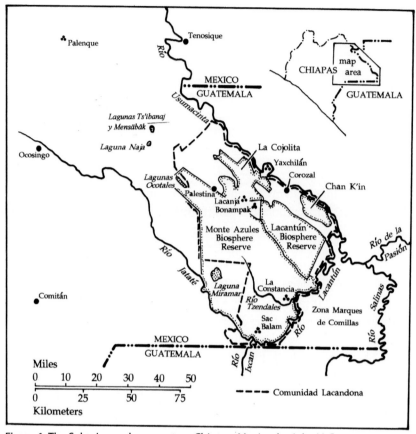

Figure 1. The Selva Lacandona, eastern Chiapas, Mexico, by John V. Cotter.

Nacional de Áreas Naturales Protegidas for information on protected areas in the Selva Lacandona and to Jesse Czekanski-Mir and the AntAsk Team of the California Academy of Science for information about leaf-cutter ants. I thank Jonathan Campbell for sharing his knowledge of rainforest reptiles.

Three particular books implored me to be accurate and honest while writing this volume: Pekka Hämäläinen's *Lakota America: A New History of Indigenous Power*, Edmund Carpenter's *Oh, What a Blow That Phantom Gave Me!*, and Paul Chaat Smith's *Everything You Know about Indians Is Wrong*.

And finally, to my mostly companion, the wise and beautiful Maryanna Kieffer: Thank you. You are my love, my love, my love.

Distances and Measurements

This book uses the metric system of distances and measurements—meters instead of yards, kilometers instead of miles, hectares instead of acres. The following list will aid readers not accustomed to these units.

Distance

- 1 meter = 1.1 yards or approximately 3.3 feet
  To convert meters to yards, divide the number of meters by 0.9144
- 1 kilometer = 0.6 miles
  To convert kilometers to miles, multiply the number of kilometers by 0.6

Surface Area

- 1 hectare = 2.47 acres
  To convert hectares into acres, multiply the number of hectares by 2.471
- 1 square kilometer = 0.4 square miles or 247 acres
  To convert square kilometers to square miles, multiply the number of square kilometers by 0.386

Notes on the Text

Phrases and words in **Jach T'an**, the Indigenous language of the Lacandón Maya, appear in this book in **boldface**, with the exception of personal names and frequently used place-names that are now part of regional geography. Lacandón Maya vowels and consonants are pronounced as they would be in Spanish, but Lacandón has vowels and consonants that require special note. The vowel **ä**, as in the name of the Lacandón community of Mensäbäk, is pronounced like the "u" in the English word "but." The Lacandón vowel **i** (with a hatch mark), as in the word for "hill," **wits**, is pronounced like the English word "wit." The letter **x** represents the English sound "sh," as in the Lacandón word **ya'ax**, which means blue or green.

The symbols **ch'**, **k'**, **p'**, **t'**, and **ts'** represent glottalized—or ejective—consonants, and they differ from the un-glottalized form by being delivered with an explosive release, popped out of the mouth without the use of the lungs.

The text uses the Spanish **j** for the English sound "h" for two reasons: It follows the alphabet approved for Indigenous languages by Mexico's Instituto Nacional de Lenguas Indígenas, and it eases the transition for literacy between Spanish and Lacandón. Lacandones who are learning to read and write today are being taught (so far) only in Spanish. They recognize **j** as the glottal fricative, the "h" of "house" in English, or the "g" of "*gente*" in Spanish. Most Lacandones read **h** as silent. With very few exceptions, Lacandón words are pronounced with emphasis on the first syllable.

Several chapters of this book are presented in the ethnographic (or historical) present, meaning that the descriptions were accurate at the time, but things may have changed through the decades.

Introduction

Lacandón Maya in the Twenty-First Century: Indigenous Knowledge and Conservation in Mexico's Tropical Rainforest is the story of an Indigenous people living at the nexus of two worlds in the largest remaining rainforest in Mexico.[1] The first world is a forest filled with wildlife, gods, and spirits, the second is a twenty-first-century world of missionaries, media, and change. The worlds coalesce in today's Lacandón communities, where families blend knowledge gleaned from centuries of life in the tropical forest with the kaleidoscopic input of a modern, globalized society.

A strong connecting thread ties the old and new worlds together. The thread is born in the forest, in the Lacandones' understanding of how it functions, and in their respect for the creatures that live there. The thread is spun from the native names of a hundred birds and from the trill of a thousand insects, from plants that cure colds and snakebites, and from the songs of gods who dance in whirlwinds through newly planted fields.

The thread connects to questions: How can Indigenous families protect their environment as they adapt to the contemporary world? How can they pass their tradition of sustainability to the children who follow behind them? How can they keep their rainforest alive in a world that seems determined to destroy it?

Lacandón Maya in the Twenty-First Century brings the Lacandón people to life through their history, traditions, environmental ethics, and adaptations to the outside world. The central message is this: With quiet and persistent resilience, Lacandón Maya are combining lessons from their ancestors with new technology and information to mold a society adapted to the twenty-first century. As the legal owners and protectors of the largest tropical rainforest in Mexico, Lacandones are following a thread of environmental tradition to become architects of a new Indigenous future, in which their respect for nature remains unbroken, and the rainforest continues as their source of spiritual and material well-being.

Who Are the Lacandón Maya?

In the early eighteenth century, a half dozen tribes of Yucatec-speaking families hid in the tropical rainforest of northern Guatemala to escape Spanish missionaries and soldiers intent on "civilizing" them. As the Spaniards intensified their search, the families slipped across the Río Usumacinta into an immense tropical wilderness left depopulated by Spanish attacks on its previous Ch'ol Maya inhabitants. The arriving refugees called themselves **Jach Winik**, "The True People," but the pursuing Spaniards called them "Lacandones" after a Ch'ol Maya settlement they had destroyed in the area a hundred years before.

As Spanish expeditions edged closer to their settlements, the Lacandones retreated farther into the forest, disappearing into dense vegetation, leaving their trails unmarked and camouflaged. Living in isolated family compounds dispersed along the rivers and lakeshores of eastern Chiapas, Lacandones tenaciously held on to their language, religion, and environmental knowledge. They fished the lakes, hunted wildlife, planted crops and trees, and only occasionally (and cautiously) approached outsiders' villages to trade tobacco, beeswax, and tree resin for metal tools and salt.

Like mysterious spirits, they moved down forest trails, long black hair flying past their shoulders, silent on shoeless feet, eyes on the forest around them. When they came upon the abandoned stone cities of the Classic Maya, by then shrouded in nine centuries of trees and hanging vines, they burned copal incense before stone carvings of the ancient rulers, whom they envisioned as gods.

The Lacandones remained within the forest for the next 200 years, emerging as the only Maya culture never conquered by invading Europeans.

But things change.

In the second half of the twentieth century, the external world literally bulldozed its way into the Lacandón rainforest in search of mahogany and tropical cedar to sell in Europe and the United States. Mexican and US logging companies took the trees and left behind roads, creating a pathway for migrant farm families and cattle ranchers to migrate into a forest that the government considered unowned and unoccupied. As the decades passed, the newcomers increased in number, and Lacandones concentrated their families into ever smaller patches of forest.

In the seventy years between 1950 and 2020, two-thirds of the tropical rainforest of eastern Chiapas, Mexico, was deforested, burned, and transformed into villages, cornfields, and cattle pasture, leaving climax forest only on inaccessible hills, in small community reserves, and in tenuously protected wildlife refuges and biosphere reserves. What was once a forest sparsely occupied by a few hundred Lacandón Maya became a landscape of towns, farms, and rural communities for 500,000 farmers, cattle ranchers, shopkeepers, and families. Today, the only large blocks of rainforest that remain are under the protection of the Lacandón Maya.[2]

During the centuries that Lacandón Maya families have lived in the rainforest, they have shown respect for their forest by embracing a life of sustainability—life for the long haul—because they know their survival depends on it. Lacandones have always lived inside the forest, rather than destroying the forest in order to live. Their children still learn time-tested techniques for producing food and shelter by helping their parents with the work of daily life: planting and harvesting crops and gathering materials from the forest for tools, housing, and ceremonies.

Their practical lessons are reinforced by fables in which animals talk to humans and ancestors talk with spirits that wander forest trails. The stories remind both children and their parents that they should protect the forest as if their lives are intertwined with it. "Because," the creatures tell them, "together they form one family."

At night, when a child convinces a tired parent to tell yet another story, she's getting more than entertainment around the fire. Stories about flying monkeys, the Wooden People, and why Lacandones never kill dogs also transmit cultural values and build a road map for survival in a sometimes hostile world. From religion, myths, and stories, children learn the place of human beings in the natural world and the rules for interacting with the creatures that live there with them.

Nature permeates Lacandón lives. Men and women learn to measure time by counting the years in **yaax k'in**, the "green year" that marks the arrival of spring rains. They determine when to plant their crops by watching the flowering of indicator plants in the forest. "When the **ek' balche'** tree (*Guatteria anomala*) blooms," they say, "it's time to plant climbing beans." Children mark their birth dates by naming the trees that were in flower on the day they were born. "I was born at the 'foot' of the mahogany tree," they say—in early June, that is, when the mahogany trees were blooming.

For generations, Lacandón Maya survived in a rainforest that seemed to go on forever. Today, Lacandón Maya families make their homes in permanently settled communities with established legal boundaries, roads, and electricity. Their children walk dirt trails to elementary schools staffed by Spanish-speaking teachers performing on-the-job training.[3] At night, young girls and boys watch television in cement block houses and text their friends on cell phones. Their teenage brothers and sisters ride motorcycles up and down a road crushed through a rainforest their grandfathers once ran through barefoot, hunting spider monkeys with bows and arrows.

But Lacandón children continue to learn about the plants, animals, and ecosystems that surround them. By the time they're adults, Lacandones know more about forest ecology than the academic scientists who come to learn from them. Hiking through the forest, even teenagers can cite the names of dozens of plants, tell you when they flower, which animals eat them, and how Lacandón families use them for food or religious ceremonies.

This book presents part of the knowledge these families utilize to protect the natural world they live in: how to conserve wildlife and forest resources, how to produce food without eradicating the natural environment, how to harvest what is needed from the wealth of the forest and leave it unimpaired. The book also describes the economic and environmental changes now impacting the forest and how Lacandones adapt to them. Along the way, the text conjures forth Maya gods who were born in flowers, spirits in limestone cliffs, and crocodiles that teach canoes to swim.

The book is the product of four decades of research—three initial years of fieldwork, two years as a post-doc, and forty years of periodic visits as a professional conservationist. These years overlapped with a major seam in Lacandón history, spanning years of cultural change wrought by waves of loggers, missionaries, colonists, and cattle. The change was wrenching for the Lacandón grandfathers and grandmothers, who lived by the old ways in a forest filled with spirits. From them, the reader learns about mammals, birds, and voices heard in sacred caves. They tell us how the ancestors balanced human life and nature in the midst of a tropical forest.

The grandparents' sons and daughters grew up as a generation whipsawed by the sharp edge of the outside world and forced to live in a world of change. From the sons and daughters, readers learn how a traditional society can adapt with intelligence, discernment, and good humor, while preserving what they can of their grandparents' ancient knowledge.

During the past decade, most books about Lacandón Maya have focused on "salvage ethnography"—vital work that has documented Lacandón Maya oral history and religious practices before it disappears. But missing from the literature is the story of how Lacandón families have adapted to the modern world and how their understanding of nature is still vividly active. How have Lacandones kept their rainforest alive in a world of development and destruction? What can they teach other Indigenous people about the protection of homeland environments? How can the outside world help them achieve this? That story is the most important message Lacandón Maya have for the modern world, and telling that story is the purpose of this book.

In their twenty-first-century settlements, Lacandón mothers and fathers still teach their children about the land, lakes, and rainforest that surround them, channeling the voices of the ancestors, reminding the rising generation to care for the forest and the creatures who live there. Persisting with grace and laughter, today's Lacandón communities are thriving, and the people seem determined to survive.

Please note that this book includes images of human remains.

I

The True People

1

Sanctuary

In the early sixteenth century, wooden ships carrying Spanish invaders appeared off the coast of Mexico, bringing a firestorm of disease and gunfire to the civilizations of the Americas. Maya families died by the hundreds of thousands as smallpox, plague, and influenza spread through their cities and settlements. Because the native peoples had no previous exposure to—and no immunity from—old-world diseases, even childhood illnesses such as measles turned lethal in the New World. Infection spread down forest trails and trade routes, killing women, men, and children before they ever saw a living Spaniard. Entire villages were wiped out, with no one left alive to bury the bodies.

In the wake of Spanish diseases came the Spanish conquerors themselves. Spanish warriors attacked and defeated depopulated Maya cities in the highlands of present-day Mexico and Guatemala, then moved on to attack the surviving towns and cities of Yucatán. Although Spaniards explored parts of the lowland rainforest during the first decades of the Conquest—Hernán Cortez led an expedition across the Guatemalan Petén—they considered the rainforest to be inhospitable. They focused instead on dominating the Maya populations of the Pacific coastal plains, Yucatán, and the mountainous regions of Chiapas and Guatemala. But even as Spaniards consolidated control there, Maya families everywhere continued to perish en masse from introduced diseases, depriving the Spaniards of their labor force. During the first 150 years after Spanish contact, native populations declined by 80 to 90 percent from their precontact levels throughout much of Yucatán, Chiapas, and Guatemala. People disappeared completely in some Maya regions. As a result, the Spaniards were forced to search elsewhere for workers to replace them (Lovell and Lutz 1990: 129).

To find these new workers, Spanish officials launched a series of expeditions into the lowland rainforest, cutting paths through the Guatemalan Petén and the Selva Lacandona of Chiapas, capturing Maya families as slaves for Spanish ranches and plantations. They attacked the Ch'olan-speaking Maya in the rainforest watershed of the Río Usumacinta as well as Yucatec-speaking Maya who lived in the drier forests of Yucatán. They marched away the survivors, leaving behind torched villages and the bodies of warriors who had chosen to fight. By the time the smoke cleared in the 1690s, most of the Ch'olan-speaking Maya in the rainforest of eastern Chiapas had been killed or forcibly relocated. The survivors hid in the forest to avoid the Spanish invaders (de Vos 1980).

Meanwhile, a half dozen groups of Yucatec-speaking Maya continued to live in settlements and villages on rivers and lakes along the base of the Yucatán Peninsula: Kejach in Campeche and northwestern Guatemala, Chinamita and Itza in the north central Petén, Mopán in eastern Petén and Belize, Xocmo in the southern Petén, and Petenacte in the western and southern Petén and likely in northeastern Chiapas. As Spanish military and missionary expeditions probed at the edges of their territories, the families recoiled. They began to migrate toward the southwest, filtering across the Río Usumacinta into rainforest territory that would in subsequent years be called Chiapas (Nations 1979; Palka 2005: 76–78).

The families that fled across the river were refugees, but they knew the river they were crossing and they recognized the rainforest on the other side. The plants, animals, and ecosystems were the same. The forest the migrating families moved into had long been the home of Ch'ol and Ch'olti Maya, but most of those populations were now dead or removed by Spaniards. The few Ch'ol and Ch'olti families who had escaped the Spaniards gradually mixed with the arriving refugees, creating a new, blended society that predominantly spoke Yucatec. Over time, this amalgamated group of families would become known as the Yucatec Lacandón Maya, the people whose living descendants call themselves **Jach Winik**, "the True People." Dispersed along the rivers and lakeshores of an immense tropical rainforest, they lived in isolated family compounds separated by kilometers of rainforest that would eventually take the name Selva Lacandona because of the families who lived there.

What little government existed in the area at the time was ill-defined, having mutated from New Spain to Guatemala, from Guatemala to Mexico, and back and forth, depending on which national government claimed the unexplored region during any particular decade (de Vos 1993). But the Lacandón families who lived in this territory were not concerned with distant governments. They were focused on more important things—staying alive in the tropical forest and staying away from everyone else.

Survival in the Selva Lacandona is a full-time task, even for people who have lived there all their life, and the outsiders who sought out the Lacandones seemed intent only on stealing their land, felling their trees, or changing their religion. Not to mention the crocodile hunters, chicle gum harvesters, and all-purpose renegades who periodically raided family compounds to abduct women and girls. In the early decades, even nonviolent contact with people from the outside world brought risks of infection— measles, influenza, yellow fever, and malaria. The Lacandones were wise to keep their heads down.

Missionaries: The First Wave

The Lacandones' early years of isolation were periodically interrupted by Spanish missionaries who continued to search the tributaries of the Río Usumacinta for new subjects for the Spanish church and crown. In 1786, a Christianized Ch'ol named Santiago de la Cruz came upon a single Lacandón Maya man eight hours south of Palenque, near an arroyo the missionary called Baglunte', which he said meant "jaguar tree."[1] The two men attempted to converse in Ch'ol, the native language of Santiago de la Cruz. The Lacandón knew enough of the language to tell the missionary that he would return to the spot and meet him again "at the next moon" (de Vos 1988: 36–38).

As agreed, Santiago de la Cruz returned to Baglunte' the following month, this time with a group that included the Catholic priest of Palenque, Manuel José Calderón. They found a small number of Lacandón families waiting in the forest. Speaking in Ch'ol, Calderón tried to convince the families to relocate to Palenque and become Christian subjects of the Spanish king. But the most the two sides could agree on was to meet again the following month.

Which they did. On the designated day, Calderón appeared on the forest trail wearing full church dress, bearing a crucifix and a painting of the Catholic saint, San José. Waiting for him were twenty-two Lacandón men and two women. According to Calderón's assistants, the Lacandones had hidden their bows and arrows in the forest. Calderón showed the Lacandones the portrait of San José and told them the saint would be the patron of their new community on this very site in the forest.

The Lacandones told Calderón they could bring their relatives out of the forest to be baptized, but they balked at Calderón's proposed site for a settlement. Instead, they suggested a place near the Río Chacamax where they had already planted crops. Calderón agreed, blessed the group, and distributed "some tools, which is what they needed," he wrote. "With that, they were very happy."

Calderón named the Lacandones' preferred site San José de Gracia Real, and during the following years, Lacandón families began to settle there to trade forest products for manufactured goods the Catholic missionaries carried in. Church documents reported that the Lacandones "sold their fruits and bought tools that were necessary for their work, salt for their food, and glass beads for adornment" (de Vos 1988: 38; Boremanse 2006: xxv).

Spanish records of the time make it clear that the families in the forest were the ancestors of today's Lacandón Maya. They spoke a version of Yucatec Maya, although they understood some Ch'ol. Families were polygynous. Men wore white tunics that reached their knees and grew their hair past their shoulders. Women wore white tunics over skirts, shell earrings, and bead necklaces. The families built their houses inside fields dispersed throughout the forest. They cultivated corn, tobacco, annatto, cotton, manioc, and sweet potatoes, and planted avocado, orange, and lemon trees. From the forest they gathered beeswax, mameys, and palm hearts and shoots. The families devoted considerable energy, the friars wrote, to hunting and fishing (de Vos 1988: 43).

It's also clear that the Lacandones' interest in the Catholics was economic. The families brought in fruit, wax, and cacao to trade for metal, cloth, and salt, which they then traded with other Lacandones still hidden in the forest. By 1793 the mission of San José de Gracia Real had grown to include a blacksmith shop and a large church with a palm-thatch roof. The Lacandones periodically brought in sick individuals to be baptized, possibly believing that San José's blessing would add to their traditional efforts to cure them.

But the Spaniards must have been frustrated with their inability to convert the Lacandones to Christianity. Despite the priests' best efforts, the Lacandones continued to practice their traditional, pre-Hispanic religion. The priests reported to church fathers that the families maintained a god house[2] on the edge of the new settlement, and one church functionary complained that the people "seemed to be addicted to their idols" (Orozco y Jiménez 1911 II: 170–171).

Spanish documentation on the mission settlement of San José de Gracia Real is extensive, but how many Lacandones lived there is less clear. In 1799, only thirty-one Lacandón Maya were living in the settlement, including "children at the breast." At that time, only eight Lacandones had abandoned the settlement and returned to live among the families still scattered in the forest (Orozco y Jiménez 1911 II: 172). By 1806, the missionaries had died or been called away, and San José de Gracia Real was abandoned to the florid vegetation (de Vos 1988; Nations 1979; Palka 2005: 110; Boremanse 2006: xxvi).

Over the next few years, other short-lived Lacandón mission settlements were established on Lake Petexbatún in the Guatemalan Petén (several families and a church) and near the Río de la Pasión. The latter settlement, created in 1814 by a Dominican priest named Manuel María de la Chica, included a small church and thirty baptized Lacandones, but after only three years an unidentified servant ended the padre's work by killing him (de Vos 1996: 42; Palka 2005: 112).

Capuchin friars from Antigua Guatemala scoured the banks of the Río de la Pasión and Río Usumacinta between 1862 and 1865, seeking isolated Maya families to baptize. They found an average of one to three settlements per day, they reported, some of them home to single families—a Lacandón man and several wives—and others with up to fifteen families. Archaeologist Joel Palka points out, "Evidence from historical sources suggests that Lacandón society had its greatest numbers and largest territory from the late 18th century to the 1870s." Added together, there may have been as many as 3,000 to 5,000 Lacandones living in the Selva Lacandona and Petén at the time of the American Civil War (Palka 2005: 103–107).

Those would have been the glory days of population size, brief as they were, because the Lacandón population has not risen to that height in the 150 years since. Instead, missionary expeditions and waves of disease continued to threaten Lacandón society. In the decades after 1870, the number of **Jach Winik** plummeted precipitously because of diseases brought into the forest by missionaries and loggers. As it had during the sixteenth-century invasion of the Maya world, the Indigenous population of the Selva Lacandona came close to disintegrating (Nations 1979; Palka 2005: 117).

Adding to the dangers, the remnants of Lacandón society suffered dramatically after 1859, when laborers organized by a Yucatec businessman cut down seventy-two mahogany trees along a tributary of the Río Usumacinta and dragged them to the river with oxen, rolled the logs into the water, and miraculously recovered seventy of them weeks later as they floated past the downriver town of Tenosique, Tabasco. With that achievement, the loggers initiated a rush for hardwood timber that would relentlessly alter Lacandón lives for decades to come.

The promise of riches to be made by extracting mahogany and tropical cedar trees prompted a half dozen foreign and Mexican timber companies to file logging claims on huge swaths of forest territory in eastern
Chiapas. By the turn of the century, the entire Selva Lacandona—most of
it still unexplored by outsiders—was legally controlled by private companies through logging concessions with the Mexican government. In 1902,
government officials transformed these concessions into the legally owned
property of seven specific timber companies based in Mexico City, Tabasco, and Spain (de Vos 1996: 260). Lacandones were "neither consulted nor
informed" about this transfer of their forest to outsider owners.[3] Through
the signatures of men they had never seen, written in a language they didn't
know, the legal documents turned the Lacandón Maya into interlopers in
the rainforest that carried their name.

In December 1902, a young anthropologist named Alfred Tozzer borrowed horses and a guide from one of the timber companies and followed a
trail into the forest in search of the elusive Lacandón Maya. He found three
families living a two-hour walk from a lake they called Petja' (which simply
means "lake" in Lacandón). Based on the cliff drawings Tozzer recorded
there, the lake was Yajaw Petja', known today by outsiders as Guineo, near
the Tzeltal Maya community of Sibal. Tozzer described the Lacandones he
found in the forest as "simple and pure" (Tozzer 1907: 6).

"When the men are not engaged in hunting and fishing," Tozzer wrote,
"they are busy in the observances of their religious ceremonies, carried on
before their incense burners on behalf of the family gods. The main object
of these rites is to cure disease and avert evils." During rituals in their god
houses, Tozzer said, the Lacandones pierced their ears with a stone knife
and used the blood to anoint the idols they worship (Tozzer 1903–1904:
56).

The natives, he said, "have very little to do with the Mexicans, as their
environment furnishes them with all their needs, with the single exception
of salt" (Tozzer 1902–1903: 47).

"No people in Mexico and Central America has been more free from
outside influence," he continued, then went on to lament, "From the heights
reached in the development of the hieroglyphic system and noted in the
remains of the ruined structures found throughout Yucatan and Central
America, we come to what we find today, a few scattered families living
out their own lives, hidden in the depth of the forest, alone and forgotten"
(Tozzer 1907: 165–167).

Tozzer was cautious about judging the size of the Lacandón population at the time. "Concerning their number," he wrote, "one hesitates in giving even an estimate, inasmuch as they are scattered over so wide a range of country." He noted though that the German linguist Karl Sapper, who hiked through Chiapas and Guatemala in 1891, had estimated the entire Lacandón population at between 200 and 300 (Tozzer 1907: 5).

Half a century later, when Frans Blom explored the Selva Lacandona in 1943, he noted, "I roughly calculate that there are about 250 of them left, and with the death rate as it is at present, they will be gone soon" (Brunhouse 1976: 173). In 1949, Blom and Gertrude Duby Blom conducted a census that counted 158 individuals, plus a few distributed in distant *caribales,* a name Spanish-speaking outsiders used for Lacandón settlements in the forest (Blom and Duby 1955; Villa Rojas 1967).

But the Lacandones did not disappear as Blom predicted, nor did they remain—as Tozzer described them—alone and forgotten. By the 1950s, timber extraction in the Selva Lacandona was a full-blown industry. Using hand labor to fell the trees and oxen to haul them to the rivers, loggers had cut down all the mahogany and tropical cedar trees they could access along the banks of the rivers. Technology gave them a second breath. They began to use bulldozers to carve roads into the Selva Lacandona in search of more trees.

Devastation followed in the bulldozers' wake, caused not so much by what the loggers took out, but by what they left behind—the roads themselves. Loggers hauled the valuable timber down the roads and out of the forest, but farmers and cattle ranchers used the same roads to infiltrate the Selva in search of new land and new lives. Goaded on by government officials touting agrarian reform, the aspiring colonists—most of them Tzeltal Maya families from the highlands and foothills of Chiapas—cleared and burned the forest to plant corn and beans for consumption and planted grass for beef cattle as a cash crop. Pigs served as self-propelled investments, eating the farmers' excess or spoiled corn. The conversion of farmland to pasture after only one or two years of crop production brought an ever-expanding need for additional forest to clear, and the agricultural frontier moved through the rainforest like a giant scythe sweeping across the landscape.

The destruction of the Selva Lacandona threatened the very survival of the Lacandón population. In 1959, Mexican anthropologist Alfonso Villa Rojas guessed the number of Lacandones at 160–170, and Roberto Bruce, an American linguist who lived with Lacandón families for a decade during the 1960s, estimated 200 Lacandones, including men, women, and children (Villa Rojas 1967; Bruce 1968: 13).

"Counting isolated families," Bruce continued, "the population can't be higher than 300 individuals, unless there are other large groups that are still unknown" (Bruce 1968: 13). Which there weren't.

The serial impact of roads, colonists, and cattle ranchers pushed the Lacandón families off land they had occupied for centuries, forcing them to concentrate into the blocks of forest that remained. As outside civilization encircled them, oil exploration roads and electrification projects pierced the perimeter of their settlements, wrenching the families into the modern world by force.

During the second half of the twentieth century, much of the dwindling Selva Lacandona was clear-cut and burned, transformed into agricultural fields and cattle pastures, leaving old-growth forest only in struggling protected areas on either side of the Guatemalan/Mexican border.

The Lacandón population barely held on to survival. Over the course of three years, 1974–1977, I compiled a census of every living Lacandón known to both Northern and Southern families, including fifteen Northern individuals at El Censo, a lone family near Granizo, and sixteen Southerners in the settlement of San Quintín. Although I met only a few of the families of San Quintín, I was able to record all their names and genealogies through close relatives living in Lacanja' Chan Sayab. The total number of Lacandones living in Chiapas at that time, in the summer of 1977: 348 women, men, and children, including babies at the breast (Nations 1979).

I say "living in Chiapas" because through the centuries the Lacandón population has periodically leaked individuals into other societies. For example, several Lacandones living at the 1806 missionary settlement of San José de Gracia Real drifted off to live in Palenque as the rest of the families slipped back into the forest.

A second example: In the early 1860s, Capuchin friars searching the rivers of the western Petén discovered settlements of Lacandones who traded with the inhabitants of Sacluc (now La Libertad, Petén) and transported them to Guatemala's Department of Alta Verapaz to be Christianized. As the families were marched away, they left behind an orphaned Lacandón boy who later was adopted by the German American anthropologist Karl Hermann Berendt in exchange for "a cow and 20 pesos." In his travels as a student of Mayan languages, Berendt took the boy, Sabino Uk, to Yucatán, then to Tabasco, and later to the United States for schooling. When

Berendt left the United States to study Indigenous languages in Nicaragua, he enrolled Sabino Uk in the School of Agriculture in Mobile, Alabama. In Berendt's absence, though, the boy fled the school and became a "vagabond." He developed an infamous reputation for acts of delinquency and when last heard from in the late 1860s was living in the environs of Mobile (Estrada 1972). Somewhere in Alabama today, there may be people who carry the genes of a nineteenth-century Lacandón.

Sabino Uk may have gotten a better deal than the Lacandón families the Capuchin friars relocated to Alta Verapaz. The friars later noted that, given the rapid rate at which the Lacandones died there, they were moved to release them once again into the forest.

In the early 1900s, Tozzer noted that Lacandones rarely abandoned the forest on their own volition, but that it did happen. "Sometimes in one of the *monterías* [lumber company camps] there is found a Lacandón who has adopted the life and customs of the Mexicans," he wrote. "His hair is short, and he is not readily to be distinguished from his fellow Mexican."

Such a desertion of the family gods was not common, Tozzer observed. "The Lacandones regard such a course as a bad breach of conduct. The seceding Indian, on the other hand, thinks it an upward move. He often renounces his family, and in some cases he refuses to understand his native tongue" (Tozzer 1907: 34).

The defectors Tozzer saw in the logging camps may have included the mestizo-like Lacandón ancestors that missionaries Phil Baer and William Merrifield heard about in the mid-twentieth century while collecting oral histories from Southern Lacandones at Lacanja' Chan Sayab. The Lacandones told Baer and Merrifield that around 1907 two men of the now-defunct White-Tailed Deer Clan visited the families living at Lake Lacanja' and inquired about potential wives.

Through history, some Lacandón women have left their families to marry non-Lacandón men, most frequently chicle harvesters or mule drivers, but many of them later returned home with mixed-race children and without their husbands (Baer and Merrifield 1971: 66; Palka 2005: 234).

People came the other direction, as well, marrying into Lacandón families. Baer and Merrifield recorded the story of a Lacandón woman who crossed the Río Usumacinta into Guatemala after the death of her family around 1888. She met and bonded with a Black man (likely from Belize or the Caribbean coast of Guatemala), who returned to Chiapas with her, took a second Lacandón wife, and became known as Box, a Lacandón word for the color "black." Unfortunately, Box got mixed up in some unspecified interfamily dispute and was ambushed and killed in a rain of arrows launched by Lacandón rivals in 1892 (Baer and Merrifield 1971: 66).

More recently, in 2016 and 2017, I met two non-Indigenous Mexican women who had married Lacandón men. One of the women had lived in Los Angeles, California, for a while and greeted me in solid English.

Throughout these years of unrest, the Lacandón Maya have protected what they could of their heritage and oral history and what they can of their forest. Their total population, which several times teetered toward extinction, is now increasing, reaching 1,740 women, men, and children in mid-2022.

North and South

Although outsiders call them "Lacandón Maya," the families know they are actually **Jach Winik**, "the True People," and that they form two related groups—Northern and Southern. Most Northern Lacandones, who number around 900, live in the forested communities of Mensäbäk and Naja', although two families (one of seven, the other of fifteen) live in isolated forested compounds near Tzeltal Maya communities in other parts of the Selva Lacandona. Around 725 Southern Lacandones live in the community of Lacanja' Chan Sayab, near the Classic Maya site of Bonampak.

As if to confuse matters though, in 1980, three Northern Lacandón families in a dispute with relatives in Naja' moved to the Southern Lacandón settlement of Lacanja' Chan Sayab. Just under a decade later, a half dozen Northern families from Mensäbäk converted to Seventh-Day Adventism (more on that in chapter 9) and moved south to form the settlement of Bethel, two kilometers east of Lacanja' Chan Sayab. Thus, the two groups, Northerners and Southerners, have begun to mix.

Northern Lacandones and Southern Lacandones differ historically and culturally, but they speak similar languages, both of which form part of the Yucatec Mayan family of languages (Hofling 2014: 1).[4] The two tongues are sufficiently different from each other that individuals from either group will say they understand "most, but not all" of what speakers from the other group are saying. Based on these differences, linguist Morris Swadesh estimated the temporal separation of Northerners and Southerners at "about 300 years" (Baer and Merrifield 1971: x).

Despite their differences, both groups of Lacandones recognize the other—as well as the Yucatec Maya of Yucatán and the related Itza Maya of Petén, Guatemala—as **winik**, "people," although they reserve for themselves the full term **Jach Winik**, "True People." Older Spanish-speaking residents of the Selva Lacandona sometimes refer to all Lacandones as "*Caribes*," a survival term from colonial Spaniards whose first encounters with New World people took place in the Caribbean, where all native families were called *Caribes*.[5] Today, the word *Caribe* survives in the Selva Lacandona in a few geographical references to *caribales*, "settlements of *Caribes*," and in Tzeltal words such as *cotón Caribe*, the name for *Poulsenia armata*, the tree Lacandones once used to make tunics from its pounded and flattened bark.

But among themselves, in their own language, Lacandones are always **Jach Winik**, and outsiders are **kaj**, "people who live in communities," or **tsul**, "foreigners who know how to read and write."

Traditionally, Lacandón men let their black hair grow past their shoulders and wear a simple knee-length tunic of white cotton cloth. Northern men distinguish themselves from Southerners by cutting bangs straight across their forehead. Northern women pull their long hair back in a single braid, which they decorate after they marry with the yellow breast feathers of toucans. Southern Lacandón women leave their hair long and flowing and dress in colorful, full-length tunics of store-bought cotton cloth, while Northern women wear a short version of the men's white tunic over a patterned cotton skirt bordered with colored ribbons. For both men and women, the longer sleeves and hem of the Southerners' tunics give outsiders a clue to their origin and provide the source of one of the Northern Lacandones' nicknames for their Southern relatives—**chukuch nok**, "long clothes." In turn, the Southern Lacandones sometimes call Northerners **naachi winik**, "far away people," or **jun tul winik**, "the other people."

Northerners also have another name for Southern Lacandones: **winik ku kinsik u bojo**, "people who kill their brothers," a reference to the feuds and wife-stealing raids that Southern Lacandones perpetrated as recently as the 1950s. Among Southern Lacandón adults, homicide was the most frequent known cause of death until 1940. Three-quarters of these deaths were the result of feuding over women, which was the consequence of high demand for marriage-age females in a small population where men aspired to have at least two wives. Until the end of the 1940s, it was not uncommon for Southern Lacandón men to raid other Lacandón settlements to abduct women and girls, although oral history indicates that almost all of the fifty-eight known Lacandón homicides were cases of Southerners killing other Southerners (Nations 1979).

Northern Lacandones heard stories of these raids, though, and well into the 1970s, Northern women would hide if a Southern Lacandón man came into their settlement. In 1975, Chan K'in Viejo, the religious leader of the Northern Lacandones, told me, "The reason Southern Lacandones aren't still killing men and stealing their wives and daughters is because there are now so many foreigners and prisons." He said that a Southern Lacandón from Lacanja' Chan Sayab with the colorful name of Pancho Villa Bor had visited him in Naja' some years back and told him stories about the murders in and around Lacanja' during previous decades. The fact that Pancho Villa Bor related these stories to a Northern Lacandón leader indicates that enough time had passed since the incidents that the man felt safe discussing them in the open (Nations 1984: 33).

Northerners' fears of Southern Lacandones also have dissipated with increased contact between the two groups. The migration of Christianized Northern Lacandón families to Southern communities during the 1980s means that some Northerners now have close relatives they visit in the south. So far, all the visitors have managed to return home safely.

Population Increase

Despite periods of low—almost extinct—population levels in the past, Lacandón Maya are increasing in number today, but the growth is a function of reduced mortality rather than increased natality. With no treatment for disease beyond prayer and medicinal plants, early Lacandones—especially children—died at the whim of the gods. Demographic data of 1870 to 1979 show that death rates for all cohorts were highest among children aged one through four. Half of all deaths during those decades occurred before the individual turned thirty. People's short life expectancy hindered population growth, because fewer than one-third of Lacandones born before 1979 lived to complete their reproductive years. (Baer and Merrifield 1971; Nations 1979: 161–163).

There also were cases of intentional death of newborns and selective neglect of toddlers and young children. With no knowledge of contraception before the 1970s, couples spaced their children's birth postnatally. Mothers did not attempt to breastfeed two children at once for fear they would lose them both. They rejected one child in a set of twins to ensure that at least one of the two would survive, and they rejected some newborns who arrived too soon after the birth of a previous sibling. Faced with that dilemma, parents either neglected the newborn outright or suddenly weaned the older brother or sister to a diet of corn dough and water. Toddlers who were rapidly weaned became susceptible to malnutrition and communicable diseases. If parents felt forced to reject a child at birth, they told other families that the baby's hands had been deformed (**me'ech u käp**) or that "they wouldn't suckle" (**ma' u chuch**) (Nations 1979: 212), which in some cases may well have been true.

The decision on which child to keep in these situations was a function of gender, sometimes male, sometimes female. Among Northern Lacandones, preference went to male children, but Southern Lacandones showed a preference for females. What determined the decision? Postmarital locality: where a couple lived after they married. Northern Lacandones were traditionally patrilocal, meaning that a son of marriageable age found a wife in another family and brought her home to live with his parents. Sometimes the groom was required to perform a year or two of bride service for the woman's parents, working in his in-laws' fields, but when his service was complete, he was allowed to take his wife to his own parents' home, where he was expected to provide the older couple with food, shelter, and protection in their later years. Hence the Northern Lacandón preference for sons over daughters.

The opposite held true for Southern Lacandones, who were traditionally matrilocal. Young women found a husband in another family and brought him home to live with her parents, providing food and security for her mother and father in their old age. Polygynous marriages among Southern Lacandones were sororal, meaning one man married a series of sisters, who, having grown up together and having brought the man into their own household, pretty much ran the show. The husband spent his early marital life working for his wife or wives' parents, and spent the rest of his life surrounded by his wife and her sisters, who also were his wives. Faced with difficult decisions in child-rearing and food distribution, Southern Lacandones had good reason to favor daughters. Postmarital residence patterns molded their decision.

The impact of the groups' variable treatment of male and female children was evident in unbalanced sex ratios in the different communities during my initial population census of 1974.[6] Not surprisingly, girls outnumbered boys among the Southern Lacandones of Lacanja' Chan Sayab and San Quintín (73 males per 100 females) (Baer and Merrifield 1971; Nations 1979: 250). In the Northern Lacandón community of Mensäbäk, boys under the age of fifteen vastly outnumbered girls (171 males per 100 females) in 1974 and rose to 214 males per 100 females by 1977 (Nations 1979: 248). In Naja', boys also held the majority (118 males per 100 females). But men who married women from Naja' tended to stay in Naja' to coalesce around the last spiritual leader (**t'o'ojil**), Chan K'in Viejo, making many Naja' couples ambilocal rather than patrilocal and relieving the pressure to raise more sons. That change in postmarital residence affected the gender ratios of the young couples' children.

Imbalanced sex ratios were more the effect of differential death rates of young children, based on gender, rather than on infanticide. The selective neglect of some children was apparent in the poor nutritional status and ineffective medical care they received. When it came to feeding the family, Northerners showed preference to sons over daughters, frequently making young girls wait while their father and brothers ate their fill and giving the girls the leftovers. By contrast, Southern Lacandón girls ate with their mother and her sisters and tended to be well cared for.

Historically, in Northern communities, selective neglect also resulted in the death of some young co-wives. An older wife forced to share her home and husband with a pubescent co-wife sometimes abused, overworked, and underfed the young girl (Baer and Baer 1952: 98; Nations 1979: 153–156).

After Lacandones came into almost constant contact with the outside world in the 1960s and beyond, improved medical care prompted an increase in population. The introduction of clean water systems, vaccines, and antibiotics dramatically decreased deaths from communicable diseases. Consistent interaction with outsiders also prompted a dramatic decrease in infanticide, selective neglect, and homicide. Only two or three murders are known to have occurred since the 1970s, mostly domestic violence of men against women among Northerners. In all communities, women are now as likely to give birth with outside medical assistance as they are at home with only the aid of their mother and grandmother. Maternal and newborn deaths have declined accordingly.

Contemporary Lacandón women, in both the North and South, increasingly make their own decisions about whom they marry and where they live. Only a few families practiced polygyny into the twenty-first century, and those relationships have now aged out, meaning that the husbands in those marriages are now deceased, and polygyny no longer exists among the Lacandón Maya. Young girls are no longer taken or traded as co-wives. Instead, Lacandón girls attend grade school (in Spanish only so far) in their community, and many go on to secondary school in neighboring Tzeltal Maya villages, returning home to be with their families on weekends. One young woman from Mensäbäk is now in her second year of dental school in the Chiapas state capital, and several others are seeking scholarships to attend college. Several Lacandón women have married outsiders, usually

Tzeltal Maya men, and have moved to their husband's community elsewhere in the Selva Lacandona. And everywhere, Lacandón women are determining their own reproductive destiny through the use of modern methods of birth control. The selective infanticide that sometimes took place during past decades has ceased.

What It's Like in the Twenty-First Century

Throughout all these changes in lifestyle and social organization, Lacandones have maintained their daily practice of forest and wildlife conservation. In contemporary satellite images of eastern Chiapas, three large, green islands of old-growth forest pop out in the midst of an ocean of pastureland and regrowth. In the northern Selva Lacandona lies the Área de Protección de Flora y Fauna Metzabok, home to the Northern Lacandón community of Mensäbäk. Thirteen kilometers south lies the Área de Protección de Flora y Fauna Naja', home of the Northern Lacandón community of Naja'. And an hour's drive farther south, the much larger Reserva de la Biósfera Montes Azules covers 3,312 square kilometers of forest and embraces the Southern Lacandón community of Lacanja' Chan Sayab, as well as the Northern Lacandón relocated community of Bethel and a mixed Southern/Northern settlement called Crucero San Javier.[7]

Lacandón Maya continue as faithful defenders of these remaining forest lands. Protection of the lakes and forest that surround their communities almost seems to be permanently rooted in their genes. This protection extends, of course, to the animals that live in the lakes and forest—and that live beside them in their homes. Lacandones' relationship with the animal kingdom is best reflected in their eternal bond with their closest animal protector: the dog. The following chapter reveals why.

2

Lacandones Don't Kill Dogs

During one of my early stays in the Lacandón Maya settlement of Mensäbäk, a dog from a neighboring Tzeltal Maya village stumbled out of the rainforest and began snapping at children and other dogs, prompting everyone to rush into their house and put poles across their door. Once the dog staggered back into the woods, the families came outside again.

A few days later, Chan K'in Pepe Castillo's dog got sick.

A ten-year-old Lacandón boy, Rafael, appeared at my door and reported that Pepe's dog had the illness that makes you bite other people if the dog bites you.

Rabies? I stood up from the bench where I was writing field notes and hurried to Pepe Castillo's house.

I found him standing in front of his house, looking down at a dog tied to a post he had stubbed into the ground. At sixty-five, Pepe was the oldest man in the Mensäbäk settlement, head of one of its original families. He and his three wives lived in a long, low house with a dirt floor and a palm-leaf roof, next to the river that flows into Lake Ts'ibanaj. A short, wizened figure with graying hair falling past his shoulders, Pepe was wearing traditional Lacandón men's clothing—a white cotton tunic that hung to his knees and no shoes.

The dog was snarling, snapping at shadows, and trying to focus its eyes. White foam seeped from the corners of his mouth. Pepe had managed to control the dog by tying a rope noose to a long stick and somehow slipping the noose over the dog's neck. He then tied the stick to the post outside his house. The dog couldn't reach the rope looped around his neck, so he bit furiously at the stick, gnawing the wood to try to escape.

I was looking at a distraught and angry dog. Not especially large—maybe half a meter high, light brown with dark streaks, a classic lowland rainforest dog with undecipherable genetic origins. Maybe part coyote, who knows?

Either way, this was one aggressive dog, and he would have angrily bitten anyone who got close enough to let him do it. I was thankful for the noose and stick and homemade fiber rope. A dozen Lacandones were standing behind me at a respectful distance, ready to run the other way if the dog managed to break the stick.

"Why don't you kill the dog?" I asked Pepe.

"No," he answered. "True People don't kill dogs."

Okay, that's strange, I thought, but I'd been visiting the Lacandones for only six months, and I was definitely not clued in on all the cultural norms.

"How about if I kill the dog?" I asked.

"That would be good, if you would kill the dog," Pepe said.

So, I walked 30 meters to the house of Juakin Trujillo, the community leader, who recently had accumulated enough money (no one was quite sure how) to build the only house in Mensäbäk with a cement floor, sawed board walls, and a corrugated tarpaper roof. He also had a single-shot .22-caliber rifle, and I asked to borrow it when I saw him leaning out of his doorway. Juakin was also dressed traditionally—white cotton tunic and long, black hair to his shoulders—but he also owned and wore a pair of black plastic shoes. He disappeared into his house and came back with a single-shot rifle, one .22 cartridge, and a small shovel.

I carried the borrowed rifle and shovel back to Pepe's house, where Pepe had meanwhile untied the dog from the pole and was using the stick and noose to hold it at a safe distance. The dog was snapping and snarling and thrashing its head back and forth in a froth. Pepe handed me the far end of the stick with the writhing dog on the other end.

With the rifle under my arm and the shovel in one hand, I used my other arm to wrestle the dog-on-a-stick up a small mound 10 meters behind Pepe's house. I tied my end of the stick to the branch of a tree and stood back. Everyone watched intently—from a distance.

I lifted the rifle to my shoulder, clicked off the safety, and shot the dog.

Poor dog.

Sorry, dog.

I leaned the rifle against the tree and, using Juakin's shovel, dug a shallow grave on top of the hill and maneuvered the dead dog into the hole and covered him with dirt, stick and all. As I walked down the hill past Pepe's house to return the rifle and shovel, everyone turned back to what they had been doing. The women disappeared into their houses. No one ever mentioned the dog again.

Except that in the days that followed, I began to ask why True People don't kill dogs.

"Poor dogs," they would say. "Lacandones don't kill dogs."

Then, a few days later, without making any reference to the rabid dog, my friend, Chan K'in José Valenzuela, told me the story of the man who married his dog. I sat by the fire and listened.

The Man Who Married a Dog

One day a Lacandón ancestor hiked into the rainforest to bleed resin from copal trees to burn as incense in his god house.[1] The man was worried, because he had not yet found a woman to marry, and he wondered how long he was going to have to make his own tortillas and eat alone. As he walked down the trail, the man's trusty dog, a female, trotted behind him. Suddenly, an agouti flashed across the trail in front of them (*Dasyprocta mexicana*). The man carefully notched an arrow to his bow, crept up on the agouti, and killed it. Right there on the trail, the ancestor sliced open the agouti and fed its intestines to the dog. Then he wrapped the animal's carcass in fresh green leaves and hid it beside the trail so he could retrieve it on their way back home.

The man and his dog resumed their trip into the forest. But a few minutes down the trail the dog whirled around and ran back toward home. The man worried that the dog might be going back to eat the rest of the agouti, but even so, he decided to let the dog keep running. He continued down the path alone, on his way to collect copal incense for the gods.

When the man returned home that evening, the dog was already in the house, lying on the dirt floor. But when she saw the man approaching, she jumped up on her hind legs and began to bark as if she were telling him something important. (Lacandones say that dogs can talk, but the words just won't come out of their throat in a way that human beings can understand.)

Amid the barking, the man looked up and saw the gutted agouti hanging from a house beam above his head. So, the dog hadn't eaten it after all. But how had the dead agouti ended up in his house, he wondered. And, wait, who prepared this corn gruel and those tortillas on the bench? Confused, but hungry, the man decided to eat the food that had miraculously appeared in his house. His dog stopped barking and sat back on her haunches and watched him eat. The man threw her a tortilla, and the dog snapped it out of the air and wolfed it down. He threw another tortilla and the dog nabbed it with both paws and calmly sat down and began to eat.

While the dog ate the tortilla, the man retrieved the dead agouti from the roof beam and lay it across the fire to barbeque it, wondering out loud, "Who brought this agouti into the house, and who ground that corn and patted out these tortillas?" It's a mystery, he thought to himself. "I'll never figure this out."

The following day, the same thing happened. The man left his house to work in his milpa garden, and the dog followed him halfway there, then suddenly turned around and disappeared down the trail. That evening when the man came home, he found that someone had again come into his house, ground corn into dough, patted out tortillas, built a fire, and cooked him food. And it happened again the next day and the day after that.

Finally, the man looked at the dog and asked out loud, "What's going on here? You hike out with me, but you always come back to the house. You must be seeing the person who comes into the house to grind corn and make tortillas."

The dog barked, as if she had something to say but couldn't get the words to come out of her throat.

The next day, the man woke up and casually said to his dog that he was going into the forest to gather more copal for his religious ceremonies. As usual, the dog followed him halfway, then whirled around and disappeared. The man stopped and waited a bit, then ran back down the trail toward his house to see who was sneaking in and preparing food.

As the man crept up on the house, he heard the rasping sound of someone grinding corn. Quietly, he snuck closer to the house and looked up to see a nude woman standing at the grinding table, vigorously crushing corn kernels into dough and singing. He looked at the woman's feet and saw that the dirt floor was covered with fur. The woman hadn't seen him, so he slowly came up behind her and reached out and grabbed her arms.

"What's this?" the woman yelled. "Why have you come back to surprise me? And you grab me and keep me from doing my work? Let me go! How do I know you'd be a good husband, anyway? Do you even have any clothing for me?"

Stunned, the man responded, "For sure I do." Suddenly he realized that the woman was his dog transformed into a human. Her hair, ears, tail, and snout had fallen off, and the dog had become a human. She was talking, and the words were coming out of her throat.

"I'll do no harm to you," the man assured her. "I'll be a great husband. And you, you'll prepare food for us, and we'll eat together and be married."

So, the dog/woman went back to work while the man rummaged through the house and found some old clothes—a skirt and a tunic, some red beads—and gave them to the dog/woman, who put them on and smiled.

She asked the man to throw away the dog hair that lay at her feet and the discarded ears and snout, and to do so without touching them. So the man used two sticks to carry the hair and dog parts into the forest while the dog/woman continued her work. By nightfall she had ground a large ball of corn dough and made tortillas. And the man and the dog/woman sat down and ate together, which meant that they were now married.

They were married for many years. As time passed, they had children— first, one (human) girl and then another. As their first daughter matured, things were good and they were happy. But things began to take a turn for the worse after the second daughter was born. The man grew crotchety and began to complain that the dog/woman relieved herself wherever she happened to be at the time, the way dogs sometimes do. She even relieved herself inside the house, in the corner of the kitchen—wherever she was when she needed to go. One day, the man found poop in his corn gruel and lost control. He hit the dog/woman with a stick of firewood.

"You stop doing that," the man yelled. "Stop pooping in the corn gruel. It makes it inedible!"

The dog/woman seemed not to understand what the man was saying and slinked off to hide on the bed where their new baby girl was sleeping. That night, when the man looked over at the dog/woman, he saw that she was licking the baby with her tongue instead of washing her with a cloth and water. The man totally lost it. He hit the dog/woman so hard that he killed her.

Poor dog/woman.

The next day, a young Lacandón man from another family—not knowing what had happened—came by to visit, hoping to ask the man for the couple's older daughter in marriage. When he saw that the man's wife wasn't there, he asked where she had gone. The man confessed to the visitor what he had done. He had killed his dog/wife.

The visitor began to scold him.

"But she was pooping in my food," the ancestor protested.

"So what," said the visitor. "Didn't she feed you? There's no reason to hit her and kill her. Didn't she cook your food? Poor dog! What kind of man are you?"

The ancestor began to cry. Not many days afterward, he died of remorse.

From that day forward, Our True Lord, Jachäkyum, never again allowed a human being to marry a dog. Jachäkyum realized that humans don't make good spouses for dogs. Also, because the dog/woman's two daughters would go on to become ancestors of human beings, Jachäkyum said that from that day forward, no Lacandón should ever kill a dog. And until this day no one is permitted to do so. They can hit them, even hit them hard, but they can never kill a dog. Any Lacandón who purposely kills a dog will be punished when they die. If someone kills a dog, the devil Kisin will burn their soul in the afterworld—forever. Any Lacandón who kills a dog will be punished just as if they had killed another human being.

And that's the end of the story.

Except for this: When a True Person dies, the family weeps and grieves, and they quickly bury the person in traditional fashion. With great reverence, they lift the dead person into a hammock and carry them to their grave site. They hang the hammock inside the grave so the body doesn't touch the dirt at the bottom of the hole. On the deceased person's lap they place a net bag that holds a gourd filled with corn gruel, some tortillas, and some candles, sticks, and wood shavings so the dead soul can build a fire and have food during its lonely nights in the underworld (Tozzer 1907: 47; Boremanse 1998: 94).

The family covers the grave with poles and palm leaves, then covers everything with earth. They build a small, palm-thatched structure over the mound and top it with four small figures of a dog fashioned from xate palm leaves (*Chamaedorea oblongata*). They put two of the dog figures at the deceased's head and two at their feet. The four dogs are the dead person's companions. The mourners then tell the departing soul: "These are your dogs. Tie them up when you go to sleep alone in the night. They will guard you" (Boremanse 1998: 94).

At the appropriate time, the symbolic dogs travel with the person's soul to the River of Tears, but they don't cross the river. Instead, if the deceased has been kind to his/her real dogs during their lifetime, the soul of one of those dogs will be waiting on the other side of the river. Recognizing its human master, the dog will leap into the water and swim across, where it will tie the dead person's wrists together and gently carry them on its back across the River of Tears into the realm of Sukunkyum, the Lord of the Underworld. Sukunkyum will accept the human's soul and direct it past the caves of K'ak', the Lacandón God of Fire, and Ts'ibanaj, the God of Writing, to the cliff of Mensäbäk, the God of Rain. There, the soul will remain until the world is destroyed and Our True Lord, Jachäkyum, creates a new rainforest.

Constant Companions

You would think that this story alone would make a Lacandón be kind to dogs. Not so much. In life, as in the underworld, Lacandones and dogs are constant companions, but people don't always treat their dogs kindly. Every Lacandón household has at least one dog, and some have four or five (as well as cats to control the mice). The rail-thin dogs hang around the family kitchen much of the day, waiting for a tossed, day-old tortilla or an occasional ball of corn dough. They're given affectionate names: Ek' Ni' (Black Nose), Barum (Jaguar), Bobby, Caruso, and Pennsylvania. But the poor dogs are sometimes tied up and left for hours or kicked when they bark. Children chase the dogs and slap them with sticks as if they were counting coup. Even the largest Lacandón dog will sometimes lower its head and whimper when a human approaches. Pick up a stick and every dog within striking distance will hightail it into the bush.

Yet when a dog gets sick, the human owner is beside himself, nurturing the poor critter as if it were a child. Dogs poisoned by chilillo berries receive special care. Chilillo (*Rourea glabra* and *Connarus lambertii,* both members of the poisonous *Connarus* family), are a favorite food of curassows and parrots, but they make the birds' intestines noxious to dogs. A hunter who kills a bird and isn't careful to keep its intestines away from his dog will end up with a sick, potentially dead, pet. A dog that eats chilillo-laden intestines will soon be moaning and whimpering, poisoned by the toxins in the berries. The family launches into action. Someone searches out the jack-bean plant called **u yoch pek'** (literally "its food, dog," *Canavalia* sp.), a leguminous vine, and cooks its beans into a stew, which the family painstakingly feeds to the ailing dog. If the dog downs the stew, it will survive to hunt another day. If not, poor dog.

Even though dogs are sometimes poorly treated, there's good reason to keep them alive—even beyond their role in the afterlife. Until the 1970s, Lacandones built their houses inside their milpas, isolating their homes a half hour or more away from one another in the forest. This dispersed settlement pattern provided a buffer zone against human-spread diseases and protected the family from kidnappers. Families living hidden in the forest used dogs as their first line of defense, an early warning system that announced approaching strangers. If need be, a barking dog provided time for a family to flee into the forest or grab weapons to defend themselves. Outsiders, including intruding chicle harvesters and Southern Lacandón men, were still sneaking up on other Lacandón settlements to steal wives and daughters as recently as the 1940s (Baer and Merrifield 1971).

There are still other reasons to keep dogs close. As Chan K'in Viejo, the spiritual leader of Najá, told me, dogs protect a family's food supply. Wild animals such as the coatimundi (*Nasua narica*) will creep into unprotected milpas in groups of a dozen or more "and eat the year's corn supply in a single night," he said.

"Coatimundis like young corn," he said. "Dogs scare them away. Otherwise, they will wipe you out. Dogs scare away other mammals as well: raccoons, pacas, agoutis, squirrels, and peccaries. And they scare away deer that eat the leaves of sweet potatoes, beans, and chayotes."

Warned by a barking dog, a Lacandón may be quick enough to kill a wild animal trying to steal food from his milpa, and if that animal is edible, like a paca or peccary, he's protected the family food supply and bagged tomorrow's dinner at the same time.

Most Lacandón families started to build their houses outside their milpas in the 1960s and 1970s, when they began concentrating into settlements of multiple families. Some did this to have access to missionaries' medicines. Others moved because their forest territory was invaded by migrant farmers and ranchers. Even in today's concentrated communities, families still depend on dogs to let them know when a stranger is approaching the house. At night, dogs scare away foxes, opossums, ocelots, and tayras that would eagerly steal the family's chickens and turkeys.

In both traditional isolated households and modern, settled communities, Lacandón hunters still depend on dogs to help them find game animals. If the family heads to the milpa to work, the dogs go with them to scout the field for agoutis and peccaries, doing perimeter patrol while the family gathers corn and squash.

A dog walking a forest trail will sometimes sniff out the entrance to the hiding hole of a nocturnal paca, frequently located at the base of a tree. The Lacandón hunter mounds dry leaves around the hole and lights them, smoking out the animal so he can chop it with a machete as it emerges. In a successful hunt, the human gets the meat, and the dog is rewarded with the dead paca's intestines.

While staying with an isolated Lacandón family on the northern side of Lake Mensäbäk in the late 1970s, I watched a dog bag a brocket deer (*Mazama americana*) basically by itself. Chan K'in Juanito, one of the family's sons, and I were fishing from a dugout canoe in the lake when we heard a rustling of brush on the lake shore. We swiveled around and saw the family dog, Capitán, running along the edge of the lake toward the commotion. The dog dashed into the trees and began to bark. Suddenly, a large male brocket deer hightailed it out of the forest with Capitán tight on his heels. The deer leaped into the lake and began swimming away from shore. Juanito immediately began paddling the heavy mahogany canoe toward the deer. Twice as we got close to it, the deer swerved away in the opposite direction. Providing a soundtrack for the chase, Capitán kept up a constant chorus of barking from the edge of the lake. If the deer got close to land, the dog would run to head it off.

After five minutes of hard paddling, we got within striking distance of the deer, now tired from struggling in the water. Juanito raised his mahogany paddle and slammed it down on the deer's neck, then reached into the water and grabbed the deer's hind leg. He held it under the water until it drowned. After the deer quit moving, I helped Juanito pull the deer into the canoe. It was a cruel but effective way to secure meat for the family. Capitán, the dog, had done most of the work.

We rowed back to the shore, tied up our canoe, and carried the deer up the hill to the house. As we approached, I counted ten deer hides hanging from the rafters near the cooking fire. That night when I asked Juanito's father, José López, about them, he said he would sew some of them into deerskin purses to carry cigars. The others he would use as mats so the family could sit on their home's dirt floor. I was sitting on a deer hide as he told me this. Juanito jumped in to say that all the hides hanging from the rafters were from deer hunted down by his dog, Capitán.

Whether they're bringing in meat for the family larder, warning the family of approaching strangers, or carrying their master's soul across the River of Tears, the Lacandones' dogs are vital companions. Following Jachäkyum's orders and their own best interests, Lacandones don't kill dogs.[2] Poor dogs. But without their dogs, poor Lacandones.

II

"Where Did We Come From?"

During the no-travel days of the 2019–2022 COVID-19 pandemic, a young Lacandón Maya friend, Cecilia Valenzuela, sent me a WhatsApp message, asking where her people had come from. It was the first—and so far only—time a Lacandón asked me what Westerners knew about their tribal history. (Normally, they're telling *me* their history.) Based on my research, I wrote a short answer to a big question:

> *Cecy, the Jach Winik have always lived in the rainforest of the Río Usumacinta, in the beginning, in the Guatemalan Petén, on the eastern side of the river, and later on the western side of the river, in the Selva Lacandona of Mexico. Families began to cross the river from east to west during the 1700s and continued into the 1960s, when the last Lacandón families crossed into Chiapas. The rainforest of the Usumacinta has always been your home, as it is today.*

Lacandones have a detailed oral history about their origins as a people, but information about geographical movement was only partially preserved from generation to generation. In the main, Indigenous people have long memories for places, people, and events, as we shall see in the following chapters, a blend of history, traditional knowledge, and fables that provide a deeper answer to Cecy's question.

3

The Ancient Ones

Lacandón Maya have lived in the forested watersheds of the Selva Lacandona for centuries, but they're fully aware they're not the first people to walk the area's trails and fish its lakes. When they clear garden plots in the forest regrowth, they find stone axe heads and obsidian blades made by people who lived in this rainforest before them. On rock faces around the lakes, they see figures painted in red ochre, and when they enter the caves hidden beneath the cliffs, they see bleached human bones scattered on the dust-thick floor.

Lacandones say these are the bones of the **chuchu winik,** "the old people," or the **nukuch winik,** "the ancient ones," who lived in the Selva Lacandona long ago. Western archaeologists would add considerable detail to that description. What the Lacandones are finding are the remains of a civilization that flourished in this forest—and throughout the surrounding territory—for 3,000 years, a civilization that was the most advanced in the Western Hemisphere when Europeans invaded it in the 1520s. The ancient Maya developed a writing system that recorded the rise and fall of dynasties, depicted great victories and defeats, and chronicled solar eclipses and the cycles of planets. They conceived the mathematical concept of zero and produced a calendar as accurate as the one we use today.

"The old people," the ancient Maya, built an entire civilization out of stone and plaster and timber, without the benefit of metal tools, draft animals, or wheels (except on toys, oddly enough). They built it without the assistance of the Egyptians, the Polynesians, or extraterrestrials. And they built their civilization in the most unlikely of places—in a lowland tropical rainforest, expertly using the elements they had in abundance: stone, plants, soil, water, fire, ingenuity, and time.

The first Maya families to make their way into the rainforest of the Usumacinta watershed likely followed the rivers upstream from coastal areas in the east and downstream from highland areas to the south and northwest. In the forest, they lived in small settlements on lakes and rivers. They hunted with spear throwers (atlatls) and spears tipped with stone points, but would not have bows and arrows for another two millennia (Ciofalo 2012; Aoyama 2021: 83). By 2000 BC, they were planting and harvesting maize (corn), and by 1000 BC, they were making pottery from clay, an indication that they were living in established locations. Archaeological excavations demonstrate that they raised dogs, turkeys, Muscovy ducks, and bees.

Over the centuries, their small settlements evolved into villages of pole and palm-thatch houses built on low stone platforms. Some of these villages eventually blossomed into Classic Maya cities such as Yaxchilán, Palenque, Piedras Negras, Tikal, and Bonampak—all known for their architecture and art, sophisticated water control, and bountiful agricultural production. At their peak population, around AD 800, as many as eight to ten million people lived in the Maya region (Coe 1993: 20, 24; Sharer 1996: 28, 40).

But it was not all peace and light. The ancient Maya experienced harsh, long-running enmity between competing powers—city against city, region against region—and lengthy periods of warfare marked by on-again/off-again alliances.

Most of the Classic-era populations in the region (AD 250–AD 900) divided into two major groups, Yucatecan and Ch'olan, so named because of the languages they spoke. Populations in the Yucatán Peninsula and along its southern edge spoke Yucatec and several related languages in the Yucatec Mayan family. To their south and southwest, other Maya peoples spoke languages from the Ch'olan Mayan family. This division into two language groups may have exacerbated competition between the two major entities.

Although Maya civilization endured for millennia, between AD 760 and AD 820, things began to fall apart. The highly populated polities of the southern Maya lowlands underwent a wave of political collapse and warfare, followed by abandonment of many urban areas and eventual demographic collapse. By the early 900s almost all of the most powerful cities were abandoned, and by AD 1000–AD 1100, the rainforest of the southern Maya lowlands was inhabited only by groups living in isolated forest settlements (Haldron et al. 2020: 29; Arnauld et al. 2021: 5; Okoshi et al. 2021; Grube 2021: 37).

Debate about the disintegration of Classic Maya civilization is the stuff that archaeologists' careers are made of. Through the decades, theories have included peasant uprisings, disease, endemic warfare, religious change, environmental degradation, and climate change punctuated by severe droughts. But research during the past fifty years indicates that "the so-called Maya collapse" was not a singular event, but took place over more than 100 years through processes that involved "many factors and multiple causes at various points in time and space" (Chase and Chase 2021: xvii; Chase et al. 2021: 349).

Among those factors and causes were political fragmentation within and among population centers, shifting political alliances, warfare, disrupted trade routes, heightened competition for resources, and "loss of credibility in the leadership expected to maintain the system" (Haldon et al. 2020: 30). Together with prolonged periods of drought, increased demographic pressure on the land, and warfare, these elements produced a systemic collapse from which Classic Maya civilization never recovered.

The disintegration began as early as AD 760 in the rainforest region of the Río Usumacinta and expanded in a swirling pattern from west to east and south to north. Cities such as Tikal and Caracol held out until the end of the ninth century, then also dissolved into the forest (Arnauld et al. 2021: 7). In the words of one research team, "From the perspective of organizational theory, the collapse of the Classic Maya city-states in the Southern Lowlands was a widespread systemic disintegration, a breathtaking network failure" (Demarest et al. 2021: 348).

For good reason, archaeologists use the term *Postclassic* for the centuries that followed (AD 900–1521), because the peak glory of the Classic Maya was exhausted. The Ch'olan-speaking peoples still holding on in the rainforest of eastern Chiapas built fortified villages on islands and peninsulas in the region's lakes and rivers, living once again in perishable structures perched on stone foundations.

Traces of some of these fortified villages are still visible in the Selva Lacandona. Archaeologists have found ruins on the Ch'olti Maya island of Lacantún in Lake Miramar, Topiltepec Island in the Río Jataté, and Pochutla Island in Lake Ocotal Grande. Near today's Lacandón settlement of Mensäbäk, ongoing archaeological excavations by US and Mexican researchers are providing clues to what these settlements of Ch'olan speakers were like.

The Mensäbäk Archaeological Project led by Joel Palka and Fabiola Sánchez Balderas has identified six archaeological sites with at least fifty-seven stone structures around two large lakes, Lake Mensäbäk (86 hectares) and Lake Ts'ibanaj (174 hectares). Smaller lakes and connecting waterways add another 36 hectares of surface water to the immediate area. The Mensäbäk region had its highest populations during two specific time periods— toward the end of the Late Preclassic (around AD 200) and during the Late Postclassic to colonial period (AD 1500–1525), Palka notes. Strangely, existing evidence suggests that the lake area was only lightly populated during the Classic Maya era, presenting the possibility that the region's families were lured away to major population centers (Palka 2014).

Despite these questions, it's clear that when the Ch'olan-speaking families built houses and stone structures around the lakes during the Postclassic years, they were reoccupying lands where their ancestors had lived more than 1,000 years before (Palka 2014: 308–309; Palka et al. 2008; Cucina, Tiesler, and Palka 2015: 146).

Palka and Sánchez Balderas report that the largest of the settlements around the lakes—a site they named Tzibanah—was likely the political focal point of the area. Located on a peninsula on the northern side of Lake Ts'ibanaj, the ruins include more than twenty-five stone structures. A half-hour canoe ride away, on the western shore of the lake, a 695-meter limestone mountain provides a high point for monitoring the site and the lakes and land that surround it. The mountain stands as a half-dome formed when the eastern face of the mountain collapsed an unknown number of centuries ago. Modern Lacandones call the mountain Chäk Aktun ("Red Rock Cliff") and say that during the old days, a **ba'alkan** ("a sky object") smashed into the mountain and knocked away one side, exposing its red interior. (No one has yet found evidence that this story records an actual event.)

Either way, the mountain has been a sacred site for Maya people since Preclassic times. During the Late Preclassic (300 BC–AD 200), they leveled the summit of the mountain to construct a plaza and temple and built thirteen terraces that cascade down the mountain to the lake below. Palka and Sánchez Balderas's archaeological team explored a series of caves on the eastern face and top of Chäk Aktun, including a large, vertical cave that has a blow hole on the summit. Standing over the narrow cavity, you can feel cool wind rushing to the surface from the heart of the mountain.

Palka notes that the cave held ceramic offerings from both Late Preclassic (300 BC–AD 200) and Late Postclassic times (AD 1200–1521). Other caves on the mountain revealed Late Preclassic to Historic (1521–present) burials with ceramic offerings. Pilgrims of the Late Postclassic (AD 1200–1521), as well as modern Lacandones, used the mountain's caves and terraces for ceremonies and left behind ceramic bowls and pots with the faces of gods molded on their rims (Palka 2014: 265, 269).

The special characteristics of Chäk Aktun have drawn pilgrims to Lake Ts'ibanaj for centuries. Even today, the mountain inspires adventurous tourists to canoe across the lake with Lacandón guides and huff up the forested trail that zigzags to its top. When they arrive at the flattened peak, they look out over a labyrinth of interconnected tropical lakes—Ts'ibanaj, Mensäbäk, Chan Petja', and K'ak'—with shores that are draped in rainforest. Today's Lacandones use this "Mirador" as an observation post to watch for looters, resource poachers, and illegal fishermen who sneak into their territory from nearby settlements.

The Mirador was likely a watch post for the ancient Maya as well, allowing lookouts to warn families when potential enemies approached. "It is possible that people lived on top of the mountain," Palka and Sánchez Balderas write, "But they would not have been many because of the small number of platforms" (Palka, et al. 2008: 816). Not to mention how far uphill they would have had to carry water.

Modern Lacandones who guide visitors up Chäk Aktun tie their canoes to trees at the base of the mountain, but in centuries past, the Maya may have docked their craft at a nearby peninsula called Paten. When they examined the peninsula during an archaeological survey, Palka and Sánchez Balderas's team found what appears to be a stone dock that could have sheltered ancient Maya canoes (Palka et al. 2008: 816).

Across Lake Ts'ibanaj, inside a cave called Säk T'at' ("white *Pomacea* snail") because of the large number of bleached-out snail shells found there, Palka and Sánchez Balderas found human remains that are carbon dated to AD 1460–1650. Most of the remains appear to be reburials, meaning that the bodies were originally interred elsewhere and relocated to the cave as skeletons. Some of the bones show clear signs of violence, including "evidence of trauma caused by sharp metal weapons." One jawbone had a piece cut from it with a sword or metal machete, another skull had marks from scalping with a metal knife, and yet another showed "blunt force trauma in the back caused by a club or from falling on a rock" (Palka 2014: 167, 293).

In a cave on a connected lake, the team found "three human skeletons with their knees drawn up to their heads, like mummy bundles" and human skulls with a growth manipulation called tabular erect cranial shaping (Cucina, Tiesler, and Palka 2015). In layman's words, it means the Maya tied their infants to cradleboards, binding their head so that as they grew, the back of the child's skull flattened, and the head bulged out slightly on the left and right. No doubt considered a sign of physical beauty, this style of cranial shaping was common in the Late Postclassic period.

The human remains found in the caves and rock shelters around the lakes indicate that the people who lived here were short—the males averaged 157–160 centimeters and the women 148 centimeters—and that they had a "demanding physical regime and intense mobility," meaning that they carried heavy loads and walked a lot. They suffered from infectious diseases and nutritional deficiencies. Some of them decoratively filed their teeth.

They likely lived in fear, at least part of the time. At two of the sites around the lakes, the archaeological team found stone walls that appear to be defensive fortifications that would have prevented raiders from penetrating the site via the lake, and one site sprouts a remnant concentration of large, spiked piñuela plants like those the lowland Maya surrounded their settlements with as a defense against raiding warriors (Palka and Sánchez Balderas 2012: 814–815).

Rounds of death from unseen disease must also have created anxiety. Chan K'in José Valenzuela told me in 1976, "At one time, people were thick around Lake Ts'ibanaj, but smallpox came and they all died. Äkyanto', the God of Foreigners, or perhaps Jachäkyum made the disease, because people were chanting to the gods to kill their enemies. The wife of Äkyanto' went and got strong medicine and cured the disease once, but then she left. The gods themselves went deep into the mountains and didn't die. But the people who got the disease all died."

Southeast of Lake Ts'ibanaj, a team from the Mensäbäk Archaeological Project mapped a related 200-hectare site called Noh K'uh, with an estimated 400 structures dating to the Late Preclassic period between 395 and 1 BC. They found minor evidence of Postclassic occupation (AD 950–1539), but no evidence of Classic period occupation (Juarez, Salgado-Flores, and Hernández 2019).

Modern visitors who travel to the settlement of Mensäbäk can usually convince one of the Lacandón residents to row them out on the lakes to see the wildlife and cliff paintings along the shores. Visitors who know about the caves and rock shelters usually ask to see them, and the Lacandones may decide to take them there.

Invariably, outsiders fall silent as their guide maneuvers the canoe along the shoreline to a hidden landing spot beneath the moss-covered cliffs. Trying to keep their balance, the visitors crouch in the canoe and scoot forward, gratefully grabbing any available tree limb to pull themselves onto dry land. Looking up, they see that the cliff face has fallen away to reveal an open, porch-like space with a limestone wall looming over it. On the dust and rock floor at their feet, piles of human skulls and long bones are surrounded by whitewashed clay bowls with humanlike faces. The bowls are the retired "god pots"[1] of Lacandones of decades past, and the bones are those of the ancient ones who still watch over the lake and the people who live along its shores today.

4

A Memory of Lakes

In the northern reaches of the Lacandón forest, the vegetation is interrupted by two large tropical lakes, Mensäbäk and Ts'ibanaj, named for the gods who live in caves along their edges. A four-hour hike to the south is Lake Naja', "Big Water" in the Lacandón language. The lake serves as the centerpiece of the Lacandón community of the same name. Ten kilometers east of Lake Naja' lies a lake with three names. Lacandones call it Yajaw Petja', "Wide Lake," and say that a limestone cliff on its shore is the home of Itsanojk'uj, the "Great God of the Itza," the Lacandón deity who guards all lakes, makes hail and ice, and controls the population of crocodiles. On maps and satellite images of Chiapas, you'll find the same lake labeled Lago Sival—not by coincidence, because the Tzeltal Maya who now own the lake and the mountains around it call their community Colonia Sival. However, Tzeltales call the lake Guineo.

The first outsider to write about Lake Itsanojk'uj/Sival/Guineo and the people who lived there at the time simply called it Petja', the Lacandón word for "lake." The outsider was Alfred Tozzer, who lived with Lacandón Maya families there in 1903–1905 and went on to publish the first ethnography of the group (Tozzer 1907). Even decades later, Lacandones remembered Tozzer's visits. During the 1960s, linguist Roberto Bruce discovered that Chan K'in Viejo, who died in 1996 at close to 100 years of age, still remembered "Don Alplelo," who he said always carried a notebook and a tak'in wich, "a metal eye," that never forgot what it saw—a camera, in other words. Chan K'in Viejo would have been a very young boy when Tozzer visited the group, but he was the son of Tozzer's chief informant, José Bor García (Bruce 1968: 120–121).

Today, the majority of visitors to Lake Itsanojk'uj/Sival/Guineo are Tzeltal Maya families from surrounding communities. They paddle canoes out to one of the lake's four islands to picnic on rustic tables built for just such occasions. Mexican and international visitors who know their history find someone from the community who, for a small price, will show them the Maya ruins hidden not far away. What they'll find is a small ancient site with three temple mounds, one of which has exposed walls that are still precariously standing. Unfortunately, an almost mature **ch'uite'** tree (*Pseudobombax ellipticum*) is growing directly out of its roof, its roots clasped around the structure like a giant hand around toy blocks. It will take only a few more years of growth and one big wind to collapse both the tree and the temple it embraces.

On a visit to the site in 2017, I listened as Minchu Valenzuela explained to his young sons, Chan K'in and Bor, that the temple is one of the homes of K'anank'ax, the Guardian of the Forest, who most frequently appears to human beings in the form of a jaguar. But a stylized, eagle-like creature painted on one of the surviving walls of the temple also depicts K'anank'ax, "the creature who will eat all the surviving human beings on the day the world ends," Minchu warned his sons.

Dressed in white tunics, the two boys approached the temple cautiously, as if waiting for the tree to fall and the world to end; as if a jaguar were about to devour them. Minchu took the opportunity to press home K'anank'ax's message of how True People must always guard the forest, as their ancestors did.

Southeast of Yajaw Petja' lie the four finger lakes called the Lagos Ocotales (Ocotal Grande, Suspiro, and two called the Ojos Azules, "Blue Eyes"). These particular lakes get their Spanish-language name, *los Ocotales,* from the ocote pine trees that grow on the hills that surround them (*Pinus chiapensis*). The trees are the source of the pitch pine, or fatwood, that Lacandón families used to illuminate nighttime trails before kerosene lamps and flashlights reached their settlements.

The largest of the Ocotales, Ocotal Grande, is known in Lacandón as u Petja' Kaj, "Outsiders' Lake," an Indigenous echo of a Spanish attack on the Ch'ol-speaking Maya families who lived there during colonial times. In 1559, 100 invading Spanish soldiers and 600 Chiapaneco Indian allies led by Pedro Ramírez de Quiñones from the Kingdom of Guatemala attacked the Ch'ol island of Pochutla on that lake. The Spaniards sought to eradicate the unconquered Maya communities in the Selva Lacandona while simultaneously seizing the families as slaves for their plantations. The Ch'ol Maya resisted the Spanish attack, and many died. Although Spanish forces eventually won the battle, it was a short-lived victory. When the Spaniards left the area, marching away the Ch'ol Maya they had captured, families who had hidden in the forest returned to the island and rebuilt their settlement on the same spot (Nations 2006: 160–161).

Older Lacandones in the communities of Naja' and Mensäbäk have a concise explanation for why they call the place "Outsiders' Lake."

"A long time ago," Chan K'in Viejo said, "soldiers came and killed all the people who lived there."

Farther south in the Selva Lacandona lies Laguna Miramar, Spanish for "view of the ocean," and as if on cue, the Lacandón name for the seventy-nine-square kilometer lake is Chan K'agnaj, "Little Ocean." Few Lacandones have seen the ocean, but they've heard of it, and they tell stories about the sharks that live there. Laguna Miramar also has an island with Maya ruins, having been occupied from the Late Preclassic through Late Postclassic times. The island is best known for its final occupants, the Postclassic Ch'olti Maya of Lacam Tun, which Pedro Ramírez de Quiñones also attacked on his expedition of 1559 (Rivero Torres 1992: 80).

Colonial scribes reported that when the Spaniards and their allied Indian warriors arrived at the shore of Laguna Miramar, they built two sail- and oar-driven war vessels and maneuvered them out to attack the Ch'olti Maya who were sheltering inside the island's fortifications. Faced with the approach of 600 Chiapaneco Indians with bows and lances, 200 Zinacanteco Maya cargo bearers, 100 Guatemalan Maya warriors, and 100 Spanish soldiers armed with matchlock muskets, many of the Maya of Lacam Tun dashed for their canoes and escaped down the Río Azul, which flows out of the lake into the Río Jataté.

But others stayed to fight, and in the ensuing battle the Spaniards and their allies killed scores of Ch'olti and captured 150. The Spaniards burned the Ch'olti houses and trashed the fortifications, then marched their captives to Guatemala where they sold them as enslaved people. The Ch'olti who escaped the battle returned to the island to pick through the remains and rebuild (Remesal 1619/1966, Vol. IVC, bk. 10, chapt. LL: 1524–1526).

Unfortunately, twenty-seven years later, in 1586, the Spaniards came back. This time, seeing that an attack was imminent, the Ch'olti burned their own houses and jumped into their canoes and fled. The Spaniards killed the Maya who stayed to fight or who were too frail to flee. Then, the chroniclers wrote, they burned the Indians' crops and cut down their orchards of cacao trees. The resulting devastation was too much for the Ch'olti, and they abandoned the island settlement at Lacam Tun and fled south.

The Spaniards also abandoned the now uninhabited island and marched off into history, but they remembered the name of the island they had attacked: Lacam Tun. The name became their code word for the Ch'olti and any other unconquered Maya who continued to hide in the rainforest. Gradually, the term morphed into *Lacantún*, then *Lacandón*, giving rise to the name of both the forest and the Maya families who live in the Selva Lacandona today as the Lacandón Maya (Scholes and Roys 1968: 41).

For the next three and a half centuries, the lake's brutal history kept the Lacandones away from Laguna Miramar. Danish archaeologist Frans Blom set out to explore the ruins on Lacam Tun island during a 1950 expedition through the Selva Lacandona, but his Lacandón guides would not follow him to the edge of the lake.

"From the confluence of the Jataté and Perlas rivers," he wrote, "the Indians tenaciously refused to accompany us to the lake. They gave signs of fear, and it would seem this had to do with the existence of a taboo among them. They told the mule drivers that once, many years ago, there had died there a great number of Caribes—the name by which they designate themselves today—by **pum pum**, firearms. The Lacandones know the lake because various times it would show itself from the nearby hills; but they completely refused to come close to its edges" (Blom 1958: 7).

How the Lacandones managed to preserve memory of events that took place on these lakes 450 years ago is a wonder. But many other stories, myths, and legends likewise have a long half-life in the oral history of the Lacandón Maya. As anthropologist Edmund Carpenter pointed out, "When a large proportion of a population is illiterate and books are scarce, memories are often tenacious to a degree outside modern European experience" (Carpenter 1973: 51).

5

The Wooden People

Human beings known as the Lok'in, "the Wooden People," once lived in the northern reaches of the Selva Lacandona. So said Chan K'in Viejo, the last spiritual leader of Naja'. His children would ask him to tell the story. And Chan K'in Viejo would begin:

"The Lok'in? The Lok'in—they were like jaguars. They ate people. But they cooked them first. The Lok'in lived near the river that outsiders call Chancalá, and they wore pumpkin squashes over their heads. Their heads were already deformed, because adults wrapped their babies' heads with strips of wild cane.[1] The Lok'in wore cotton tunics just like the True People, except when they were hunting for human beings to eat. Then, they wore jaguar skins to frighten their victims out of their wits."[2]

When the Lok'in captured human beings, they didn't kill them in the forest. They carried them back to their village so they could decide which captives they would eat and which they would take as mates. If a Lok'in took a fancy to someone, they kept that person alive and treated them as they would treat a spouse. But if they decided to eat someone, they plastered the victim's eyes with beeswax and shoved cloth into their mouth so they couldn't scream. They scalded them in water, then gutted them, and cut them into quarters. Then, they boiled the pieces in a pot. They used a separate pot to cook the intestines, liver, heart, and lungs "because they ate those parts first."

Then, they divided the cooked meat among their companions. "They were all very hungry and eager to eat," Chan K'in said.

Chan K'in Viejo went on to tell his children that many years ago his father and uncle came upon a group of Lok'in in the forest.

"They saw two men and one woman. It was on the shore of Yajaw Petja' (Lago Sival/Guineo), close to the home of K'anank'ax, the Guardian of the Forest. My father and uncle were hunting animals there, but what they found were the Lok'in."

But the Lok'in didn't attack his father and uncle. Instead, they talked with them. The Lok'in told the men they were fleeing their village. They said Ladinos had killed their companions and they were escaping to the west to stay alive. But Chan K'in's father suspected otherwise. He felt that the Lok'in were lying so that the two Lacandones wouldn't kill them with their bows and arrows. After a while, the two groups parted ways without any problems.

The next day, when Chan K'in's father told his own father about the encounter, the older man yelled, "You let them get away? Let's go find them. Let's kill them, because they'll come back and eat us if you let them get away!"

So, Chan K'in's father and uncle ran into the forest to look for the Lok'in. But they were nowhere to be seen. The Lok'in had disappeared.

"I don't know what happened to them," Chan K'in Viejo admitted. "I don't know if they went somewhere else or if they just quit eating people. Maybe they became Ladinos. But there aren't any of them around anymore."

Who could the Lok'in be? Chan K'in Viejo's story has a foothold in history. During the sixteenth and seventeenth centuries, as detailed in chapter 1, Spanish military expeditions scoured the Selva Lacandona for Maya communities that had resisted Spaniards' attempts to subjugate them. When the soldiers found such a group, they perfunctorily offered the families the opportunity to submit by reading aloud a document—in Spanish—from a nearby hill. If the families didn't agree at that moment to become Christians and subjects of the Spanish king, the soldiers attacked. They killed anyone who physically resisted and enslaved those who surrendered. The Lok'in may have been one of the Ch'ol or Ch'olti Maya groups that hid in the Selva Lacandona during the colonial era to escape the Spaniards' wrath—at least initially.

In 1646, two Franciscan friars heard a story told by a Yucatec Maya-speaking man in the Selva Lacandona village called Nohha, where Spaniards had concentrated 300 individuals rounded up from the forest (Boremanse 1998: 16; Palka 2005: 75). The man told the missionaries, Hermenegildo Infante and Simón de Villacís, that in the northern rainforest he had visited villages occupied by a Ch'ol-speaking people whose name the friars transcribed as "los Locen." The Locen lived in seven or eight villages, the man told them. The largest of the villages had 800 houses (Cogolludo 1955, bk. 12, chapt. 7: 347).

Another clue came fifty years later, in 1695, when a Spanish scribe wrote of a Ch'olti Maya man captured by Spanish soldiers near Lake Miramar.

The scribe recorded that, like most Ch'oltis of the time, the captive wore his hair to his waist and had wooden ear spools and a pierced nose into which he inserted a vanilla bean. His clothing consisted of a simple loin cloth and a sleeveless shirt of cotton. The captive told the Spaniards that many years ago the inhabitants of five villages around Lake Miramar had fled north along the bank of the Río Usumacinta—twenty hours walking—to escape the harassment of Spanish forces. These Ch'olti-speaking families, the captive said, settled in the northern Selva Lacandona, the same region where the seven or eight villages had been reported decades earlier (Ximénez 1901/1973, bk. 5, chapt. 57: 309).

The Lok'in?

Perhaps. Either way, the group disappeared from history, and their villages—even their identity—were subsumed by the vegetation of the Selva Lacandona.[3] Except in Lacandón oral tradition, where the Lok'in still roam the forest, pumpkin squashes on their head, dressed in scary jaguar skins, searching for a meal of human flesh.

6

The Story of the Stolen Skulls

(As Related by K'in Enrique Valenzuela, May 2018)

In the territory of the Lacandón Maya, rainforest spills over white limestone cliffs that surround a series of crystalline blue-green lakes. In the afternoon, women wash clothes along the water's edge, and children swim and laugh in the shallows. After everyone leaves for home, there is only the gentle slosh of waves where water meets forest.

Fissures in the cliffs along the lakeshores hide caves that Lacandones say are the homes of Maya gods. For centuries, Maya peoples have used these caves as the resting place for ancestors' bones and sacred objects.

Inside the caves, bleached human skulls and long bones are piled behind clay god pots that pay homage to the deities.[1] For as long as they can remember, Lacandones have climbed into the caves to pray for plentiful crops and freedom from disease. Hunkering in the darkness, they burn sticky balls of copal incense, using the flames and smoke to carry their prayers to the gods. Hundreds of ceremonies over hundreds of years have blackened the cave walls and created stalagmites of melted incense bonded to the limestone floor like last night's candles. Thin obsidian blades lie in the dust, left by supplicants who offered their blood in payment for answered prayers.

The lakes, the rainforest, and the Lacandones began to attract adventurers even before logging roads connected the Lacandón settlements to the outside world. With the easy access of the twenty-first century, visitors began to appear almost weekly in the northern Lacandón settlements of Mensäbäk and Naja'. Sometimes a Lacandón man or his teenage son can be convinced to row outsiders across the lakes to see the bones hidden in the shadows of the caves. Under careful watch of their guide, the visitors are allowed to take photographs, but are reminded not to touch anything.

The Lacandón families of Mensäbäk were not surprised, then, when two students from the Universidad Nacional Autónomo de México (UNAM), a man and a woman, drove into their community in 2005 and set up camp by the river that feeds into Lake Ts'ibanaj, named for the Lacandón god of writing and art. Curious children watched the two build a fire and make dinner. The woman told them her name was Elena. The students didn't ask to visit the lakes or the caves. Instead, after hiking several days in the forest, they got into their car and drove away, waving goodbye. But they returned several months later, and came again the following month, always spending their days exploring the forest.

During their third visit, they finally told Enrique Valenzuela, the community president, that they were searching for something—the remains of guerrilla fighters said to have been killed by the Mexican army somewhere around the lakes during the mid-1970s.

"Someone told us they died near the community of Mensäbäk," they said. At least one Mexican soldier had been killed "and both of the guerrillas." The bodies of the guerrillas had never been recovered, and the students were hoping to find them and take them home for burial. They told Enrique, "One of them was our relative."

The guerrillas were likely members of the Fuerzas de Liberación Nacional (National Liberation Forces, FLN), a pro-Cuban group founded in northern Mexico during the late 1960s. In 1972, the FLN established a training camp in the Lacandón rainforest to prepare fighters for an armed rebellion against the Mexican government (Shapiro 2000; Chiapas Support 2015).

But the Mexican army and federal police discovered the camp and in early 1974 attacked it as part of Operación Diamante, named for a Ladino ranch a few kilometers northwest of Mensäbäk. The army and federal police killed at least five guerrilla trainees and leaders, and the rest scattered into the forest. The army pursued them and killed them in firefights whenever they found them.

The attack almost eradicated the FLN in Chiapas, but the individuals who survived eventually morphed into the Ejército Zapatista de Liberación Nacional (EZLN), the internationally known Zapatistas who led a widespread Indigenous uprising against the Mexican government in Chiapas on New Year's Day 1994.

Enrique told the two visiting students that he was too young to remember the firefight of 1974, but he walked them to the house of his father,

Chan K'in José Valenzuela, who did remember the incident and who told them what he knew.

"I didn't see it happen," Chan K'in said, but he had heard the gunshots across the lake—rapid fire from inside the forest. Chan K'in suggested they talk to Pepe Ramos, his oldest son and a half brother to Enrique, who knew more about what happened. When the students found Pepe Ramos, he told them that he and a friend, Antonio, from the Lacandón community of Najá, had come upon the site where the fight took place. Several days after the battle, they had paddled across the lake, tied their dugout to a tree, and walked into the forest. They found a place where the vegetation was disturbed—saplings broken, bushes flattened—and blood on some leaves. Leather military boots were piled together in the undergrowth.

"We didn't find any bodies," Pepe said, "but later we saw vultures circling the sky over Jot'on K'ak," a lake due east of Lake Ts'ibanaj.

After hearing the story, the students stayed in the community several more days, searching the forest near Jot'on K'ak'. Enrique gave them some advice about the skulls and bones in the caves. "Those aren't from the fight," he said. "Those are our ancestors. But if you find the bones of your relatives in the forest," he said, "you can take those."

After a fruitless search in the forest, the students drove to several of the Tzeltal Maya communities that border Lacandón territory and asked the families there if they knew anything about the firefight, the fallen guerrillas, or the missing remains. They were looking for any information they could find, they said.

The Lacandones would later hear that in the Tzeltal community of Esperanza, two men—Pedro Cruz and Alfredo "something"—listened to the students' story and approached them.

"We know where the guerrillas' bones are," they said. "We saw them in the forest. But for us to take you there would take a lot of time and work. You'd have to pay us $30,000 pesos"—about US$3,100 at the time. "Twenty thousand up front and 10,000 more when we show you the remains."

Excited, the students said they'd find the money and return, which they did. A few weeks later, the two Tzeltales led them into the rainforest, headed in the direction of Mensäbäk. Enrique later heard that the students and their guides dragged back into the community late that night, looking exhausted, and left early the next morning. That was all anyone could say about what had happened.

Daily life in Mensäbäk returned to normal, but two months later, a new group of visitors appeared and asked to visit the lakes. Enrique's older brother, Minchu, rowed the group across Lake Ts'ibanaj and into the connecting Lake Mensäbäk. Minchu disembarked and helped the tourists climb into the cave. As his eyes adjusted, he saw, "All the bones in the cave— skulls, leg bones, ribs—were gone. Someone had sneaked into the cave and stolen them."

The Lacandón families in Mensäbäk speculated about the theft at length, but no one had a clue about who had taken the ancestors' bones. After another three months, the government-provided satellite phone rang in Mensäbäk's community office. Enrique, the community president, picked up. Although he is Lacandón through and through, Enrique speaks Spanish fluently, the result of time spent in Mérida for medical treatment as a boy.

On the phone was an official from the Procuraduría General de la República (PJR, the Attorney General of Mexico) in the regional office of Ocosingo, Chiapas. The official told Enrique that the head of the PJR office in Mexico City wanted him to travel to Ocosingo to provide some information.

Enrique said the call made him anxious. "Why do they want to talk with me?" he asked.

"Nothing to worry about," the official told him. "It's an old problem. Something about bones."

At the PJR office in Ocosingo the following day, the staff set up a phone call between Enrique and PJR officials in Mexico City. As Enrique listened, one of the officials said he was trying to clear up confusion about people who apparently had died near Mensäbäk thirty years ago. It was known, the official said, that Mexican army soldiers engaged a group of guerrillas in the rainforest near Mensäbäk several decades ago.

"One soldier died, and two were wounded," he said. "But we have no information about how many guerrillas died. And if any died, we don't know where their remains are."

The official told Enrique he was sending a team to investigate. He asked Enrique to wait for them in Ocosingo. The officials would come to him.

The next day, fifteen PJR officials flew into the state capital, Tuxtla Gutiérrez, loaded into three Suburban vehicles, and drove four hours to Ocosingo, where they found Enrique waiting at the regional office. The team included a mix of federal and state officials and two archaeologists from Mexico's National Institute of Anthropology and History (INAH). With them were the two students who had come to Mensäbäk to search for their relative's bones.

The officials took Enrique to lunch and told him the story: The two students had filed a legal claim for the skeletal remains of individuals they had found in the forest near the Lacandón community of Mensäbäk. The students showed the PJR officials photographs of the site in the forest and of the bones—four skulls and several long bones.

"We found them in the forest near a lake," the students said. In their legal claim, they were seeking official permission to recover the bones and take them to Mexico City.

"That's not right," Enrique said. "I know the place in these photos, and there are no bones there."

"But," he went on, "we do have bones missing from a cave on one of our lakes."

"Really? You have photos of the missing bones?" the officials asked.

"I do," Enrique answered. "But they're back in the community."

The individuals most interested in seeing the photographs, Enrique said, were "*los peritos*," the specialists who dig up bones—meaning the government archaeologists.

"Let's go see the photos," one of them said. With that, the group loaded into the Suburbans and followed behind Enrique to the community of Mensäbäk, a three-hour drive. When they arrived, Enrique brought out the photographs his brother, Minchu, had taken. One photo showed the entrance of the cave beneath Mensäbäk cliff, the home of the God of Black Dust and Rain. In a second photo, the officials could see god pots lined along the cave walls and skulls and long bones in a pile on the floor.

Enrique pointed to the photographs the students had taken of the bones the Tzeltales from Esperanza had shown them. One of the skulls in the photos had visible signs of trauma—a jagged hole in the crown. Then he pointed to the photo of the missing bones when they were still inside the cave. One of the skulls had a jagged hole in the exact same spot.

The archaeologists and PJR officials looked up.

"We need to see the cave," one of them said.

The group decided to divide into two teams. Enrique, the archaeologists, and half of the PJR officials would cross the lakes to the cave of Mensäbäk. The other team would drive to the Tzeltal community of Esperanza to find the men who had guided the students to the bones in the forest.

Lacandón men from Mensäbäk helped Enrique paddle the officials across Lake Ts'ibanaj and Lake Mensäbäk. When they arrived, they stood at the mouth of the cave. They could see the same arrangement of fallen trees visible in Minchu's photographs. The photographs showed multiple skulls and bones on the cave floor inside, but when the teams entered the cave, they found it empty. There were no skulls, no human bones.

The archaeologists dug a small test pit in the floor of the cave and found a human rib and vertebrae. They asked Enrique for permission to take the bones for testing in Mexico City.

Meanwhile, the other half of the PJR team was in the Tzeltal community of Esperanza interviewing the men who had led the students on the search for bones. The PJR team leader asked the men to take them to the place where they had shown the students the human remains, and with the two Tzeltales as guides, they started down the trail.

"They hiked out of Esperanza early in the morning, and they were gone all day," Enrique said. "When they hadn't returned to Mensäbäk by early afternoon, the other officials started to get worried."

Finally, at 3:00 p.m., "They drove into Mensäbäk. Inside their Suburban, they had a cardboard box. They didn't show me what was inside it."

When the PJR officials, the archaeologists, and the students left in the Suburbans the next day, they took the cardboard box and the human rib and vertebrae with them. They gave Enrique a receipt.

Life in Mensäbäk went back to normal. After a month, a phone call came from Mexico City.

"We've just about finished studying the bones," one of the archaeologists reported. "Looks like they are not from 1974."

Another month and a half passed before the archaeologist called back. "We've finished the study, and it proves the bones are not from the guerrilla fighters. The two students from Mexico City are in trouble. The bones are pre-Hispanic. They're 400 to 500 years old. They're the bones stolen from your cave."

"And don't worry about them," the archaeologist said. "We're sending them back to Mensäbäk."

And he told Enrique the rest of the story: In the search for the bones that day, the Tzeltales from Esperanza took the PJR team on a torturous ramble through the rainforest, up and down hills, around the lakes, "trying to get them tired so they would give up." But the officials persisted, and the Tzeltales "began to realize the heaviness of the situation." Finally, they led the team to the spot where they had shown the students "the bones of the guerrillas." In a shallow grave, the PJR team found four human skulls and some leg bones. They cleaned them off and carefully placed them in a cardboard box.

"The whole thing about finding the guerrillas' remains was a lie," the official said. "The two Tzeltales made up the story just to get the money."

A month later, one of the officials from Ocosingo drove into Mensäbäk, removed a cardboard box from his vehicle, and handed it to Enrique. Inside, carefully packed, were four skulls and a half dozen human bones. The ancestors were home.

"So," Enrique said, "We rowed the bones across the lake and put them back in the cave. I don't know what happened to the two students from Mexico City, but they must have been very sad they never found the bones of their relative. I know that they got cheated out of 30,000 pesos. And nothing happened to the liars, as far as I know."

"We never pressed charges against anyone, because the bones are back where they belong. They're still here. Nothing is lost. All I know is that our ancestors had no idea they would end up flying in an airplane to Mexico City."

III

Creating a Culture from a Forest

7

How to Eat a Rainforest

José Camino Viejo[1] and his wife, Josefina Koj, moved north from Sa'm in the mid-1960s, one of a dozen Lacandón Maya families forced to abandon their homes when a well-connected Mexican woman sold the logging rights to the rainforest that Lacandones had lived in for hundreds of years. The families were told that the forest they had grown up in now belonged to someone else.

José and Josefina, both around fifty-five years old at the time, carried their few possessions a several day's walk through the forest to a site just east of Lake Ts'ibanaj, where they selected a well-drained plot of black and red earth and built a small pole and palm-thatch hut to live in while they cleared land to plant crops.[2] Using only a machete and axe, José spent ten days clearing the forest undergrowth—vines, palms, and small trees—and another twenty days felling the larger trees. Then he built a large palm-thatch house and a god house on a 1.5-meter-high mound within the field while the couple waited for the felled vegetation to dry in the tropical sun.

Just before the rains began in May, José swept a 2-meter-wide firebreak around the field and set fire to the dried vegetation in a slow, carefully controlled burn that left a 6-centimeter carpet of gray ash on top of the soil. The ash concentrated the plant nutrients that, before the burn, had been held in the rainforest vegetation.[3] Once the area had cooled, José and Josefina began to plant fast-growing root and tree crops—chayotes, sweet potatoes, macal, manioc, papaya, bananas, and plantains—to capture the nutrients released by the fire and to prevent the exposed soil from eroding with the coming rains.[4] When clouds began to threaten the horizon, José moved methodically through the ash-covered field with a heavy wooden staff, punching holes in the soil and dropping in kernels of seed corn (*Zea mays*), which would soon germinate and turn the field green with promise.[5] Corn would be the couple's staple food, but they would add dozens of other crops and useful trees to the field during the coming months. While Josefina planted tomatoes, onions, chilies, and sugarcane, José moved through the field pulling up weeds that might compete with their crops. When the corn began to sprout, José chanted in the god house for a good harvest and his wife's health.

The site José and Josefina selected was hardly new to the Lacandón Maya. Their ancestors had lived in this part of the forest on and off during the past 200 years, returning every few decades to occupy sites their predecessors had cultivated years ago. Long before Lacandones migrated into the Selva Lacandona in the late 1700s, Ch'ol Maya families had farmed this same land for at least 2,000 years. The mound that José and Josefina built their house on was, in fact, scattered with building stones from the foundations of homes where countless families had lived before them.[6]

A Cultivated Landscape

During the following three years, José and Josefina planted, weeded, and harvested a cornucopia of food and fiber from their clearing in the forest. Stalks of corn dominated the area, but long vines of pumpkin squash radiated among the mounds of corn, and other crops sprouted in bunches every few meters: patches of pineapples here, manioc a few steps beyond, swatches of green onions, tomato vines, peanuts, more pineapples, five kinds of chayote, clusters of mint, a sudden mini-forest of carrizo cane for making arrows, and a shock of colorful zinnias out of nowhere. Zinnias in the middle of a cornfield? "I like its flower," José said.

A score of banana trees (plump red bananas, huge plantains, tiny finger bananas, and tasty *guineos*) ran in a long row down the middle of the field, planted in one- to two-month intervals so that every month bore fruit. Here and there among the vines and ground crops, José tended trees—limes, two kinds of oranges, papayas, guanabanas, gourds, and a solitary lemon tree that José said had sprouted by itself from a seed tossed out the door.

The planting times for some of the crops were keyed to seasonal signals, usually the flowering of natural forest species.[7] When the flowers of the mahogany tree fell, for example, José knew it was time to plant corn. The flowers of wild tamarind (*Dialium guienense*) and **ek' balche'** (*Guatteria anomala*) trees indicated the days to plant tobacco, and the flowering of the **sak'ats** tree (*Licania platypus*) marked the time to plant bottle gourds and garlic. Following these indicator species, the couple seeded their crops according to local conditions rather than by a fixed, foreign calendar.

In one section of the field, between the blackened skeletons of felled trees, José tended several dozen tobacco plants that he and his wife would roll into cigars or bind into cone-shaped bundles to sell to Tzeltal Maya who lived an hour away through the forest.

And one very important thing: There were no weeds anywhere.

Having built their home inside their agricultural field, José was constantly on site to pull up any errant weed that sprouted. The field was **paakaj**, José said, a Lacandón word that means "clear, clear, clear, with not a weed in sight."

A clear field meant his crops had less competition for water, light, and nutrients from unwanted plants and that when José planted tobacco, the plants would put forth large, healthy leaves. José piled the pulled weeds onto partially burned tree trunks inside his field, and at the end of each year's corn harvest, he added dried corn stalks and other crop debris and burned the piles in small, low-intensity fires. Then he scattered the ashes over the soil around his crops.

The couple occasionally recognized sprouting weeds as plants they could use, some of them edible, such as mamey, sapodilla, wild pineapple, or wild dogbane, and others like balsa or corkwood, ideal for making bark beds, twine, and rope.[8] They allowed those species to grow alongside their cultivated crops.

At night, animals from the surrounding forest crept into the field to sample the bounty of food crops, and if his dogs alerted him to the intruders, José emerged from the house to scare them away. He killed the edible animals—brocket deer, tepesquintle, and peccaries—with his bow and arrows, a weapon he would continue to use into the 1990s.

In a very real sense, José and Josefina had transformed their field into a combination produce market, meat larder, and hardware store that provided grain, fruits, vegetables, meat, and construction materials—all just outside their door. José and Josefina had created an edible landscape in the middle of a tropical rainforest.

After three years of harvests on the couple's original site, José cleared a second hectare of forest on the northwestern edge of his field. Again, he cut and burned the trees, then built a new pole and palm-thatch house and god house in the middle of the newly cleared field. As they had at their previous site, José and his wife planted the area in corn and several dozen other crops.

But they did not abandon their original field.

Instead, as the area regrew in natural forest species, the couple continued to care for some of the crops they had planted there. Sweet potatoes, peanuts, and manioc were still producing underground, and the half dozen orange trees and solitary lemon tree were still bearing fruit. José and Josefina called the area their **paak che' kol**, a stage of plant succession that Spanish speakers would call an *acahual* and which English speakers usually refer to as a "fallowed field." For Lacandón Maya, **paak che' kol** is an agricultural field that has been cleared of vegetation, kept absolutely clean while it produces crops, then allowed to fallow and regrow in natural forest species.

Here and there, tree crops broke through the regenerating weeds of the **paak che' kol** to offer yet another year of fruit. José cleared weed-free perimeters around the trees, but left the rest of the area to be absorbed by secondary vegetation. Gradually, the remaining root crops disappeared in the growing mass of vegetation, giving cover to coatimundis and raccoons during surreptitious visits in the night. By day, birds foraged for food in the regrowth, depositing undigested seeds from fruit they had eaten elsewhere, and field mice searched for tidbits of food left over from last year's crops. Snakes slithered in behind the mice in search of a warm meal, and a crested eagle (*Morphnus guianensis*) kept watch from overhead, eager to snatch either the snake or the field mice it was pursuing. On some mornings, flocks of **k'acho** parrots (*Amazona farinosa*) landed on the remaining stalks of corn, gleaning kernels from the husks of molded ears.

After four years of cultivation in his second field, José extended the area once again, clearing another hectare of forest in line with the previous two. He did the same thing three years after that, creating an extended rectangle of producing fields marching into the forest, one hectare always in corn, the others following behind in sequential stages of regrowth. The couple built a new house less often than they changed fields, but they were always within sight of their active cornfield, living quietly in a small clearing surrounded by a world of forest.

Fifteen years after they had made their home in the rainforest near Lake Ts'ibanaj, José and Josefina were the de facto proprietors of five hectares of cleared land, three of which were already regenerating as natural forest. And they would use those lands again. By the time they had cultivated their fifth hectare of forest for three years, the regenerating forest on their original field had grown tall enough that the couple could return there and begin the cycle anew.

José recleared their original plot's fifteen-year-old trees, dried and burned the cuttings, then once again planted corn and other crops. He found that the soil was even more fertile than the first time he had planted it. Some of the trees—avocado, **balche'**, and rubber—were still alive and growing, and José carefully cleared fire breaks around them before he burned the field for a new round of cultivation.

Although José's land-use pattern might have looked like a linear progression into the rainforest—previous plots regenerating as José cleared a new one—the actual process was more like a circle. Clear and burn a plot of forest, grow crops for three to four years, then fallow the field as a "cleaned tree garden" and allow it to regenerate as secondary forest. At the appropriate stage of growth, clear the vegetation and begin the circle again.

Well into the twenty-first century, the skilled work of José Camino Viejo and Josefina Koj continues to reverberate. Although Josefina died in the mid-1990s, followed a year later by José, the land they cleared and cultivated continues to produce for their nephews, Minchu and Enrique Valenzuela, who inherited usage rights to the clearings when José died.[9] Today, Minchu and Enrique's corn crops sprout from soil that José carefully tended for three decades, rotating food crops, tree crops, wildlife, and forest. Nothing is left of the houses that José built, but where his last god house stood, a dozen ceramic god pots lie buried to their rims in black earth, as if offering prayers for an eternity of bountiful harvests.

Minchu and Enrique say the soil is the best anywhere in the area.

Recycling the Rainforest

The traditional Lacandón Maya farming system evolved during centuries of daily experimentation as families worked to produce a sustainable supply of food and fiber without disrupting the regenerative power of the tropical forest. In fact, traditional Lacandón agricultural practices enhance the forest, making it more productive for human use, while conserving its biological diversity.

José and Josefina's farming practices cycled food crops, animal protein, and tree crops on the same small plots of land, with only slight—and temporary—impacts on the tropical forest. Lacandones transform a section of rainforest into a field for food crops, which gradually morphs into an orchard-garden, which grows again into tropical forest, which can then be cleared again for food production, and so on through a farmer's lifetime. By using controlled, low-temperature fires, aggressively weeding their crops, and enhancing forest regeneration by planting specific trees, Lacandón farmers can cultivate the same site for years, while simultaneously increasing the fertility of the soil. The farmer's descendants inherit the right to step into the cycle and continue to harvest the same plots of land their ancestors cleared decades ago.

Not all Lacandones followed José Camino Viejo's pattern. He and Josefina remained in the forest near Lake Ts'ibanaj for three decades, but most families periodically moved from site to site. Chan K'in Viejo of Naja' said that his father, José Bor García (1880–1932), moved in a circuit among lakes where he or his relatives had previously settled. During those decades, Lacandones had the freedom and the forest to go most anywhere they wanted in the vast Selva Lacandona.

"He would live only a few years in one place before migrating to a different place several hours away," Chan K'in Viejo told me. "We usually moved from one lake to another. Lake Marona to Lake Naja' to Lake Itsanojk'uj, and back again to the same places.[10] We moved when the cockroaches got too thick in our house."[11]

Other ecological factors likely played a role as well. In addition to moving to allow harvested fields to fallow and mature into forest, families changed locations when too many weevils infested their corn or tobacco lice attacked their tobacco crop.[12] The wisest course of action in such cases was to relocate to a distant, uninfected site. Relocation also allowed wildlife populations to recover from hunting, promising plentiful meat protein when the family cycled back to that location.

"Once he had enough **paak che' kols** on the different lakes, my father never had to cut large trees again," Chan K'in said. "He cut regrowth forest in places we had lived before."

In the past, the amount of old-growth forest a Lacandón farmer cleared was a function of his age and agility and how much help he had from sons or sons-in-laws performing bride service. In 1977, for example, Chan K'in José Valenzuela, age forty-two at the time, was healthy, had two wives, three sons, and one daughter, and was only midway into his agricultural career. His practice in those days was to clear two milpas each year—one from secondary forest and one from old-growth forest. He did this so he would have sufficient secondary forest to recycle by the time he grew old, but he also grew tobacco, which requires a weed-free site in order to prosper.

"The corn comes up the same in both fields—whether cleared from **paak che' kol** or from forest," Chan K'in José told me one morning as he selected tobacco leaves for harvest. "But tobacco grows better in a field cleared from forest, because fewer weeds grow there. If I plant tobacco and keep the field weeded, I can plant corn again and more tobacco the next year. But I can't plant the same field three years in a row. The corn grows well, but the field gets too weedy for tobacco."

After two years of corn and tobacco harvests, José fallowed his milpas and allowed them to regrow until pioneer trees such as balsa and shield-leaf pumpwood reached a height of 7 meters.[13]

"I don't cut a **paak che' kol** after only one year of regrowth," Chan K'in José Valenzuela said, "because the vegetation isn't thick enough. The cuttings won't burn well, and weeds would begin sprouting immediately."

"If I let the field continue to grow for more years, it turns into brush and trees. When I finally cut it and burn it, the fire kills the weeds and their seeds and the weevils."

José Valenzuela pointed out that his relative, José Camino Viejo, kept his field absolutely cleaned of weeds and was able to produce crops in the same field for up to four or five years in a row, "but his corn got weevils because he stayed in the same place for so long."

By the late 1970s, Chan K'in José Valenzuela had eleven fields in various stages of regrowth. When his oldest field had regenerated to a sufficient height, he returned to clear it again, knowing it would produce good yields of both corn and tobacco.

"I don't cut mature forest anymore," he said. "I don't have to. I have enough fallowed fields that I can cut and plant just those. It's less work for me and my sons."

Lacandón farmers say they prefer to cut agricultural fields from regrowth vegetation rather than old-growth forest for a simple reason: Clearing a 1-hectare plot of mature forest requires thirty–forty man-days of hard and dangerous labor.

"It wears out your hands," said Chan K'in José Valenzuela.

By contrast, clearing the same area of regrowth takes only eight man-days. In the decades before they began to live in fixed communities, farmers cleared as few as 10 hectares of mature rainforest during their entire agricultural career, from the ages of seventeen to seventy years (Nations and Nigh 1980). Since 1988, families have ceased to clear mature forest at all, instead recycling their crops among previously used plots.

The Underlying Science

What to call the traditional Lacandón system of food production is still up for grabs. In their native language, Lacandones simply call it **kol**, "agricultural field." But a lexicon of Lacandón terms qualifies and amplifies that simple word: soil classifications, names for the stages of crop growth, descriptions of the forest that regenerates on a fallowed plot. For example, of the seven different soil types in the northern Selva Lacandona, Lacandones consider only three arable: **k'änk'aj** (yellow-bitter), **chäk** (red), and **ek'** (black) soils are prized; **säk** (white), **k'än** (yellow), **sa'm** (sandy), and **k'an** (clay) soils are rejected (Nations and Nigh 1980: 9).

Agronomists and ecologists who actively study Lacandón agriculture variously label the system "high-performance milpa" (Ford and Nigh 2016: 65); "polyculture milpa agroforests" (Falkowski et al., 2019); "orchard-gardening," "intensive agroforestry" (Ford 2020); or "multi-stage swidden agroforestry" (Falkowski et al. 2016). By any of these names, it is a well-developed system that agroecologist Ronald Nigh describes as, "Far from being a destructive force in the forest . . . is an efficient tool for maintaining and restoring biodiversity and creating fertile anthropogenic soil."

Take a closer look at the Lacandón system, from the beginning.

Like forest farmers throughout the tropics, Lacandones create agricultural fields by felling and burning vegetation to create a nutrient-rich ash to nourish their crops. There's good reason for this seemingly destructive process. The majority of nutrients in a tropical rainforest are suspended in the leaves, stems, and trunks of the standing vegetation rather than held in the soil. Organic litter that drops to the forest floor is quickly decomposed by fungi, insects, and microscopic creatures, then reabsorbed into the vegetation through interconnected networks of roots and mycorrhizae. Clearing the vegetation from a plot of land without burning the dried cuttings would expose a soil only minimally capable of growing crops. To make the nutrients available, the farmer releases them with fire. Burning the vegetation also temporarily scours the plot of insect pests and weeds.

Lacandones set an intense, "hot" burn in a field only once—when they clear it of mature rainforest for the first time. Even then, they're careful to burn only the area they intend to cultivate. They clear 2-meter firebreaks around the perimeter of the felled vegetation to prevent the fire from escaping into the surrounding forest.

"If you burn the forest around your field," said Amado Seis, a sixty-year-old farmer in Mensäbäk, "your crops become infested with weeds. The weeds reseed the area of burned forest and then move into your field. You don't want to burn the forest except where you want to plant."

The initial "hot" burn nonetheless results in incomplete combustion, leaving behind charred tree trunks and branches that will continue to deteriorate and release nutrients into the soil during the following months and years. As the farmer pulls or chops weeds from his field, he piles them on the remaining, partially burned tree trunks to dry. After he harvests his corn, he adds the dried corn stalks and other crop debris to the piles and, before seeding a second corn crop, burns the piles in a half dozen low-intensity, "cool" fires that leave behind additional charred material. The farmer scatters these ashes over his field, adding to the existing nutrients and black carbon in the soil.

"Black carbon has a dramatic, positive effect on soil fertility," writes Nigh, "providing surface area for microbial activity and the fixing of nutrients." Burning vegetation at a low temperature produces high levels of black carbon residue associated with higher levels of phosphorus and the increased ability of soils to capture and hold nutrients that crops require. The process not only promotes quick regeneration of forest when the field is fallowed, "but assures agricultural productivity in future cycles as well," Nigh says. "Repeated intensive cycles of cultivation and regeneration can actually lead to enhanced soil fertility" (Nigh 2008: 239–240).

Even more, black carbon stored in agricultural soils can persist for long periods of time, resulting in what agronomists call Anthropogenic Dark Earths, the famous *terra preta* or "black earth" sites that indicate previous—sometimes prehistoric—occupation; for example, along the banks of rivers in the Amazon Basin, where Indigenous families have occupied and cultivated the same sites repeatedly over centuries (Hecht 2003).

Benefits of Polyculture

To capture the nutrients released by burning, and to get a head start on weeds and insects, traditional Lacandón farmers plant fast-growing tree crops and root crops—chayote, papaya, bananas, plantains, manioc, sweet potatoes, and a New World tuber called *macal* (*Xanthosoma*) (Dickenson 1972: 219). As these crops take root, the farmer and his wife plant other food and fiber crops between and around them. Corn is the primary focus, but families plant dozens of cultivars in the same field simultaneously: avocados, beans, chilies, cacao, coriander, cotton, garlic, ginger, grapefruit, guavas, lemons, limes, mint, onions, parsley, pineapples, plums, rice, squash, sugar, tobacco, tomatoes, and watermelons, among others. The result is an agricultural polyculture, a multiplicity of crops.

Westerners are accustomed to seeing monoculture crops—huge fields of the same plant species like corn or wheat—stretching to the horizon, the classic "amber waves of grain." Raising monoculture crops makes it easier to use tractors and combine harvesters, but also creates ripe opportunities for plant pests and plagues that prey on particular species, making chemical pesticides and herbicides a necessity. Instead of monocultures, Lacandón Maya farmers plant multiple crop species in the same field, dispersing them to avoid large clusters of any particular cultivar, thus minimizing plant diseases and insect infestations.

Even corn is widely distributed throughout the field. Lacandones plant corn in mounds rather than in rows. Walking through his burned field, a farmer punches holes in the earth with a 2-meter tall, wooden dibble stick. As he punches each hole, he reaches into a woven bag or armadillo carapace sewn into an open-topped container and selects a half dozen or so corn kernels—his seed corn—and drops them into the hole. He buries the seeds by sweeping soil into the hole with his foot as he slowly works his way across the field.

"I plant seven seeds in each hole," said Amado Seis. "But each person knows best. There are people who plant four or five seeds in a hole. But never ten. Ten is too many," he said. Agronomists Stewart Diemont and Jay Martin point out that planting multiple seeds of corn in the same mound ensures effective cross-pollination of the crop, improving the chances for a well-developed yield (Diemont and Martin 2009: 257).

Gilberto K'in Faisán of Lacanja' Chan Sayab told me that he mixed corn and squash seeds together before planting his field, so that even he didn't know which combination of plants would sprout from which mound. To prevent rats and mice from digging up the seeds, some Lacandones scatter extra kernels over the surface of the field as a distraction (Baer and Merrifield 1971: 179).

Once the corn germinates, the farmer bunches dirt around the young sprouts to create 20-centimeter-tall mounds throughout the field. As the cornstalks develop, the farmer and his wife or wives plant climbing beans at their base. The vines of the climbing beans wrap around the cornstalks and use them for support as they mature. As nitrogen-fixing plants, the beans also add a key nutrient to the soil, benefiting the corn. The family may also plant bush beans elsewhere in the field.

Over the course of the year, the farmer creates a diverse, polycultural garden of useful plants. In the 1990s, José Camino Viejo's active cornfield contained two dozen crop species: long rows of banana and plantain trees, clumps of onion, five kinds of chayote, peanuts growing among vines of pumpkin squash, a sudden shock of sugarcane, then cherry tomatoes, sweet potatoes, manioc, gourds, chilies, and bushes of scarlet runner beans. Nearby, his previous fields, his **paak che' kols**, were still producing tree crops and holdover plants such as pineapple, rubber, and 6-meter tall arrow cane (*Gynerium sagittatum*).

A traditional Lacandón field gradually becomes a living mass of food-producing plants occupying the entire cleared area both above and below the soil. Citrus trees mix with clusters of papaya, bananas, and plantains. The vines of squash, sweet potatoes, and jícamas cover the ground between the hills of corn. Beneath the surface, root crops lie at varying depths: taro and sweet potatoes a few inches beneath the soil, manioc below them, and yam tubers below the manioc, utilizing the available space, water, and soil nutrients in a highly efficient manner (Nations and Nigh 1980: 11). Gradually, the diversity of the field begins to emulate the diversity of the tropical forest that surrounds it.

Down in the Weeds

The farmers' crops have competition, however. Extraneous plants begin to sprout in the disturbed and exposed soil of the field shortly after it is burned. Wind and wild animals bring in seeds from the forest and nearby secondary growth, threatening the farmer's crops. To avoid the proliferation of weeds in their fields, some Lacandones demonstrate an attitude of care that approaches reverence. The trail to the field of José López (chapter 10), for example, passed over a small stream, where he and members of his family would pause to wash any stray seeds from their feet before they stepped into their cornfield. They asked visitors to do the same. (Also, no smoking while working in the field, they told me once as I stubbed out my cigar. "The gods do not like it.")

Frans Blom observed similar behavior among both Northern and Southern Lacandones in 1943. "Their milpas are very clean," he wrote, "not a weed, not a blade of grass, and if one throws a fruit peel or the like on the floor of the milpa, they immediately pick it up and carry it outside the milpa. They clean their feet before stepping into the milpa, as they do not want to bring in seeds of weeds which may stick to their feet" (Brunhouse 1976: 173).

Lacandón farmers say that aggressive, almost daily, weeding is the key factor in their ability to cultivate the same agricultural field for up to five (or even as many as seven) years in a row. By actively minimizing weeds in their fields, farmers can increase the number of sequential corn crops they produce on the same plot of land. In fact, Lacandones move to a new field not because of a decline in soil fertility, but because the amount of labor required to control weeds eventually outpaces the amount of work required to prepare a new site.

If he plans to grow corn in a field for a second (or third or fourth) year in a row, the farmer must keep his field well weeded. If he fails to do so, he must by necessity fallow the field before planting it again. A farmer who plans to fallow a field after the current harvest ceases to weed his corn crop after he doubles the ripened cornstalks. He allows the weeds to take over the field, though he may chop the weeds around tree crops that are still producing. Some farmers in both the northern and southern Selva also plant specific trees at this time to bolster the field's recovery.

Forest Enhancement

As he works in his field, a farmer may recognize some "weeds" as plants he can use. Some forest trees that sprout voluntarily in the field—a bits' tree (*Inga vera*), or red mamey (*Pouteria sapota*), for example—produce tasty fruit, and the farmer welcomes their presence. When this happens, he spares the intruders and allows them to grow alongside his crops, even to the point of clearing weeds from around them.

Lacandón farmers select for—and protect—up to twenty different tree species that sprout naturally in their fields. A few examples: The milk tree (*Sapium lateriflorum*) acts as a phosphorus pump, pulling the vital nutrient to the surface. Mastate (*Poulsenia armata*), tropical cedar (*Cedrela adorata*), and cabbage bark (*Lonchocarpus guatemalensis*) increase the amount of available phosphorous, nitrogen, and organic matter in the soil, thus improving crop yields (Falkowski et al. 2016: 212).

Although Lacandones may not fully understand the chemical interactions taking place (neither do I, I admit), they recognize that these particular trees improve the performance of their crops. They say that the trees "give food" to their crops or "provide vitamins" to their roots (Falkowski et al. 2016: 212).

The type of forest that regrows in a fallowed field is determined by the mix of species that reseed and dominate the area. Rather than leave this to chance, some Lacandón farmers intervene in the early stages of regeneration through "enrichment planting," planting tree crops that produce food or useful fiber or have positive impacts on future crop production. By enhancing the early stages of regrowth, Lacandones ensure the rapid recovery of forest on a fallowed site and simultaneously increase the density of tree species they can use. The farmer's purpose, as agroecologist Nigh puts it, "is to influence the eventual structure and function of secondary vegetation in a way that favors human subsistence." The initial goal is canopy closure, Nigh says, "though this may require soil fertility restoration as a prerequisite" (Nigh 2008: 231).

To augment forest regeneration and soil fertility, some farmers actively seed native trees in their fields as they transition them into **paak che' kols**. One key species used in this practice is balsa (*Ochroma pyramidale*). Some Lacandones protect naturally sprouting balsa trees in regrowing fields, and others deliberately cast balsa seeds onto a field as they fallow it, in order to increase organic matter and enrich the soil, a process known in Western regenerative agriculture as "sheet mulching." Balsa trees control weeds and grasses by maturing into a dense, continuous canopy over the regrowing plot. The trees grow rapidly and can produce canopy closure in one or two years, shading out invasive species such as the aggressive bracken fern (*Pteridium aquilinum*).

Balsa also inhibits nematodes in the soil and attracts bats and kinkajous (*Poto flavus*), which bring in seeds of desirable long-lived trees such as breadnut ramón (*Brosimum alicastrum;* **ox**), hog plum (*Spondias mombin*), Santa María (*Calophyllum brasilense*), and majagua (*Heliocarpus appendiculatus*) (Diemont et al. 2005; Nigh 2008; Douterlungne et al. 2010; Cheng, Diemont, and Drew 2011; Levy-Tacher and Golicher 2004; Diemont and Martin 2009).

The results of Lacandones' intervention in natural forest succession, say environmental scientists, "support the claim that the Lacandon Maya are actively engineering their agroecosystems to enhance soil fertility based on long-term trial-and-error experimentation and close observation of vegetation responses to different management techniques" (Falkowski et al. 2016: 216).

With its mix of natural and semidomesticated tree species, the fallowed milpa begins to take on the aspect of the surrounding forest, populated by myriad young saplings stretching through the weeds for sunlight. When the trees reach a suitable height, the farmer may return to the site and clear and burn its vegetation to begin the cycle anew. If he allows the field "to cool" (as Lacandones say) for several decades, the end result is "reestablishment of long-lived mature canopy trees on the once-cultivated parcel" (Ford and Nigh 2016: 43; Nigh 2008: 235).

Abundant Harvests

The traditional Lacandón agricultural system is productive as well as eco-logically sound. In a good year, a single hectare can produce more than 2,000 kilograms of shelled corn, easily providing the 5 kilograms that the average Lacandón family prepares daily to make tortillas, tamales, and corn drinks, plus occasional balls of dough tossed to the family dogs. Corn spoiled by weevils or corn fungus is fed to household chickens and turkeys (Nations and Nigh 1980; de la Cruz Guillén 2004: 8).

Most Lacandón farmers plant a corn crop in April or May and harvest it in August or September, depending on weather conditions, and many plant a second corn crop in the same field in November/December—a crop called **päten när**, "first corn," because they harvest it the following March, making it the first corn of the new "green year." Some farmers plant only once per year, but plant two fields at the same time.

As we have seen, farmers' fields and **paak che' kols** also produce root crops, vegetables, and fruit, creating a steady volume of food that meets a family's nutritional requirements in most years. Not every harvest is a good one, of course. Regional droughts and the opposite—hurricanes and floods—periodically hit the Selva Lacandona, and there have been lean years. During a 1950 stay among the Southern Lacandones of San Quintín, Frans Blom and Gertrude Duby Blom learned of starvation conditions among the families living not far away on the Río Jataté.

"For several years their crops had failed," Blom wrote, "too much rain when burning the clearings and scorching sun when the maize grew up. They are emaciated, weak, with hungry bellies. Their small children are skeletons in a sack of skin." Mexican officials responded to the Bloms' re-quest for help and packed in food and medicines to the suffering families (Brunhouse 1976: 213–214).

But in most years, the fields produce an ample supply of food, and fami-lies supplement their crops with bushmeat and foods gathered in the near-by forest. Baer and Merrifield noted, "The corn tortilla and corn gruels are the essential elements of the Lacandón diet, and when there is a plentiful supply of corn many other potential sources of food may be ignored" (Baer and Merrifield 1971: 172).

In the past, when a food crisis struck, the backup plan included hearts of palm, snails, crawfish, crabs, fish, edible fruits gathered in the forest, and tortillas made from ramón nuts.

Animals in the Garden

In addition to producing food from plant crops, Lacandón agricultural fields carry another benefit: hunting in cultivated and fallowed fields provides meat protein. Animals attracted to a farmer's milpa during the night may end up as food for the family the following day. To accommodate predation by animals, some farmers plant extra quantities of the animals' favorite foods. At night, hunters wait for the animals to enter their field, then shoot the edible ones with a .22-caliber rifle or bow and arrows. Research in the Latin American tropics indicates that the presence of garden plots in a tropical forest can actually expand the populations of certain wild animals by increasing the animals' food supply (Linares 1976; Denevan 1992: 375).

Lacandón farmers also have techniques for deflecting pest animals from their food crops. When their corn has ripened, farmers double the corn-stalks by whacking them head-high with the back of a machete blade and bending the stalks to point the ears of corn downward toward the ground. Doubling the stalks prevents rain from entering the gap at the top of the enveloping husks, minimizes mold, and helps prevent losses to high winds and flocks of parrots. It also helps prevent coatimundis and raccoons from climbing the stalks and using their body weight to bring the corn stalks to the ground so they can devour the ears. To prevent animal marauders from raiding the family's corn supply, some farmers purposely leave a section of corn stalks undoubled along one edge of their field. Lacandones normally do not eat either coatis or raccoons,[14] but say that allocating this "obligatory margin" to the animals decreases overall crop loss. In that sense, the milpa garden is also a form of wildlife management, and crops designated to feed wild animals are an investment in future food supplies.

Evolution and Adaptation

The earliest descriptions of Lacandón farming, hunting, and food collection—reports from the late 1790s and 1800s—still held true into the 1960s, when Lacandón families began to concentrate into permanent settlements in reduced areas of forest. Even today, Lacandón families continue to practice the essential aspects of the traditional agricultural system, though many have had to adjust to changes in their physical and economic environments.

A quick overview: Southern Lacandones in Lacanja' Chan Sayab live today in household clusters dispersed, like nodes in a neural network, along the few dirt roads that run through their community. Family groupings are separated from one another by agricultural fields and small parcels of forest. The Northern Lacandón families who migrated in the 1980s from Mensäbäk and Naja' to Bethel and San Javier—only a few kilometers from Lacanja' Chan Sayab—established a more tightly packed community than their neighbors. A few families have milpas near their houses, but others walk or drive to their fields. As one Southern Lacandón man said about these northern cousins, "They bunch people together."

In the northern settlements of Naja' and Mensäbäk, Northern Lacandones live in concentrated settlements of extended families spread along the one road that leads to—and in the case of Naja', through—their community. Instead of living inside their fields, as their grandparents did, they walk or drive motorcycles or pickups to access them.

Both Northern and Southern Lacandón farmers still cultivate corn, beans, squash, chilies, and root crops in their fields and plant fruit trees in house gardens around their homes. But few families live inside their active milpas, and farmers weed their fields less frequently than their parents and grandparents did. Instead, they periodically chop weeds with machetes, a practice that can disperse weed seeds and cause additional weeds to sprout. Rampant weed growth requires farmers to rotate fields more frequently and leads to shortened fallowing periods and lessened crop production.

Agricultural practices have also changed in reaction to Lacandones' conservation of their tropical forest. Since 1988, when the families of Mensäbäk and Naja' declared their territories Flora and Fauna Protection Areas (see chapter 19, "Saving a Rainforest"), Lacandones have chosen not to clear milpas from old-growth forest. Instead, they clear only recuperated fallowed fields.

The 450 families in Naja' have access to an average of 4 to 7 hectares of **paak che' kol** per family. They rotate fields frequently, planting two crops per year per field for one to three years. Naja' farmers carry out only minimal weeding—in May, June, and August—piling up and burning the weeds and crop debris before they plant another corn crop in the same field. They fallow a field for four to seven years before cycling back to plant it again.

In Mensäbäk, where only 173 people live in a territory almost as large as Naja', farmers average ten-plus **paak che' kols** per family. Like the families of Naja', they tend to plant the same field for one to three years and conduct only minimal weeding—at two months and just before harvest if the milpa will be planted again. If they don't intend to plant a field again that year, they stop weeding after they double the corn in late July or August and allow the field to fallow for nine–fifteen years.

In the more expansive territory of Lacanja' Chan Sayab and nearby Bethel and San Javier (population ±1,095, mid-2021), farmers have access to twice as much secondary forest. They tend to cultivate a field for four to six years, then fallow it for seven to twelve years (Levy-Tacher and Golicher 2004: 497).

Weeding and burning extracted weeds and crop debris pay off for only so many harvests. As Minchu Valenzuela said, "Once the weeds take over a milpa, you can't find your root crops like sweet potatoes anymore. They're hidden in the regrowth. Also, they get eaten by animals that come at night. They use the weeds as cover to move in and eat the leaves. After the third year," Minchu added, "the native grass begins to invade, and I fallow the plot and let it regrow. I don't plant other trees. After four or five years of fallowing, I go back to that field and burn it and start over."

Under twenty-first-century conditions, Lacandones also have changed the number and variety of crops they plant. Modern Lacandón farmers plant fewer crops than their ancestors did. Field research in Northern and Southern Lacandón communities during the late 1970s and early 1980s produced a list of fifty-six cultivars growing in active Lacandón milpas, plus another two dozen species in **paak che' kols** and house gardens (Nations and Nigh 1980). Thirty years later, researchers identified thirty-seven species in milpas and another eleven in house gardens within the community of Naja' (Contreras and Mariacas 2016: 57). Only twenty-six species and varieties were growing in milpas at Lacanja' Chan Sayab (Diemont and Martin 2009).

Most families have abandoned the cultivation of tobacco and cotton entirely, because they can buy commercial substitutes in nearby towns and cities. Lacandones formerly planted and harvested tobacco in their milpa gardens to sell to neighboring Tzeltal Maya and itinerant middlemen who bought the harvest and funneled it into the regional tobacco market. Today, fewer smokers, the development of industrial tobacco manufacturing, and the easy availability of cigarettes in local stores have almost eliminated tobacco as a cash crop. A few Lacandón men continue to plant tobacco, but mostly to sell to visitors as ready-roll cigars at US$1 per stogie. For most families, tobacco is no longer a viable source of income. The change has impacted modern agriculture, because Lacandones who don't grow tobacco have less incentive to aggressively weed their crops, leading to shortened fallow times and a loss of crop productivity.[15]

Most families have also dropped the cultivation of cotton, because they can buy commercial bolts of cloth in nearby towns and cities. As recently as the 1990s, a few Lacandones (Chan K'in Viejo among them) still planted cotton to be spun and woven into ceremonial tunics for religious ceremonies. But the practice has fallen by the wayside. As early as 1907, Tozzer noted that, "Every [Lacandón] Indian along the Usumacinta still has his cotton patch," but also that, "There is some fear that the arts of spinning and weaving, long since vanished from Yucatan, will also disappear among the Lacandones in another generation. They now buy the cotton cloth of Mexican manufacture for their commonest clothes" (1907: 55).

Today, new crops are taking the place of tobacco and cotton. Being much more integrated into the cash economy than their predecessors, twenty-first-century Lacandón families need money to buy gasoline, books and supplies for their children's education, and foods such as oil, sugar, and salt. Growing chili peppers, coffee, and xate palm can provide needed sources of income.

Some Lacandones now depend on the sale of chili peppers into commercial markets. Chili cultivation frequently entails the use of pesticides and is labor intensive at harvest, but families can produce a profitable crop on as little as one-eighth to one-quarter hectare of land.

Shade-grown coffee is also important. As a major export crop from the State of Chiapas, coffee already has established commercial networks and requires only 1 to 2 hectares of active land to be lucrative, when coffee prices are normal. Coffee is a perennial crop and is compatible with forest conservation, because farmers grow arabica coffee under the shade of mature, natural forest cleared of undergrowth or beneath the shade of mature **paak che' kols** cleared of weeds.

Several Lacandón farmers are experimenting with xate palm production. Lacandones already gather naturally-occurring xate palm fronds in the rainforest, taking care not to kill the palm trees, because xate is a renewable natural resource. Harvesters can cut one or two fronds from the same palm every two to three months if they are careful to leave the plant alive. They sell the harvested fronds to middlemen who appear periodically in the Lacandón communities to truck them to Tenosique for sorting and sale into the international floral market. A few Lacandones now plant xate palms in half-hectare plots beneath mature forest cleared of undergrowth or, as in the case of coffee, beneath the regenerating trees of fallowed milpas.

The hard, hot work of agriculture prompts some Lacandones—those who can afford to do so—to hire Tzeltal Maya as day laborers to help them clear vegetation, plant corn, and weed their fields. Cash income from the sale of chilies, coffee, xate, and handicrafts, as well as salaries as forest guards and guides, allows them to pay decent wages. Many of the laborers they hire are sons of landless Tzeltal Maya families who arrived in the Selva Lacandona after all communal lands had been distributed.

Although Lacandón Maya farming practices are changing under outside pressures, most Lacandón farmers still practice sustainable, organic agriculture for food crops, reserving pesticides for the chili peppers they sell to middlemen in the regional marketing network.

"I don't put chemicals on anything but the chilies I sell," said Minchu Valenzuela. "I plant chilies in one part of my field, and if the plants get infested with insects, I spray those plants and nothing else."

Researchers Levy-Tacher and Golicher noted this change in their detailed study of Lacandón traditional ecological knowledge. "Older members of the Lacandón communities," they wrote, "have a rich understanding of vegetation properties. This knowledge includes a complex classification system for patterns and processes that occur as the vegetation cover develops following disturbance through slash and burn. However, many younger members of the community have adopted simplified but economically more profitable farming methods in which soil fertility and weed control are obtained through the use of chemical inputs" (Levy-Tacher and Golicher 2004: 497). Similarly, Contreras and Mariaca reported that some Lacandón farmers of Naja' have begun to use Paraquat on weeds in their cornfield (Contreras and Mariaca 2016: 64).

A few families in Naja' have ceased to plant and harvest fields altogether. Instead, they purchase corn from relatives and buy additional food in stores using cash earned from other sources, especially the sale of handicrafts such as seed necklaces, carved cooking spoons, and clay animals (Tatiana Villalpando, personal communication, March 2021). With access to vehicles and roads, some Lacandón families in both northern and southern communities periodically buy groceries in supermarkets in Chancalá, Ocosingo, and Palenque. In Palenque, families shop at Bodega Aurrerá, a big-box supermarket owned by Walmart, which is now Mexico's largest food retailer (Jacobs and Richtel 2017: A15). They purchase rice, cooking oil, pasta, and sugar, as well as flashlight batteries, medicine, and school notebooks.

Despite the changes and challenges, the Lacandón Maya agroforestry system is still more protective of biodiversity, less consumptive of natural resources, and provides a more varied diet than most of the food- and income-producing techniques utilized by other Indigenous groups in today's Selva Lacandona—especially the production of beef cattle.

Tzeltal and Ch'ol communities in the Selva Lacandona have dedicated the majority of their holdings to milpas and cattle pasture, leaving little land in forest. Cattle ranching eliminates forest regeneration, because deforested plots end up as pastureland and stay that way. If the farmer/rancher overgrazes the pastures, they devolve into scrub growth that even the cattle disdain.

At the same time, two factors—population density and the restriction of agriculture to specified zones within their territories—threaten Lacandón agricultural production in the future. Researchers note, "Lacandon ecological knowledge has the potential to facilitate the restoration of degraded tropical forests in Chiapas, Mexico," but add that, "our findings also demonstrate that shortening fallow periods will undermine the ecological integrity of this traditional system" (Falkowski, Diemont, and Douterlungne 2016; Falkowski, Chankin, and Diemont 2019).

Still, the researchers say, the Lacandón system "underscores the potential of Lacandón agroforestry management to provide rural smallholder farmers in the Lacandón rainforest with food sovereignty while maintaining nearby forest cover to conserve biodiversity and other ecosystem services" (Falkowski, Chankin, Diemont, and Pedian 2019).

Conservation Impacts of the Traditional Farming System

The Lacandón system of food production and forest regeneration has drawn serious attention from ecologists and agricultural researchers, producing a flurry of detailed publications on the functions and benefits of its elements and impacts. Conservation biologists point out that among fast-growing populations in regions of the tropics that are being devastated by deforestation and ecological degradation, systems like that of the Lacandón Maya promise highly positive potential benefits for farmers and their families.

As Diemont and Martin put it, "The effects on biodiversity and soil ecology, coupled with productivity for agricultural subsistence, indicate that Lacandón traditional ecological knowledge may offer tools for environmental conservation that would provide for a family's basic needs while maintaining a biodiverse rainforest ecosystem" (Diemont and Martin 2009).

"Lacandón agricultural knowledge," adds Ronald Nigh, "may offer options for regional restoration and conservation efforts where attainment of environmental goals must include methods to provide resources for local inhabitants. The knowledge and skill revealed in Maya milpa agroforestry are invaluable tools for conservation of tropical biodiversity" (Nigh 2008: 232).

So far, Lacandón agricultural practices are still supporting families in all three major Lacandón communities, while simultaneously preserving old-growth tropical rainforest. Moreover, ongoing scientific research within the communities—with the cooperation and input of Lacandón farmers—promises new understanding and adaptations that may aid Lacandones and other farmers throughout the Selva Lacandona.

On another positive note, Lacandón resilience and innovation continue unabated in the face of twenty-first-century changes. Armando Valenzuela, born in Mensäbäk, earned a university degree in forest engineering, but declined offers to manage coffee plantations elsewhere in Chiapas to return to Mensäbäk to oversee a community nursery of hardwood trees established with the assistance of the Mexican federal government. He is now joining other community farmers in experimenting new ways to enhance the forest, taking advantage of a federal reforestation program called Sembrando Vida, "Sowing Life," which pays farmers in nineteen Mexican states US$250 per month to reforest up to 2.5 hectares each of previously cleared land (Bloomberg News 2021). Stand by for new developments as Lacandón farmers continue to combine traditional Lacandón ecological knowledge with new ideas and financial incentives.[16]

Looking backward, we know that during at least two centuries in the rainforest of northern Guatemala and eastern Chiapas, Lacandón families lived in family compounds of a dozen or so women, men, and children, all closely related by blood and marriage. A family's nearest neighbors lived a half-hour to a day's hike away down forest trails purposely camouflaged against detection, a self-induced social distancing that was a reaction to the dual threats of disease and potential violence perpetrated by outsiders.

Families built their houses inside their agricultural fields, hunted the surrounding forest, and worked the same fields until weeds or insect pests became too prolific to continue on that site. They changed fields, and sometimes complete locations every two to five years. When they did move, the families returned to lakeshores or riverbanks where they or members of their families had previously cleared old-growth forest and left behind secondary regrowth. As a small society in an enormous tropical forest, Lacandones made almost no visible impact on the natural ecosystems they depended on for survival.

In the twenty-first century, Lacandones live in concentrated communities and are adapting their agricultural traditions to changes in their social, economic, and physical environment. They remain, nonetheless, key players in the future of agricultural production and rainforest conservation in Mexico's largest remaining tropical rainforest.

8

Farming with the Ants

Farming in the rainforest is no walk in the park. The goal is to transform soil, rain, and forest vegetation into an edible garden of corn, beans, squash, root crops, and fruit. Yet through hundreds of years of trial and error, passing information from generation to generation, the Lacandón Maya have finessed this challenge, developing a farming system that is wildly productive and precisely adapted to their forest environment. Luckily, they have leaf-cutter ants to help them.

Leaf-cutter ants (*Atta* spp. and *Acromyrmex* spp.) are the indefatigable cargo bearers you've watched on forest trails, long lines of them scurrying along a path through the leaf litter, each ant carrying a tiny piece of serrated leaf like a tiny wind sail over its head. Like the Lacandones, leaf-cutter ants are also farmers. When the ants arrive at the mound that houses their colony, they carry the leaf pieces through the entrance tunnel into an underground maze of passageways. They deposit the leaves in designated chambers, where their fellow ants use them as fodder to grow a specific fungus under precisely regulated temperature and humidity. Other groups of ants harvest the fungus and feed it to the colony's larvae.

To the Lacandones, leaf-cutter ants can be either a benefit or a threat.

First, the benefit: Leaf-cutter ants gather food for the colony's fungus farm by climbing rainforest vegetation and using their specially adapted vibrating jaw to scissor out slices of leaf. Because a colony may have as many as a million individual ants—along with the important queen, who births the ant larvae—a colony can defoliate a sizable section of forest in short order. For centuries, the Lacandón Maya used this impact to their advantage.

Imagine having to clear a hectare-sized section of mature tropical forest. You're facing buttressed trees up to a meter in diameter decorated with hanging lianas and crowded by saplings, ferns, and vines. All of it dense, tough, and tenacious. And your only tools are stones. No metal axe, no machete, just flint or arduously hand-ground jadeite axes tightly bound to a hardwood handle with homemade twine or rawhide. Now, go clear the forest.

Maybe the ants can help. Before Lacandones acquired metal tools in the 1700s, they established forest garden plots by seeking out mounds of leaf-cutter ants. After all, the ants had already defoliated a plot in the forest, opening a gap of incoming sunlight that the farmer could expand to cultivate crops. (Where there were no ant mounds, they sought out gaps created by fallen trees.) Leaf-cutter ants create mounds up to 30 meters across and 7 meters deep. The soil is rich in organic matter—the perfect place to begin a garden if all you have are stone tools.

Like modern Lacandones, the ancestors preferred to plant their milpas in a secondary forest, places they or a previous generation had already farmed, because regenerated plots are easier to clear than mature forest, and crop productivity is just as good or better. Fortunately, leaf-cutter mounds are more common in secondary forest than in mature forest due to greater availability of palatable forage, pioneer species in particular (van Gils and Vanderwoude 2012: 914–915).

Whether planting in regrowth or mature forest, the ancestors of today's Maya farmers didn't try to fell every tree on the plot. Instead, they girdled the trees, incising the bark completely around the circumference. Removing a strip of bark around the trunk kills the tree and dries it out. Using a leaf-cutter ant mound as the epicenter of a new garden, farmers expanded their cultivation area with concentric rings of girdled trees.[1] After two to three months, farmers burned the dried vegetation with a slow, controlled fire to produce a nutrient-rich ash in which to plant their crops.

The process was made easier for Lacandones after they secured metal tools by trading with other Maya groups or directly with Europeans. The first recorded incident of Lacandones acquiring such tools came in 1786, when the servant of a Spanish priest exchanged metal blades and axe heads for beeswax, fruit, and cacao carried by Lacandones approaching the town of Palenque (Boremanse 1998: 4). Metal tools were highly prized, because they transformed the work of cutting firewood, carving canoes, and clearing land for agriculture.

But wait. Even with metal tools, the farmer still faces a challenge from leaf-cutter ants. Ants harvest vegetation to grow fungi to feed their larvae. What's to keep the leaf-cutter ants from chewing their way through a farmer's corn crop? Truth be told, unless the proper ceremonies are performed, leaf-cutter ants threaten the Lacandón farmer, because leaf-cutter ants will slice up corn, manioc, and other crops as quickly as they will natural forest. In fact, Lacandones say that leaf-cutter ants will even eat the seed corn the farmer drops into dibbled holes unless he first performs specific rites.

The first step is acknowledging the ants' plight. Traditionally, a Lacandón farmer offered a prayer to the leaf-cutter ants before planting a milpa, asking forgiveness for burning the vegetation and growing crops on the ants' mound.

After the prayer, things got serious. To convince an ant colony to abandon their mound and relocate, the farmer would grab a tree branch and pound on the mound's main entrance.

There's a reason for this.

As Chan K'in Juanito López told me, "Leaf-cutter ants, they have a lord, and he understands language. If you strike the ant mound with a branch, the little lord will come out of the entrance and look up at you. You talk with him. You tell the ant lord, 'I'm planting my corn here, don't eat it. You eat tree leaves! Eat regrowth! If you eat my corn, I'll hit you.'"

The little lord goes back into the mound and gathers the rest of the ants, and they move somewhere else.

"If they don't leave," Chan K'in Juanito continued, "you light a fire on top of their mound and toast them." With that, they will definitely leave, he concluded.

In the Lacandón community of Naja', Robert Bruce learned of a last, desperate measure to rid a milpa of leaf-cutter ants: Plant cocoyam (macal, *Xanthosoma mafaffa*), a native root crop similar to taro, on the mound. The fine roots of the cocoyam penetrate the ants' subterranean passageways, blocking their movement. If the ants bite the roots, the plant releases a sticky resin that is deadly to them. Lacandón farmers told Bruce that planting cocoyam on the mounds of recalcitrant leaf-cutter ants quickly reduces the ants' activities above ground and causes the colony to migrate or die (Bruce, Robles, and Ramos 1971: 150).

Anthropologist Didier Boremanse and linguist Suzanne Cook both recorded a fable about leaf-cutter ants that reminds Lacandones they should not harm the ants unless they have good reason (Boremanse 2006: 284–286; Cook 2019: 398–404).

According to the story, many years ago leaf-cutter ants filed into a Lacandón ancestor's corn crib and began carrying away his corn. To fight back, the farmer burned the ants' path through the forest and yelled at them: "I have nothing else to eat, but you have forest leaves for your food."

The ants paid no attention to the ancestor and continued to haul away his corn. This made the man so angry that he grabbed a tree branch and began to pound on the ant mound. Suddenly, the lord of the ants appeared.

"Now this!" said the ant lord. "You're always burning up my children and now you're destroying their home?"

The farmer explained that the ants had stolen his corn and now he had nothing to eat.

"That's certain," said the ant lord. "My children are thieves. They've eaten all your food. But you have to quit burning their mounds. Poor things."

"That's for sure," said the Lacandón man. "The ants have to eat, but right now I'm the one left with nothing."

Considering this, the ant lord promised that the man would be compensated. "The ants will return what they've taken from you."

"But," he told the man, "you must move your home into your milpa. If you do, my ant children will build you a house there and give you back your food."

"Agreed," said the man.

The following day, the man hiked to his milpa and, to his surprise, saw that his crops were totally free of weeds. The ants had removed every single weed from his field. And, as the ant lord had promised, they had built a house and a corn crib, which was now chock-full of corn.

The ancestor was still standing before the corn crib, bewildered, when one of his relatives walked up.

"It looks like you have food to eat," the relative said. "What have you done to have such a beautiful milpa and so much corn?"

"I didn't do it," the ancestor insisted. "The leaf-cutter ants weeded my field and brought me this corn."

The ancestor went on to describe what had happened: The ants had stolen his corn, and he had burned their mound and destroyed it. But the ants nonetheless cleaned his milpa and brought him back his food.

"Well, then," said the visitor. "I'm going to do the same thing."

The Lacandón ancestor protested that such a plan might not work, but the visitor ignored him. Instead, he sought out an ant mound and began to pound it with a branch. Then he built a fire on top to destroy it. As the ants fled the mound, the ant lord suddenly appeared.

"Quit burning my children," he yelled at the man. "What have they ever done to you?"

"They didn't bring me food," the man replied. "I have nothing to eat. You can see that they stole all my corn—look at the kernels they left on the trail there."

But the ant lord had seen the man scattering kernels of corn along the ants' trail, and he knew the man was lying about what he had done.

"The ants didn't steal your corn," the ant lord said. "It was you who scattered corn kernels along their path."

"No," the man protested, "the ants robbed me." And he demanded reparation.

"Enough," shouted the ant lord. "The ants will give you what you deserve. Go to your milpa tomorrow and you'll see your food there."

The following day, when the man walked to his milpa, he saw that it was still full of weeds. The ants had not cleared any of them. But when he walked to his corn crib, he was happy to see that it was totally filled with corn.

"Ah, at least I've got food to eat," he thought.

But it wasn't corn he was looking at. It was a nest of wasps that the ants had carried into the corn crib. When the man reached in to grab some corn, the wasps attacked him. They stung him so many times that he spent the rest of the day in bed with a fever.

As the man lay there, suffering, the ant lord appeared to him and said, "Don't burn the leaf-cutter ants if they've done nothing to you. Don't destroy their nests without reason."

And from that day forward, the ants never again worked for this man in his milpa. Instead of bringing him corn, they had brought him wasps out of revenge. The man who burned ants for no reason had been taught a lesson.

Western science backs up what the Lacandones say about leaf-cutter ants and milpas. (The little lord may be a stretch, but who knows?) Research in the rainforest of southern Colombia revealed that leaf-cutter colonies exposed to full sun either relocate or die. Removing all the forest canopy over a leaf-cutter mound produces microclimatic changes that include higher soil and air temperatures and lower soil moisture. These changes prompt the ants to relocate to sites that are still covered with forest (van Gils and Vanderwoude 2012: 919).

Deforested nests within 50 meters of natural forest relocate and survive, while colonies farther away die out. If there are no suitable forest sites nearby, the ant colonies are wiped out completely. Add to this the impact of the fire the farmer uses to burn the cleared vegetation, because a milpa fire also wreaks havoc on air and soil temperatures within the mound. Little wonder that the ants move somewhere else.

Bottom line: Science supports the Lacandones' traditional ecological knowledge about leaf-cutter ants. Even more, their oral history promotes conservation of the ants and their natural activities. Don't harm leaf-cutter ants unless you have reason to, the story teaches. Otherwise, you could end up with a fistful of wasps.

9

Teaching a Canoe to Swim

"If I don't have other work, a relative and I can carve a canoe in 15 days," Chan K'in José Valenzuela said.

For centuries, the Lacandones have crafted dugout canoes from giant trees in the Selva Lacandona. Using nothing more than axes and machetes, two Lacandón men can carve a large canoe from a tree trunk in surprisingly short order.

Preparations for making the canoe begin much earlier, of course.

A man who needs a new canoe must first find a suitable tree not far from the lake or river where he lives. The premier choice is a large mahogany tree (*Swietenia macrophylla*), but in a pinch a Santa María tree will do (*Calophyllum brasiliense*). A mature tree of either species has a large, straight bole that can be fashioned into a long, wide canoe. (Truth be told, in decades of visiting Lacandón settlements, I never saw a canoe made from a Santa María tree, but they tell me it can be done.)

Mahogany trees grow up to 45 meters in height, with trunks that exceed 3–3.7 meters in diameter. They have a long, clean trunk that can climb 25 meters upward before extending its first limb, a quality that makes it possible to carve a huge dugout canoe capable of carrying fifteen to twenty people (Shono and Snook 2006; Tozzer 1907: 55).

On his fourth voyage to the Americas, Christopher Columbus and his men encountered an ocean-going Maya canoe off the coast of the Bay Island of Guanaja, Honduras. They described it as "eight feet wide, all of a single trunk" with a crew of twenty-five and amidships "a canopy of palm leaves" under which were children, women, and all the baggage and merchandise (Sauer 1969: 128). That's a big canoe, one of many in a fleet the Maya utilized to ply the coast of Yucatán from the Gulf of Mexico to the Bay of Honduras.

But most Maya canoe traffic was inland, on the large rivers of the lowland rainforest and dozens of minor tributaries that radiate like capillaries through the forest. Up and down these jungle rivers, the Maya, both before and after the Classic period, traded honey, tobacco, tree resins, bird feathers, animal pelts, obsidian, ceramics, cacao, and captured warriors.

They traveled in carved mahogany canoes. The internal wood of the mahogany tree is dense and uniform and resistant to rot and mold, making it ideal for a water environment. When a mahogany tree dries after being felled, it shrinks uniformly, maintaining shape both width-wise and length-wise, preventing the wood from warping.

So, following direct observation and a description by Chan K'in José Valenzuela: Two men and one giant tree, now felled and seasoned for up to a year where it crashed to the forest floor. Each man stands beside it with a metal axe in his hand, mentally conceptualizing the canoe that's hidden inside.

The men decide how long the canoe should be, given the tree's length and width, and begin by blocking off the desired section with their axes. Once the section is hacked free from the tree's crown, they chop off and lift heavy blocks of mahogany wood from the area that will become the open top of the canoe. They will later carve some of these mahogany blocks into tables that their wives will use for corn grinding and food preparation. They will craft other pieces into paddles and short-legged tables for patting out tortillas.

With the top level of the tree trunk removed, they begin to dig out the inside of the canoe, chop, chop, chopping to create the hollow where the family will sit.

Some Indigenous groups in South America set small fires inside canoes at this point to save themselves days of excavating the hollow of the log. Lacandones don't burn the inside of the canoe. They chop. For days. And days. Until the inside looks like a place where you could stand, dig your paddle into the water, and push yourself across the lake.

With the inside of the canoe taking shape, the men begin to focus on the outside.

The goal is to carve a canoe that is light and buoyant enough to maneuver, but sturdy enough to support the weight of passengers. To carve the outside of the canoe, the men use their axes to shear off the tree's bark and taper the front and back. The hull must be slightly rounded to slip through the water, and the canoe must come to a point at the bow and stern to minimize drag.

When those jobs are complete, the men are looking at a canoe that can be refined into the finished product. Shape the bow a little, stand back, take a look down the length, shape a bit more, stand back. Just a bit more off that side. Definitely a canoe now—one that will last a decade.

Getting the finished canoe to the water is the next challenge. Recognize that, even with the bark removed and the inside carved into a hollow, this is still a singularly heavy object, weighing much more than anyone can pick up, even with lots of help. How to get it to the lake?

Archaeologists puzzle over the fact that the Maya—even at the height of the Classic era—utilized the wheel on children's toys, but not as a tool for transportation. But there are ways to mimic the effect of wheels. Two men want to move this heavy canoe through the forest to the lakeshore. Here's the trick: they lay a series of small limbs crossways on the ground in a path that leads from the forest to the lake. Laid perpendicular to the length of the canoe, the limbs serve as a stationary conveyor belt, over which the two men push the canoe down the path. Maybe they enlist a couple friends to keep the momentum going.

Lacandones also use this method to portage canoes over peninsulas of land. Lake Ts'ibanaj and Lake Mensäbäk, for example, link directly to one another when the lakes are full, but during the rest of the year, when lake levels are lower, a small peninsula of land divides them. Travelers who want to cross from one lake into the other lay 2.5-centimeter-wide poles in a path across the section of land and push the canoe over the limbs from one lake into the other. And go back to paddling.

This is not a new trick. While searching for the archaeological site of Yaxchilán in 1882, the British explorer Alfred Maudslay encountered evidence of the same system. Seeking to visit a settlement of Lacandones 3 kilometers into the forest from the Río Usumacinta, Maudslay wrote that he and his bearers "followed a narrow path into the forest marked by two jaguars' skulls stuck on poles, and here and there by some sticks laid across the track, over which the Indians had probably dragged their small canoes" (Maudslay and Maudslay 1899: 236).

Once the Lacandón canoe builders have rolled the newly carved canoe to the lake and slipped it into the water, they might be tempted to step into it and see how it feels. But no: An important step comes first. The canoe must learn to swim.[1]

To do this, the Lacandones ask the animals for help.

Their first step is to tie the new canoe to a shoreline tree. Then they go fishing.

"You have to catch a bunch of fish and carry them back to the new canoe," Minchu Valenzuela told me. "You attach one string of fish to the front of the canoe and another string of fish to the back. Then, you go home for the night."

As night falls, turtles and crocodiles approach the new canoe and recognize it as a relative. They gently coax the canoe to go out into the water "so it can become family with the lake." The fish hanging from the canoe's bow and stern are the animals' payment for their work.

"The crocodile is the older brother of the canoe," Minchu said. "He shows the canoe how to glide through the water."

"And turtles know how to swim," he went on. "They teach the canoe to swim."

The following morning, when the canoe owner returns to the canoe, he finds that the fish are gone, eaten by the crocodiles and turtles, and the canoe—now an accomplished swimmer—is ready to travel. The man and his family climb in and paddle off for a turn around the lake.

In the Lacandón version of "the quiet game," the father admonishes his children not to talk while he paddles, because too much chatter will cause K'echem, the Wind God, to stir up waves and dump them unceremoniously into the lake. The children zip their lips, and dad smiles as he digs his paddle into the water.

10

Fibers, Vines, and Fire in the Night

In the beginning, the gods created plants. And stone. And animals. And soil. And water. And fire.

Those are the gifts the gods gave the Lacandón Maya to work with. Plants, stone, animals, soil, water, and fire. Living in a tropical rainforest, if you wanted to plant a milpa, harvest corn, build a house, chop firewood, make clothing, or light your path through the forest at night, the only materials you had to work with were plants and stone and animals and soil and water and fire. But if you knew how to put those elements together, they provided everything you needed from the material world.

Clearing forest to plant a milpa meant you girdled the trees using a stone axe, chopped the vines with a club-like sickle studded with pieces of chert, and let nature help you out. After the sun dried the felled vegetation, you torched it in a carefully controlled fire that left a nutrient-rich layer of ash lying on top of the soil. Using a long, hardwood stick, you punched holes in the soil and dropped in five or six dried corn kernels and two or three beans, then covered them with a swish of your foot. On to the next hole, and the next, until the entire milpa garden was planted. You seeded other crops between the hills of corn and beans. And you waited for the spring rains. When they finally arrived, you weeded your crops every day until the milpa burst forth in an explosion of food and fiber—corn, beans, sweet potatoes, manioc, chili peppers, squash, cotton, tobacco. Using a bow and arrows made from plants and stone, you protected the fruits of your labor from forest animals, killing and eating the ones you found tasty. Finally, you harvested your crops, thanked the gods, cooked your meals over a wood fire, and ate with your family, sitting on the floor of a house made entirely from plants from the forest that surrounded you.

Plants, stone, animals, soil, water, and fire.

For centuries, these elements served as the foundation for Lacandón life in the lowland rainforest. During the 1970s, they were still the basis for the lives of most Lacandón families. Among the most traditional of these families were those who lived on the northern shore of Lake Mensäbäk in the northern Selva Lacandona.

The families moved to the lake from an area to the south that Lacandones call Sa'm, "sand."[1] In the 1970s, a Ladino family forced a half dozen Northern Lacandón families (including José Camino Viejo and his wife, Josefina Koj, featured in chapter 7) to abandon the area, because they intended to log their forest for mahogany and tropical cedar trees. The female owner of the land told them that if they didn't leave Sa'm voluntarily, "Soldiers would put them on trucks and drive them away" (Nations 1979: 109–110).

The Mexican family that claimed ownership of the forest justified the forced relocation by pointing out that the Lacandones were outside the Comunidad Zona Lacandona, a new land area established by the Mexican government in 1974 to control colonization in the Selva Lacandona and concentrate the Maya population into defined communities. The Lacandón families were told that, if they moved, the government would provide them with services such as schools and medical clinics. Faced with little choice, the families migrated to the shore of Lake Ts'ibanaj, a large tropical lake that is home to the Lacandón God of Writing. The lake is connected to two others—Joton K'ak', home of the God of Fire, and Mensäbäk, home of the god who makes the black powder that produces rain.

The family of José López and two closely related families had already been living on the shore of Lake Ts'ibanaj for fifteen years when the first wave of displaced Lacandón families began to arrive from Sa'm. Although the three families knew the newcomers, they were not happy with the idea of living in a dense settlement with other people. In reaction, José López and the two other established families packed their possessions into canoes and paddled an hour across Lake Ts'ibanaj to the northern shore of Lake Mensäbäk, essentially moving as far away from the others as they could while still remaining within the newly designated territory of the Mensäbäk community. The two older families no longer had children living at home, but José and his young wife, Juanita, filled the new settlement with children. They had seven, ranging in age from five to mid-twenties, six of them still living at home.

The three families built houses a half hour's walk from one another, on low hills connected to a prominent limestone cliff. Everything about the houses—inside and out—came from the forest, with the exception of a few purchased tools. The families had metal axes and machetes for clearing milpas and cutting firewood; a few aluminum cooking pots and spoons; glass gallon jugs called "ear bottles," because their handles look like human ears; single-shot .22-caliber hunting rifles and ammunition; highly prized hand-cranked aluminum corn grinders; tunics sewn from bolts of store-bought cotton cloth; and a single wood and plastic record player powered by six D batteries. Everything else in the houses—and in the families' possession—came from the forest around them.

Inventory

I visited these families a half dozen times, and in 1976 I stayed for a week in the home of José López and his family. Swinging in one of José's hand-woven hammocks one morning, I wrote down an inventory of the natural materials the family used, based just on the things I could see from where I was sitting.

I started with the plants that went into creating the house. Constructing a traditional Lacandón house begins with four upright corner posts cut from the trunk of a logwood tree, known in Lacandón as **ek'**, "black" (*Haematoxylon campechianum*). The tree grows in dense stands in seasonally inundated areas along the shores of the lakes. Despite its native name, "black," a reference to the color of its outer bark, logwood produces a deep red dye that was once exported from Belize to Britain for the clothing industry. The dye is still used today to make biological stains for medical labs.

Logwood is a gnarly tree with sharp spines and a trunk that looks like multiple young trees fused into a single bundle. The trees max out at 8 meters high, providing ample material for making house posts. The trunk is waterproof and so dense that Lacandones say that only an axe—not a machete—will cut it. (I can testify to this.)

Logwood also has an important role in Lacandón kitchens. Families build their traditional cooking hearth by placing three lengths of logwood nose to nose to create what Boy Scouts call a "star fire." As the fire consumes the ends of the logs, the cook periodically pushes them toward the center, feeding the flames and creating a convenient three-point platform to support a bean pot or flat clay griddle for cooking tortillas. The fire is also long-lived.

"A logwood fire won't go out," Amado Seis of Mensäbäk told me. "The wood burns very slowly."

At the same time, he continued, "You have to be careful when you cut **ek'** for firewood—or any other reason—because it will color your clothes red if it touches you." But there's an added benefit: "If there are no **sits'** plants around to paint red stripes on your god pots—red is the gods' favorite color—you can paint them red with **ek'**."[2]

Logwood trees pass several months each year with their roots submerged in water along the lakeshore, while their branches reach into the heat of the tropical sun. Mexican novelist Pablo Montañez described them as "the only vegetation that can live with its feet in water and its head in hell" (Montañez 1972). Lacandones prize logwood for house construction precisely because of the wood's resistance to moisture and rot. They say a logwood corner post will support a house for seven to ten years without rotting in the soil.

For a traditional house, families cut four forked logwood trunks to size and bury the ends partway in the ground. They connect the corner posts to one another with long poles that become roof beams, then frame an A-shaped roof structure above them by tying smaller poles to the roof beams. Onto this frame they attach fronds of guano palm (*Sabal mauritiiformis, Sabal morrisiana*), monkeytail palm (*Chamaedorea* sp.), **kun** (*Cryosophila stauracantha*), or **ak te'** (*Astrocaryum mexicanum*), overlapping them as if they were shingles. The result is a thick blanket of palm leaves that cascades toward the ground to create a waterproof roof. Because the palm fronds almost reach the ground, there is no need for house walls. After the 1970s, when Lacandones were forced to construct their houses in concentrated settlements, they began to build external house walls of roughly hewn planks of wood tied together.

These external house walls are made of boards split with an axe from an **ek' balche'** tree (*Guatteria anomala*), a species endemic to Mexico and neighboring countries. Lacandones use this particular tree because the wood splits straight along its grain, allowing them to fit the boards tightly together to repel rain and wind. They attach the wall boards to a pole framework with lengths of pimento vine (*Clematis* sp., **nikte' ak**), the same vine used to tie the secondary roof poles to the roof beams. The vine is known in Spanish as *Palo Santo*, "sacred stick," because a cross section of it reveals the form of a Christian cross. Lacandones also cut and boil sections of the vine to make a tea that, with a bit of added honey or sugar, is the tastiest beverage to be had in the Selva Lacandona, hot or cold.

Historically, Lacandón houses were divided into sections by internal walls made of split poles from lightweight, balsa-like trees. At one end of the house the families created a bedroom by laying sheets of flattened bark on pole platforms. At the other end, they built a covered porch with no walls where they lay the cooking fire directly on the floor. Here, the women cooked meals and the family ate together. The floors of the house were dirt, which the family periodically swept with palm fronds or with fans made from the wing feathers of the black curassow (*Crax rubra*).

Each family compound also had another structure with no walls and an untrimmed, low-hanging palm-thatch roof. These smaller structures were dominated by a thick chunk of meter-long mahogany wood hacked with axe and a machete into a corn-grinding table, elevated waist-high on four legs made from the trunk of a logwood tree. The families attached an aluminum corn grinder to one edge of the table to crush boiled corn kernels into dough for tortillas, tamales, and gruels.

Most house compounds also had another, smaller structure, the god house, made of poles and palm leaves, but with no walls, and with a long wooden shelf inside one of the eaves. On the shelf, facing into the center of the small house, were a dozen or more god pots, physical expressions of the deities who control the universe and whose work is visible everywhere in the surrounding landscape.

Fiber

One of the most ubiquitous items in the Lacandón inventory was the inner bark of two tree species known as **jarol** in Lacandón, in Spanish as *majagua,* and in English as the broadleaf moho (*Heliocarpus donnelli-smithii* and *Heliocarpus appendiculatus*). Both species are plentiful in the Selva Lacandona and are among the quickest to regrow in a fallowed milpa. If left alone, the trees can reach 15 to 25 meters in only a few years. Both species have lightweight, balsa wood–like trunks—one of the keys to their importance among the Lacandones. Families fell young **jarol** trees and slice the trunks in half lengthwise to make walls, and they use round poles from immature trees to make tepee-like structures that provide nighttime protection from predators for otherwise free-roaming chickens and turkeys.

As a pioneer species on disturbed land, **jarol** trees also aid Lacandón farmers by shading the soil of a fallowed milpa and keeping it moist while rainfall and nitrogen-fixing plants revitalize its nutrients.

But the trees' most important benefit—and the reason they rise to the top of the list of useful products—is their inner bark. Lacandones use the internal bark of the trees for more products than any other plant in the rainforest.

They begin by soaking armloads of felled **jarol** tree trunks in the water of a nearby lake or river. Once the trunks are saturated—after a month or more underwater—they peel off the outer bark and begin stripping long, thin sheets of continuous fiber from the trees' inner layers. The yellowish fiber, called **jol** in Lacandón, is strong and pliable, and when it dries, it becomes the raw material for a veritable hardware store of products. They braid the fiber into ropes to tie up a canoe or to use as a leash for an angry dog. They weave it into thin twine to hang their rifle from the ceiling or to weave a hammock. And they roll it on the calf of their leg to make strong, thin string to attach feather fletching to arrows for use in hunting or for sale to tourists. Just for starters.

Lacandones use a heavy band of **jol** as a tumpline to carry firewood and harvested crops. They tie a circular loop of **jol** fiber to the load they want to carry and hoist the other end of the loop across their forehead at the hairline. Using their neck and back muscles, they can easily transport loads of up to 50 kilos.

I tried it once. After a day of harvesting corn with a family in their milpa, I hoisted a full net bag onto my back, placed the tumpline on my forehead, and struggled to my feet. I was able to stumble 10 or 20 meters down the trail before collapsing.

In my defense, consider that Westerners grow up relying on their arms and shoulders to haul loads on their back. I schlepped a heavy backpack in and out of the field dozens of times, but never on my forehead. By contrast, Maya train from childhood to align the strength of their head, neck, back, and legs to carry loads with a tumpline. Once, facing a three-hour hike through the forest with a backpack and duffle bag of gear and medicines, I hired a Tzeltal Maya headed in the same direction to carry my backpack. I figured he would find the backpack's shoulder straps and lightweight aluminum frame an easy carry. Instead, he did the natural thing for a Maya farmer who grew up in the rainforest. He borrowed a **jol** fiber tumpline from one of his buddies, wrapped it around the bottom of the pack, then stretched it across his forehead and started up the mountain.

Lacandones use peeled bark from other rainforest trees to make beds and clothing. Although they spend much of their downtime hanging out (literally) in hammocks woven from **jol** bark or sisal (more on that in a minute), nighttime will usually find a family climbing onto bark beds covered with blankets (they used handwoven cotton cloth or animal skins in the old days). They make bark beds by driving Y-shaped corner posts into the dirt floor of their house as supports for a low platform of thin poles. On top of the pole platform they spread flattened sheets of bark from the **chäk tao** (*Trema micrantha*) or **jach tao** tree (*Belotia mexicana*), both of which are common regrowth species in fallowed milpas. To make these sheets, Lacandones fell the trees, soak the trunks in the lake, then peel away the bark in 1-by-1.5-meter rectangles that flatten out and stay that way. The pieces are pliable, sturdy, and durable. Flattened sheets of **tao** bark are the Lacandones' plywood—useful for making beds, house walls, and movable floor mats.

Families use a similar fiber, **ak jun** (*Poulsenia armata*), to make bark cloth for clothing. The fiber comes from a tree the Tzeltal Maya call *cotón Caribe*, "Lacandón cotton," because Lacandones formerly stitched sheets of the pounded bark into tunics to wear on a daily basis, saving their hand-woven tunics of homegrown cotton for religious ceremonies and special occasions. They also made tunics from **chimoj jun**, the inner bark of the amate fig tree (*Ficus maxima*), which is either closely related to—or is—the material on which the four known ancient Maya codices were painted more than 1,000 years ago. A few Lacandones still make and sew bark cloth tunics, but these days they sell them to tourists and museums.

Lacandón men formerly wore headbands made from **chimoj jun** bark during **balche'** religious ceremonies, when they gathered to drink fermented sugarcane juice flavored with the lightly hallucinogenic bark of the **balche'** tree (*Lonchocarpus longistylus*). They made these ceremonial headbands by pounding the bark flat, then cutting it into long, 2.5-centimeter-wide strips. At specific points during the ceremony, they tied the strips across their fore-head like a sweatband and dotted the bands and their tunics with a red dye made from crushed annatto seeds and water to simulate blood. After the ceremony, they carried the strips to one of the sacred caves that surround the Lacandón lakes and left them there for the gods.

From where I sat, I could see a half dozen strips of twine that some-one had thrown over one of the house beams. They were braided from sisal (*Agave sisalana*), another important fiber in Lacandón households. Families harvest the fiber from the pointed leaves of the sisal plant, which is closely related to henequen. Sisal is used in Western societies to make agricultural twine, macramé cordage, doormats, and cat-scratching posts. Lacandones fashion it into a dozen useful items: string for binding the feather fletching to arrows, woven bow strings, cordage for hammocks, and thick rope for tying things together. When Lacandones carry loose objects such as ears of corn, they first load them into a net bag woven of sisal. Chan K'in Pepe Castillo of Mensäbäk was so adept at braiding sisal fiber that he could make thin fishing line from it.

Human Figures and Rubber Balls

Lacandón religious ceremonies inspired a need for another natural product from the forest—natural rubber (*Castilla elastica*). The men of José López's compound created small, humanlike figurines from rubber latex bled from rubber trees in the forest. They burned the figures in their god pots along with copal incense to serve as soul substitutes for living members of their families.

Chan K'in Viejo, the spiritual leader of Najá, said that when **Jach Winik** die, they enter the afterworld to serve Jachäkyum, Our True Lord, by patting out his tortillas and bringing him food and corn gruel. Sacrificing rubber figures when a family member is ill prevents Jachäkyum from calling that person to their death, Chan K'in said, "because the rubber human arrives in the afterworld and serves Jachäkyum in their place."

In historical Northern Lacandón ceremonies, a man seeking intervention from the gods made rubber figures in his god house and, when the god pots were blazing with copal incense, whispered to them, "Wake up. Be alive!" He then dropped the rubber humans into the flames of the god pot. Smoke from the incense carried the man's prayers to the gods, and the human figures traveled into the Sky of the Gods, where they took the place of a True Person on earth (McGee 1990: 61).

Anthropologists Virginia Dale Davis and Jon McGee reported that Lacandones once painted the small rubber figures with their own blood, but at some point began to substitute annatto (*Bixa orellana*) (Davis 1978; McGee 1990: 91).

In 1978, Chan K'in José Valenzuela told me the recipe he used to make these figures. "First you bleed sap from the trunk of a rubber tree—without killing the tree," he said. "The latex comes out white. You pour the rubber into a cup made from a gourd and add water. Then, you add juice from the **jut ki'** vine and mix it with the rubber and water." **Jut ki'** (*Ipomoea alba*) is a night-blooming, tropical morning glory with white flowers, sometimes called "moon flower."

"The juice lets you mold the rubber," said Chan K'in, "so you can make little humans. The figures are still white, but when you lay them in the sun, they darken."

The Classic and Postclassic Maya made rubber balls for the traditional Maya ball game from the same rubber tree, *Castilla elastica*. Sixteenth-century Spaniards described the rubber balls and commented on their lively bounce. Spanish scribes of the time reported that the Maya mixed rubber latex with morning glory juice to produce the white blobs they shaped into these balls.

In the late 1990s, researchers from the Massachusetts Institute of Technology analyzed rubber artifacts found in Maya archaeological sites and verified the Mayas' recipe (*Science News* 1999: 31). Morning glory juice, they found, contains sulfur compounds that modify polymer molecules in rubber by creating cross-links, or bridges, between individual polymer chains, giving the rubber a pronounced bounciness. The modern process of vulcanization, patented by Charles Goodyear in 1844, produces the same effect. Today, we use Goodyear's process to make automobile and airplane tires—and bowling balls (Hosler, Burkett, and Tarkanian 1999).

Vines

The inventory of José López's household items also included squat, round baskets called **xak**, named for the vines the baskets are made from (*Monstera* spp.). *Monstera* vines have large leaves with holes in them, giving them the name, in English, of swiss cheese plant or split-leaf philodendron. **Xak** vines grow as hemi-epiphytes on the trunk of a tree—meaning that they have roots in the soil but also sprout roots that cling to the tree. The vines attach to the outside bark of the tree and use it for support, but they don't poach nutrients from the tree nor harm it the way parasitic plants do.

Lacandones strip **xak** vines from a tree, peel away the vine's outer covering, and use the long, cord-like stem inside to weave baskets about 18 centimeters high and 30 centimeters in diameter. A **xak** basket is a vital tool for rinsing corn that's been soaked and boiled in water and lime (calcium hydroxide), an action that removes the translucent outer hull—the pericarp—of the kernels. Boiling and soaking corn in lime also enhances the corn's food value. Lacandones use the basket to carry boiled corn to a lake or river to rinse away the pericarps before grinding the corn into dough.

They also weave **xak** vines into pear-shaped fish traps that have a trap door on a hinge. Lacandón children place small balls of corn dough inside the trap and lower it into the water by the lakeshore. Then they wait until unsuspecting minnows swim into the trap and begin to nibble on the corn dough. When enough minnows have entered, the child jerks the string attached to the trap door and snaps the trap door shut, capturing the minnows. They use the minnows as bait to catch larger fish on hand lines, or they scale the minnows and fry them in oil—guts and eyeballs and all—for a tasty fish (very small fish) dinner.

Gourds

Also omnipresent in José López's house were gourds—lots of them. Gourd cups and bowls lay on the floor near the cooking fire, a gourd colander hung by a string near the corn-grinding bench, and dozens of gourds were stored in a woven bag hanging from the rafters of the god house. Lacandones use two major kinds of gourds. The first is a grapefruit-sized, hard-shelled tree gourd called **luch** (*Crescentia cujete* and *C. alata*), which families cut in half, deseed, and dry to make drinking cups for water, corn gruels, and **balche'**. **Luch** gourds also become storage containers for small items such as beads, arrow points, and feathers. Women strain corn gruels by drilling several hundred small holes in a gourd when it's green and—once it has dried—using it as a colander. In the past, Lacandones made gourd rattles by partially filling a dried gourd with stones or hard seeds and attaching a wooden handle. Because **luch** tree gourds have so many uses, most Lacandón home gardens have at least one gourd tree. You'll find them growing in fallowed milpa gardens as well.

There's a second type of gourd: Lacandón families use bottle-shaped calabash gourds (*Lagenaria siceraria*) as water canteens and kitchenware. They harvest the gourds from vines planted in the milpa, then deseed and dry them. They make excellent water canteens if you carve a hole near the top of the gourd's neck and insert a corn cob as a plug to keep the liquid from spilling. Tie a piece of fiber twine around the gourd's elongated neck, strap it over your shoulder, and you've got a ready supply of water to mix with ground corn to make a refreshing drink while you work in your milpa.

In the Lacandón room of the Museo Na Bolom in San Cristóbal de Las Casas, Chiapas, you'll find a Lacandón guitar made with fiber strings stretched across the neck of a large bottle gourd. Lacandones also harvested honey from stingless bees they cared for in large bottle gourds inside the god house.

A pumpkin-shaped variety of the same calabash gourd produces wide, flat bowls called **lek**. Lacandones cut large, squat gourds, about 28 centimeters in diameter, into wide-mouthed bowls that are perfect for holding the huge tortillas Lacandón women pat by hand on a low mahogany table. Men and women also place a large **lek** gourd on their lap to catch corn kernels as they degrain corn cobs with a broken piece of machete blade.

The Maya have been using tree and calabash gourds for millennia. The tree gourd is native to the Americas, but the long-necked bottle gourd comes originally from Africa. Archaeological research indicates that the species passed through East Asia around 11,000 years ago and wound up in Polynesia, China, and Peru, "earning the title of most widely distributed pre-Columbian domesticated plant" (Nuwer 2014). Bottle gourds dating to at least 10,000 years ago have shown up in archaeological sites in Mexico. Analysis revealed a direct link between the DNA of bottle gourds from Africa and that of gourds from the Americas, implying that the species floated across the Atlantic to the New World, a trip that would have taken around nine months, given the movement of ocean currents (Nuwer 2014). Fortunately, bottle gourds can spend up to a year in seawater without losing their fertility. As a result of this global travel, long-necked bottle gourds hang from the rafters in Lacandón kitchens.[3]

Stone

On the dirt floor near the cooking fire in José López's house, I noticed two large, smooth stones. Someone may have carried them home after finding them in the milpa, or they may have been worn-out artifacts from José's god house. For centuries, the Maya ground corn and tubers by pulling a stone pestle over a block of limestone, granite, or basalt rock to mash boiled corn into dough for tortillas, gruels, and tamales. They used the same stones to mash manioc and chili peppers into paste for food and flavoring (Cagnato and Ponce 2017). The pestle (*mano*) is a long, cigar-shaped stone, and the grinding stone (*metate*) is a rectangular block that develops a smooth depression in its center after years of having the pestle dragged back and forth over its face. Doing fieldwork among the Lacandones between 1902 and 1905, anthropologist Alfred Tozzer noted that the one utensil found in every household was "the stone *metate* for grinding corn" (Tozzer 1907: 19).

Into the twenty-first century, Lacandones still used these grinding stones to prepare foods intended for the gods. Lacandón gods always received the first taste of harvested crops, and food for the gods had to be prepared in the traditional way. Women ground the "first fruits" of the harvest in a ceremonial kitchen built near the god house. During the ceremonies, men spooned corn gruel from the milpa onto the lips of the deities represented on the god pots. Once the gods had eaten their symbolic meal, the families were free to enjoy the leftovers and the rest of the year's harvest.

Today, Lacandones grind their corn with hand-cranked aluminum grinders purchased in Palenque, Ocosingo, or San Cristóbal. As they crank the handle on the side of the grinder, they pour boiled corn into a funnel that feeds into two opposing metal plates that mash the kernels into soft dough. The dough extrudes from the machine's spout onto the wood grinding table. Since electric power lines reached the Lacandón communities in 1991, several families have attached electric motors to their corn grinders to ease a task that has to be carried out every day, year-round.

Along with remnants of ancient grinding stones, Lacandones find stone axes in the soil of their milpa gardens. They call them "axes of the gods' lightning," and say they were created when the gods hurled lightning bolts at the earth (or at evil spirits such as Subín; see chapter 14, "The Snake in the Lake.") Most adults know these are actually stone axes used by the Maya who lived around their lakes before metal tools were introduced.

Bows and Arrows

Stone is still an important element of Lacandón life, but increasingly its role comes in the manufacture of bow and arrow sets, a source of income for many Lacandón households. Lacandones hunted with arrows tipped with stone well into the twentieth century, and a few still do. But today, men sell bow and arrow sets to tourists who visit their communities or tour the archaeological site of Palenque, where Lacandón men from Naja' display their wares outside the entrance gate.

The original Lacandón Maya hunting bows were long, fearsome weapons crafted from the guayacán trumpet tree (*Tabebuia guayacan*), known in Lacandón as **jach chulul**, "true bow." In contrast, bows made for the tourist trade are crafted from the chicle tree (*Manilkara zapota*), which has wood that is softer and easier to shape. In the post-9/11 world, the hottest sellers in the bow and arrow trade are miniature models that can be packed into a suitcase or backpack for international travel.

Pepe Castillo told me that the wood of a true hunting bow is extremely dense and difficult to work. "But it has poison in it to better kill animals when you use it to launch an arrow," he said. "The poison in the wood is so powerful that you have to be careful when carving a bow, because its dust will make you cough, as if you had a cold."

Making a traditional bow begins with the archer shaping a long, carved dowel of wood using an axe and a machete, then straightening the bow by heating it over an open fire for half an hour. As the heat hardens the tree resin in the wood, the craftsman straightens the bow with his hands. He then polishes the bow by pulling and pushing it back and forth over a whetstone rock. After three days of polishing and shaping, the archer has a 1.7-meter, perfectly tapered "self" bow, meaning that it is almost straight; it curves slightly away from the archer when properly held, rather than bending into the U-shape Westerners associate with a hunting bow. When drawn back, the bow's density produces energy that, when released, transforms a cane and hardwood arrow into a fast and deadly projectile.

Lacandones make arrows by inserting a short, hardwood foreshaft into a long, lightweight shaft of cane. They tip the foreshaft with chert or flint and fletch the other end with feathers. Then they wrap the junctions of the arrow with string made by rolling **jol** tree fiber on the calf of their leg, then blackening it with a mixture of beeswax and soot from copal or pitch pine to make it sticky and prevent it from unwinding.[4]

Lacandones make arrow shafts from the flowering stems of a six-meter-tall grass (*Gynerium sagittatum*) cut to the proper length. They chop down the desired number of canes and slice off the white-flowered stem to produce long, straight lengths of cane that make ideal arrow shafts. The shaft has a hard exterior, but is filled with soft, white pith. The archer inserts a carved hardwood foreshaft deep into the pith at one end of the cane, then ties feather fletching on the other end. (The foreshaft allows the arrow to strike its target without splitting, as the cane alone would do.)

Arrows intended for spearing fish have a foreshaft with a sharpened wooden tip and no stone point; those for birds have a cone-shaped "bird bolt" tip of carved wood; and arrows for all other purposes have wooden foreshafts tipped with stone points. Lacandón arrows designed for hunting monkeys have a stone projectile point inserted into a hardwood foreshaft that is notched with seven or eight barbs along each side. Chan K'in José Valenzuela explained: "If we don't carve barbs on the foreshaft, a wounded monkey will pull out the arrow and disappear into the trees" (see chapter 13, "Lord of the Monkeys"). Monkeys shot with barbed foreshafted arrows bleed, weaken, and eventually fall to the forest floor to be taken home, barbequed, and eaten. Monkeys are one of the Lacandón gods' favorite foods, and the gods needed tamales made of monkey meat several times per year. (Fortunately—for the monkeys, if not for the gods—Lacandones no longer hunt monkeys, but focus instead on conserving them.)

To make arrow points, Lacandones chip chert or flint stone into the desired shape, but they will eagerly use obsidian if they can find it. Chert and flint are forms of fine-grained quartz; obsidian is volcanically produced glass. Lacandones find chert and flint in streambeds and road cuts in the Selva Lacandona, but the obsidian they find came originally from Guatemala or the Valley of Mexico. Lacandón farmers find obsidian blades while working in their milpas, where the stone has lain for hundreds of years, having been imported into the Selva Lacandona by ancestral occupants of the area. In the old days, Lacandones prized obsidian over chert because, as Chan K'in José Valenzuela reported, "Obsidian causes heavy bleeding, because it is very sharp. A flint arrow point will usually kill, but an obsidian point always kills."

Recent research backs up what Chan K'in José says. Scientists using scanning electron microscopes found that obsidian blades are 100 to 500 times sharper than steel scalpels used in modern hospitals—to the point that some surgeons have used obsidian blades for delicate cosmetic surgeries and eye operations. While a metal scalpel cuts through individual cells, obsidian blades are sharp enough to actually cut between cells. Viewed under a scanning electron microscope, the edge of an unused medical scalpel looks like a saw, with jagged teeth along its length. By contrast, an obsidian blade is so sharp that its edge fades into single molecules and disappears (Pant 2014). In the past, the Maya imported obsidian in large quantities to produce tools for defense and sacrificial bloodletting, and for use in butchering animals and preparing food (Aoyama 2021: 83).

Made from either kind of stone, Lacandón arrow points are unique in their manufacture. Lacandones are the only Indigenous people in the world who still knap stone arrow points using indirect percussion, the same technique used by the ancient Maya. Most arrow points are made by striking a hunk of flint (the "core" stone) with a second rock called the "hammer stone." Striking the flint's edge with a hammer stone cleaves off a blade (a flake twice as long as it is wide) that can be further shaped into an arrow point or spear point.

In the technique of indirect percussion—again, the Lacandones are the only people who still do this—the flint knapper places one end of a 7.5-centimeter-long deer antler against the edge of the core stone and strikes the other end of the antler with the hammer stone, much the way you would carve wood using a chisel and mallet. A properly executed blow slices off a narrow blade 7.5 centimeters long and 1.2 centimeters wide. The blades can then be further retouched into arrow points, knives, or whatever sharp stone tool is required. While showing me the technique in 1980, Chan K'in José Valenzuela told me that the antler punch has to be the unbranched antler of a young deer, what we called a "spike buck" when I was growing up in West Texas. "If the antler has a second point," José explained, "when you strike it, it will break where the antler divides."

Traditionally, Lacandones knapped stone in the morning, before breakfast, and always inside the god house. José Valenzuela said, "If I eat before I knap stone, the blades won't break right." Flint knappers sometimes recite a stone-working chant as they work, ritually calling forth birds of the rainforest (Bruce 1976: 24–25; Cook 2016: 362–363).

After striking blades from the core stone, Lacandones use a piece of broken machete blade to crunch a pointed tip on the blade. Before they had metal tools, Lacandones used knuckle bones from large mammals or long flint pebbles to shape the points. For even finer projectile points, they carefully knapped the point into shape with a pointed deer antler in a process archaeologists call "retouching."

Once the craftsman is satisfied with the stone point, he chips a flange on its base and inserts the completed stone into a forked notch he has carved in the end of the hardwood foreshaft. Then he pushes the foreshaft into the soft, inner pith of the cane and wraps the joint with fiber string. Finally, he ties feather fletching to the base of the arrow to guide it in flight. The end product is a cane shaft with a hardwood foreshaft and a point that differs according to the specific purpose of the arrow (Nations 1981; Nations and Clark 1983).[5]

The modern Lacandón weapon of choice is a .22-caliber single-shot rifle, but a few men still use the bow and arrow. Chan K'in Juanito López of Mensäbäk told me in 2017 that he had recently encountered a tepesquintle eating his sweet potatoes and shot it with his bow and arrow.

"It took two arrows," he said, "but they killed the tepesquintle, and we ate it. It was delicious."

Today, conservation-minded Lacandones kill wild animals only when they find them eating their crops, but if the marauding intruder is a tasty tepesquintle, so much the better.

Fire: From Fatwood to Halogen Bulbs

When the sun went down, José López's family lit small kerosene lamps to light the night, as did all Lacandón Maya families into the 1990s. The kerosene lamps were made from tin cans with a cloth wick emerging from a cone soldered on top, as if someone had inverted a small funnel on top of a discarded tin can—which is essentially what the lamps were. Lacandones purchased the lamps in Ocosingo or Palenque and filled them with kerosene carried home down forest trails in glass gallon jugs inside a net bag. They called kerosene **u ya'alij k'ak'**, "its liquid, fire." A piece of a worn-out cotton tunic became the wick sticking out of the funnel. The lanterns put off a yellow light equal to several candles, as well as a steady stream of black smoke, making them useful for both illumination and for voiding the area of mosquitoes.

Before they had these metal lamps, Lacandones lit their homes and their path through the forest with **täte'**—what we call pitch pine or fatwood in English (*Pinus oocarpa, P. caribaea*). **Täte'** is sap-rich pine wood that burns easily and consistently when lit. A 15 centimeter stick will put out steady illumination for ten minutes or more, burning like a candle from one end to the other. Alfred Tozzer noted Lacandones' use of fatwood for this purpose during fieldwork at the turn of the twentieth century.

"A pitch pine is used for light in making journeys at night," he wrote. "It burns with a slow steady flame" (Tozzer 1907: 20).

Lacandones obtain pitch pine by hacking away part of the bark and inner wood of a living pine tree, then waiting several weeks for the tree to concentrate resin in the wound. When the wound is dense with sap, the harvester cuts out usable chunks of the wood and allows the tree to heal, beginning the process anew. Pine trees grow in areas of higher elevation around Naja' and near the Lagos Ocotales (now part of the Montes Azules Biosphere Reserve), making it necessary for Lacandones from the other settlements to trade for pitch pine with families from Naja' or periodically travel to harvest the trees (Cook 2016: 248).

Before the days of kerosene, lighting also came from wax candles that Lacandones made by drying **jol** bark fiber into long, thin strips and twisting it into string by rolling it on their leg. They repeatedly dipped the resulting lengths of string in beeswax gathered from the nests of stingless bees and liquefied over a fire. The wax strings gradually became long, stiff wicks that could be cut into smaller sections and lit like a candle. According to Rafael Tárano, the waxed fiber was so stiff that fathers were known to use it to threaten misbehaving children. Not that anyone ever used it on him, he said.

These were the ways Lacandones illuminated their houses until the Mexican federal government stretched electric power lines into the Selva Lacandona in 1991 and families began to hook up incandescent lights for the first time. Prior to the arrival of power lines, the only electricity used by Lacandón families—beyond battery-powered flashlights, radios, and record players—had been short-lived experiments with gasoline-powered generators brought into the communities by the government or by missionaries. None of the generators lasted past the first couple of mechanical breakdowns.

The electrical power lines introduced during the 1990s ended the days of fire-based illumination and brought major changes to Lacandón daily life. Electric light meant working inside after dark, staying up later in the evening, and eventually, watching television at a neighbor's house instead of sitting around the fire, regaling the children with fables and stories. The transmission of oral history suffered for it.

The Skill Is Still Alive

In 1986, José López and his wife moved to Naja' to join their son, Atenacio, who had married into the family of Chan Bor, a Naja' elder. José died a few years later, reportedly from a disorder associated with his chronic headaches, from which he had constantly prayed for relief in his palm-thatched god house. Most of his other children married and moved away, ceding the house site on Lake Mensäbäk back to the gods of the forest.

On a visit to the Lacandón communities in 2017, forty-one years after writing down the inventory of José López's house that day, I returned to the site of his compound, almost by chance. I had joined Minchu Valenzuela and two other men from Mensäbäk on one of their periodic conservation patrols, and we ended up on the northern shore of Lake Mensäbäk. We disembarked from the canoe and hiked up a forest trail to the hill where José López and his family had lived decades before. I was pushing through the regrowth, searching for signs of the house, when Minchu identified two large avocado trees and a tall **pakai che'** tree (*Hymenaea courbaril*) that once shaded José's house.

"That tree was already growing here when José López built his house here years ago," Minchu said. "My father told me the ancestors brought the seeds here from Sayaxché, Petén." The tree was still standing strong.

A little farther on, in a clump of chest-high palm trees, we found the stumps of four posts poking through the moist soil.

"These held up the corn-grinding table," Minchu said.

While I grubbed around in the dirt looking for signs of the other structures, the Lacandones found a patch of disturbed vegetation and began to discuss what had caused it.

"Right here," one of them finally said, "a jaguar caught a deer and dragged it—right through here, to right over there." The other men examined the paw prints in the dirt. They looked at the loose soil and traces of broken palm stalks and agreed: a jaguar had chased down a brocket deer (*Mazama americana*) on that very spot.

They declared this with confidence, based on the clues they could see in the soil and vegetation. Impressed by their ability to decipher the signs, I pulled out my notebook and wrote down their conversation. I ended with the words, "The skill is still alive." I later learned that, not far from the site, in 2008, biologists and veterinarians had used wildlife cameras to capture images of a jaguar cautiously walking through the forest.[6]

We continued another 100 meters into the forest above José's old house and came upon a 4-meter wide deforested strip that cut a straight line through the trees. It was the cleared dividing line between Mensäbäk and Cristóbal Colón, a Tzeltal Maya community directly to the north. Communities in the Selva Lacandona clear strips through the forest to delineate their territory and minimize land disputes between neighbors. Everyone knows where one community ends and the neighboring community begins.

Minchu said that on the other side of the deforested strip, the Tzeltales of Cristóbal Colón had left a 1,000-meter swath of forest as a conservation buffer zone, rather than clearing the trees right up to the legal dividing line, as many Tzeltal communities have done.

"They're learning to guard the forest," one of the Lacandón men said.

We finished the patrol in late afternoon and rowed back to the settlement of Mensäbäk. I climbed out of the canoe, hid the paddles in a safe place in the logwood forest along the shore, and said goodbye to the rest of the team. Then I walked down the dirt road that bisects the community and headed toward the rustic tourist cabin that was my home for the week. Passing by the cement block house of Enrique, the community president and Minchu's brother, I could hear the sound of a television.

Inside the house, Enrique's Tzeltal- and Spanish-speaking children (he married María, a Tzeltal woman from El Tumbo) were watching the Disney channel in Spanish, as they do many evenings after finishing their chores.

As I walked past, I nodded to the fact that new technologies are edging in to coexist with the old ways, sometimes discordantly, sometimes with welcomed acceptance. During a visit the year before one of Minchu's daughters had taught me to use the WhatsApp function on my cell phone, and since then I've been exchanging monthly messages with Lacandones in the communities. They send me pictures of tropical birds and lakes, and I send them pictures of my dog romping in winter snow.

Most recently, Minchu sent a photo of a crocodile swimming along the lake shore with a dead anteater (*Tamandua mexicana*) grasped in its jaws. The anteater apparently had come to the edge of the water to drink, and the crocodile—submerged just under the water with only his eyes sticking out—had flashed from the water with jaws agape and grabbed the unlucky critter by the neck.

Poor anteater.

As the Disney program ended with a musical flourish in Enrique's cement block house and the children began to chatter, I imagined a hungry jaguar moving through the forest on the northern shore of Lake Mensäbäk, silently searching for its next meal.

Figure 2. Northern Lacandón brothers Bor and Chan K'in stand in front of their family's elevated cooking hearth. Photo by James D. Nations, 2017.

Figure 3. Minchu Valenzuela, age nine, drinks from a water vine on a rainforest trail. Photo by James D. Nations, 1977.

Above: Figure 4. In a mahogany dugout canoe, Andres and Rafael paddle across the river to visit the family of Manuel Chilolo. Photo by James D. Nations, 1974.

Left: Figure 5. Pepe Castillo and Ek' Ni', "Black Nose," carve a mahogany canoe. Photo by James D. Nations, 1976.

Above: Figure 6. Chäk Aktun
mountain overlooks Lake
Ts'ibanaj, Chiapas, Mexico.
Photo by James D. Nations,
2009.

Right: Figure 7. Minchu Valenzuela spears fish with a bamboo
lance. Photo by James D. Nations, 1976.

Above: Figure 8. Elías Tárano stands on Chäk Aktun mountain, overlooking Lake Ts'ibanaj and Lake Mensäbäk. Photo by James D. Nations, 2009.

Left: Figure 9. Ancestors' skull and bones cover the floor of a sacred cave, Lake Mensäbäk. Photo by James D. Nations, 2017.

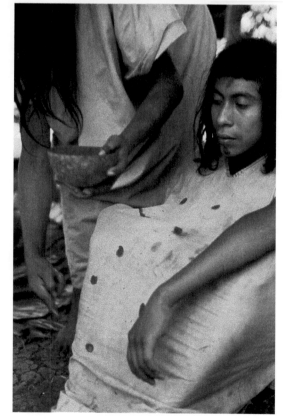

Above: Figure 10. Rafael Tárano holds the skull of a Maya ancestor. Photo by James D. Nations, 2018.

Right: Figure 11. To represent blood sacrifice, Gustavo paints spots of annatto (*Bixa orellana*) on Amado's face and tunic during a **balche'** ceremony. Photo by James D. Nations, 1977.

Left: Figure 12. In Lacandón oral history, a coatimundi (*Nasua narica*) saved an ancestor from the fearsome Jwan T'ut' K'in. Photo by James D. Nations, 2002.

Below: Figure 13. At low water, a carving of the water creature, Subín, graces the cliff of the god Ts'ibanaj. Photograph © by Rafael Tárano Gonzáles (Lacandón Maya).

Right: Figure 14. Chan K'in José Valenzuela surveys a recently burned agroforestry field (*milpa*). The larger tree trunks are remnants from a past year's burn. Photo by James D. Nations, 2009.

Below: Figure 15. José Camino Viejo examines his milpa. Note the tobacco plants growing between the partially burned tree trunks. Photo by James D. Nations, 1977.

Figure 16. Chan K'in Pepe Ramos walks through a fallowed milpa, with regrowth vegetation and old growth forest in the background. Photo by James D. Nations, 1977.

Figure 17. Chan K'in Pepe Ramos and his father, Chan K'in José Valenzuela, sort corn from an early spring harvest. Photo by James D. Nations, 1976.

Right: Figure 18. Chan K'in José Valenzuela chops a felled tree trunk to carve a canoe with a steel axe. Photo by James D. Nations, 1977.

Below: Figure 19. Pepe Castillo and his son, Chan K'in José Valenzuela, carve a canoe from a large mahogany tree. Photo by James D. Nations, 1977.

Figure 20. Juanita ties a net bag from tree bark fiber near her home on the shore of Lake Mensäbäk. Photo by James D. Nations, 1977

Figure 21. Pepe Tal uses shredded mahogany bark and water to tan a deerskin shoulder purse, part of Lacandón Maya men's attire. Photo by James D. Nations, 1977.

Figure 22. Chan K'in Juanito López stands in front of his family's house near Lake Mensäbäk. Note the deer hides, gourds, and plantains hanging from the rafters. One of Chan K'in's daily tasks is to chop firewood in the area to his left. Photo by James D. Nations, 1976.

Figure 23. A Lacandón Maya rice dehusker and mortar sits on a house porch along with gourds, baskets, and a metal bucket. Photo by James D. Nations, 1976.

Left: Figure 24. Luís Cortinas binds feather fletching to arrow shafts for the tourist trade. A stream of balsa fibers, used to make the binding string, hangs from the rafters behind him. Photo by James D. Nations, 1974.

Below: Figure 25. Hidalgo González makes a bow of chicle wood (*Manilkara zapota*) for the tourist trade. Authentic hunting bows are made from the denser wood of the guayacan trumpet tree (*Tabebuia guayacan*). Photo by James D. Nations, 1975.

Right: Figure 26. Cattle graze on cleared and burned rainforest land in the northern Selva Lacandona. Photo by James D. Nations, 2003.

Below: Figure 27. Enrique Valenzuela communicates via walkie-talkie with other Lacandón resource guards while on conservation patrol, Lake Ts'íbanaj. Photo by James D. Nations, 2018.

Above: Figure 28. Lacandón Maya resource guards and state police patrol the lakes of their home community. *Left to right*: Humberto Salórzano, José Angel Salórzano, Gustavo López, Freddy Valenzuela. Photo by James D. Nations, 2018.

Left: Figure 29. After earning a bachelor's degree in forest systems engineering, Armando Valenzuela (*left*) returned to Mensäbäk to work in his home community. His relative, Amado Seis, knows the name and uses of scores of tree species in the Selva Lacandona. Photo by James D. Nations, 2015.

Right: Figure 30. José Pepe takes home a grey-headed dove (*Leptotila plumbeiceps*). Twenty-first-century Lacandones harvest wild animals when they find them eating their crops. Photo by James D. Nations, 1977.

Below: Figure 31. Naja' residents Chan K'in Atenacio López; his wife, María; and infant son visit relatives on Lake Mensäbäk. Photo by James D. Nations, 1977.

Left: Figure 32. Nuk María Patrona uses banana leaves to keep the dough from sticking to her mahogany table as she pats out corn tortillas. Photo by James D. Nations, 1975.

Below: Figure 33. Chan K'in José Valenzuela carves a bird bolt arrow point from funeral tree wood (*Quararibea funebris*). The broad point of the bird bolt is designed to kill a bird without cutting its wing feathers. Photo by James D. Nations, 1976.

Figure 34. Note the regrowing vegetation from prior years' use of the agroforestry field of José López, Lake Mensäbäk. Old growth rainforest is visible in the background. Photo by James D. Nations, 1976.

Figure 35. Manuel Mendoza and his family, Tzeltal Maya, El Tumbo, Selva Lacandona, Chiapas. Photo by James D. Nations, 2019.

IV

Mysterious Spirits

11

Flying Monkeys

One of the ways human societies teach behavior—sharing food, caring for others, coordinating tasks, accepting social norms—is through storytelling (Greenblatt 2017). Lacandón Maya use stories to teach children how to survive in the tropical forest. Messages passed down through fables, myths, and chants counsel young Lacandones to care for the forest and for the creatures that live there. The stories speak of spirits that live inside trees and of gods who remind human beings that animals should not be made to suffer. Disguised as entertainment, narratives such as "Flying Monkeys," the Jwan T'ut' K'in, and "the Lord of the Monkeys" caution children to be mindful of animal behavior, not to harm animals that don't harm them, and to kill only animals they intend to eat. Other stories teach young Lacandones that it is immoral to hunt for the sheer pleasure of killing.

"Myths," as anthropologist Robin Fox noted, "are coded messages" (Fox 1975: 293). Lacandones are taught, for example, that animals have a **yum**, a lord, who protects them. To avoid offending these lords, people must follow certain protocols. If they don't, punishment can be harsh.

No wonder, then, that Lacandones tell stories of mysterious spirits that move about in the forest. An example: In the old days, creatures called the Maya Kimin flew through the forest and appeared at all hours of the day and night. If you heard them moving overhead, you stopped cutting firewood or whatever you were doing and remained absolutely silent, hoping they wouldn't see you.[1]

"They're like monkeys," Chan K'in Viejo said when telling the story. "They fly through the air, calling out. They pass by and come and go, here and there, and then they fall to the ground."

The Maya Kimin come from above like monkeys do, he said. But they don't come from the trees. "It's like they have wings, but they don't."

"They fall to the earth and bring death. When they fall, they can't run or walk, and they get upset. They yell like monkeys. And then they die."

"When a Maya Kimin falls," Chan K'in said, "it brings disease, high fever, and vomiting. No one survives. Our ancestors were very afraid of them. If they see you or if you touch them, you'll die too, of fever and vomiting. Your children as well. That's what the Maya Kimin do."

The creatures' name is a clue to the danger they represent. "Maya," of course, are the Maya people, although it's the only instance where Lacandones use the term. *Kimin* means "death." So, "Maya death."

In the story, a Lacandón ancestor rushed into her house yelling, "I saw a Maya Kimin. It was like a monkey."

The woman's husband grabbed his bow and arrows. "We'll kill it and eat it," he said, and he moved toward the door.

"No," his wife yelled. "We'll die if you kill it."

The man rebuffed her and ran out of the house to hunt it down.

Later, he came back with the dead Maya Kimin. "I killed it," he said.

While his wife watched, the ancestor lay the creature across the cooking fire to scorch off its hair, then gutted it and skinned it. Resigned to her task, his wife roasted the carcass over the coals, and the two sat down and had a good meal of Maya Kimin.

By midnight, both of them were sick. They felt very cold.

By the time the sun came up, they were both dead.

After hearing the Maya Kimin story in Naja', linguist Roberto Bruce wrote that, "Remembering that in relatively recent times, howler monkeys were vectors for yellow fever in the Selva Lacandona and that contact with them caused many people to die, it seems possible to suppose that this creature could have had its origins in that memory, now incorporated into mythology" (Bruce 1976: 132).

Bruce is onto something here, because monkeys play an important role in spreading sylvatic yellow fever, an acute viral hemorrhagic fever brought to the New World with enslaved Africans during the sixteenth century. Yellow fever causes high fever and vomiting, fatigue, and jaundice (hence the "yellow"). Even today, the disease is endemic to Central and South America and Africa, although for those with access to preventative care, a single dose of vaccine confers lifelong immunity. Modern Lacandones recognize the role of monkeys in spreading the disease. One of the names for yellow fever in Northern Lacandón is **u yaji u lubej ma'ax**, "the falling monkey disease."

Monkeys don't actually transmit the disease—mosquitoes do, specifically *Aedes aegypti,* the malaria mosquito, and those from the genus *Haemogogus*. But infected mosquitoes bite monkeys and turn them into—not vectors—but mobile amplifiers of the disease. Mosquitoes that feed on infected monkeys pick up the virus and spread it to other monkeys and to human beings when they bite them. The disease spreads wherever monkeys and humans come into contact with infected mosquitoes and with each other (Tranquilin et al. 2013).

Lacandones still talk about the epidemics.

"It was a long time ago, but my father told me about it," Rafael Tárano said. "The howler monkeys fell from the trees, and everyone got sick and died. If people touched the monkeys, they died. You couldn't eat them."

Yellow fever epidemics have plagued the Maya region multiple times since the disease was brought to the Americas. The first recorded wave began in 1638 in the Lesser Antilles and spread to Campeche and Mérida, then southward through Yucatán, Guatemala, and Mexico (Zinsser 1971: 62). The fierceness of one epidemic prompted a Yucatec Maya scribe to note stoically in the *Chilam Balam of Chumayel*: "1648. Yellow fever occurred and the sickness began" (Roys 1968: 120). In some towns, probably half the population died in yellow fever epidemics (Scholes and Roys 1968: 304).

The U.S. Center for Disease Control reports waves of yellow fever in tropical areas of the Americas in the decades since 1730, including as recently as 1950, when the disease spread throughout Central America, "finally stopping near the border of Guatemala and Mexico," precisely the location of the Selva Lacandona (CDC 2018). Lacandón stories about the Maya Kimin indicate that the disease jumped the Usumacinta River and spread through their rainforest settlements.

Crystallized into oral history as a fear of flying monkeys, the cultural memory of Maya Kimin served as a warning to avoid areas where diseased monkeys were falling from the trees. Generation after generation, myths and fables carried lessons that the True People were wise to listen to. This story is one of many that illustrate how cultural knowledge is transferred from parent to child to promote survival in a traditional society.

12

The Jwan T'ut' K'in

A long time ago, a Lacandón ancestor was in the forest gathering wild honey. The man climbed a tree and cut a hole in the trunk to harvest honey that wild bees had deposited there. But the man didn't know that someone was watching him.[1]

When the man climbed down from the tree with the honey, he heard a voice. "What do you see?" the voice asked.

The ancestor whipped around. He had no idea where the voice had come from.

"Nothing," the ancestor said. "It's honey to sweeten the corn gruel I'm going to offer to the gods."

"Good," said the voice. "Give it to me so I can eat it."

"No, I can't," the ancestor said, still wondering where the voice was coming from. "It's for my corn gruel ceremony."

"It's mine," said the voice. "There's plenty of honey. You'll find another bee's nest."

With that, a humanlike being appeared from behind a tree and grabbed the ancestor's honey and began to drink it. Then he ate the beeswax and the bee larvae, cell by cell, while the ancestor watched anxiously with wide eyes.

The ancestor realized he was looking at a Jwan T'ut' K'in, an evil creature that takes human form and devours True People. The ancestor stood back and said, "Eat all you like." And he looked around at the forest, wondering how to get away as quickly as possible.

To distract the Jwan T'ut' K'in so he wouldn't eat him, the ancestor pointed to the canopy of the forest and said, "Look, there's all the bee nests you'll ever need right up there: **k'ojo'** bees, **k'änik** bees, **chi'** bees, **yuus** bees, and **k'än sak** bees." [All of them stingless bees that nest in tree cavities and produce delicious honey.[2]]

But the Jwan T'ut' K'in had a different idea. He pointed to a tall, smooth-barked tree and told the ancestor, "Climb that tree and get some of that good honey for your corn gruel ceremony. When you get up there, I'll pass you the axe so you can chop out the hive."

The tree was so tall and its bark so smooth that the ancestor had to climb it by grasping the single liana that hung down from the tree's crown. When he finally managed to struggle onto a limb high above the forest floor, the Jwan T'ut' K'in suddenly reached out and slashed the liana with the axe, leaving the ancestor stranded in the top of the tree with no axe and no way to get down.

And with that, the Jwan T'ut' K'in disappeared into the forest.

The ancestor realized he was trapped and suspected that the Jwan T'ut' K'in would soon return to devour him.

The ancestor sat on the limb high above the forest floor and began to cry.

But then, just as the sun was disappearing over the horizon, he looked down to see an agouti (*Dasyprocta mexicana*) walking past the base of the tree.

The ancestor yelled down to the agouti. "Help me. The Jwan T'ut' K'in made me climb up here and now he's going to come back and eat me."

"Poor you," the agouti answered. "But I'm an agouti, and agoutis can't climb trees. It looks like you're stuck." And the agouti continued his walk through the forest.

The ancestor was dejected. Later that night, he saw a tepesquintle (*Agouti paca*) walking beneath the tree. The man called down, "Help me, I'm stuck up here, and the Jwan T'ut' K'in is going to come back and eat me."

"Yikes, too bad," answered the tepesquintle. "But I can't help you. I'm a tepesquintle, and tepesquintles can't climb trees." And he walked on through the forest.

The same thing happened with a brocket deer (*Mazama americana*) and a kinkajou (*Potos flavus*) and a dozen other animals of the forest. They would hear the man calling out and they would listen to his sad story, but then they would say there was nothing they could do. And they would continue on through the forest.

At dawn, a coatimundi (*Nasua narica; pisote*) appeared at the base of the tree, licking the tasty fruit that had fallen from the branches overhead. "What are you doing sitting up there?" the coati called out. The ancestor told the coatimundi his story, as he had to all the other animals.

"That's bad," the coatimundi admitted.

At that moment, a pale-billed woodpecker (*Campephilus guatemalensis*) landed on the branch the man was sitting on. The woodpecker asked what the man was up to and heard his sad story.

"I'll help you down from there if you'll pay me," the coatimundi yelled.

"I'll help too," the woodpecker said. "I'll peck holes in the tree trunk so the coatimundi can get a foothold and climb up to help you."

"Good," said the ancestor. "I'll pay you if you help me."

They had to act fast, though, because the sun was beginning to rise, and the Jwan T'ut' K'in would soon be back to eat the ancestor for breakfast.

The woodpecker flew off and soon returned with a flock of other woodpeckers. The coatimundi ran into the forest and came back just as quickly with a gang of his friends. Everyone set to work: The woodpeckers drilled a line of holes up the length of the smooth tree trunk, and the coatimundis began to climb the tree using the holes the woodpeckers had drilled.

When the coatimundis reached the limb the ancestor was sitting on, they told the man to climb on to their backs and hold on to their upright tails. Working together, they began to descend the tree.

Just then, they heard someone moving through the forest, playing a guitar and singing (as Jwan T'ut' K'ins are wont to do). Several large, snarling hunting dogs ran through the forest before him.

"Hurry," the woodpeckers cried. "They're coming."

As the coatimundis and the ancestor made their way down the tree, several of the coatimundis casually began to eat the fallen fruit at the base of the tree. The Jwan T'ut' K'in's dogs ran up to them and began to bark and snap at the coatimundis. The coatimundis leaped onto the tree trunk, then turned and attacked the dogs, slashing their throats with their claws.

The coatimundis killed all the dogs.

Just then, the Jwan T'ut K'in appeared on the scene. "What have you done? You killed my dogs and now you've let my prey down from the tree!"

"We killed your dogs because they tried to bite us," the coatimundis yelled. "And prey? We never saw any prey. What prey?"

"You'll pay for this," the Jwan T'ut' K'in screamed. "I'll cut you into pieces!"

But when the Jwan T'ut' K'in raised his machete to slash the coatimundis, one of them leaped onto his chest and slashed his throat with his claws.

The Jwan T'ut' K'in fell to the forest floor, shivered once, and died.

"Come look, come look," the animals cried. "We've killed the Jwan T'ut' K'in!"

The Lacandón ancestor, now safely down from the tree, was relieved.

The woodpecker and the coatimundi who had organized the rescue looked up at the man and said, "Time to pay up."

"True," said the ancestor. "What do I owe you?"

The coatimundi replied, "For me, corn. You'll clear a milpa and plant it in corn, and after it's grown and you've performed a harvest ceremony for the gods, then come back and tell me, and I'll come eat as much corn as I want."

"Do I gather the corn for you?" the ancestor asked.

"No, we'll go into the field and climb the cornstalks and eat the ears," the coatimundi said.

"And for you, woodpecker, how do I pay you for your help?" asked the ancestor.

"For me, honey," he replied. "When you go into the forest to harvest wild honey, tell me where you've found it. I'll come eat what I want of it. When I've drunk it up, you have to find me another bee's nest and more honey."

"One other thing," the woodpecker added. "Tell all the True People what happened here today—that because we had pity on you, you're still alive. From now on, they're never to shoot at us with arrows."

"Agreed," said the ancestor. "I'll tell all my relatives never to harm you."

And the ancestor happily returned home to his wife and children and told them the story of the Jwan T'ut' K'in and how the pale-billed woodpeckers and coatimundis had saved him. When the new green year came, he cleared a plot of regrowth and planted corn. Then he went into the forest and searched for the tell-tale sign of bees making honey high up in the tree trunks. He found a lot of beehives.

When the corn had grown and the man had offered the first ears to the gods, he went into the forest to tell the coatimundi and the woodpecker.

"Everything's ready for you," he called out. To the coatimundi he said, "Do you want me to double the cornstalks for you? Or gather the ears?"

"No, I'll climb up the cornstalks and bring them to the ground with my weight," the coatimundi answered.

"Eat, eat," the man told him. "The corn is there for you. And there's another milpa if you need more."

"No, that's plenty for me right there," the coatimundi said.

Then the ancestor walked into the forest with the woodpecker flying above him. "Here are all the bee's nests," he said as he pointed to them high on the tree trunks.

"Very good," said the woodpecker. There were nests from many kinds of bees. The woodpecker was pleased.

And since that day, the story goes, woodpeckers have pecked at tree trunks to open up bees' nests and drink the honey inside. And coatimundis have come into the True People's milpas, climbed up the cornstalks, and eaten all the corn ears they wanted.

All because the woodpecker and the coatimundi took pity on the ancestor and saved him from the Jwan T'ut' K'in. That's why the man stayed alive. And that's why True People don't kill woodpeckers or coatimundis.

The message of this story may simply be an explication of rainforest ecology. Woodpeckers and coatimundis are not prey animals among the Lacandones; they eat neither. But the story does tell listeners which kinds of bees produce edible honey, which animals can climb trees and which cannot, and how to find hidden caches of wild honey by watching where woodpeckers linger.

Lacandones learn that they can use woodpeckers as indicators to find honey and that they will lose part of every corn crop to marauding coatimundis. Those animals that are edible, such as tepesquintles or peccaries, Lacandones will kill if they find them eating their corn. The coatimundis and woodpeckers they leave alone. Perhaps it's because of the day those particular animals saved their ancestor from the Jwan T'ut' K'in.

13

The Lord of the Monkeys

In the old days, animals were abundant in the forest, and it was not difficult to find them.[1] One day, an ancestor came upon a troop of spider monkeys and killed them all. He did so in a very brutal way. He shot the monkeys with straight arrows instead of arrows made with barbed foreshafts. Because the arrows had no barbs, the monkeys were able to pull them out of their bodies with their hands, and the open wounds caused the monkeys to bleed to death—very slowly. The ancestor didn't even eat the monkeys he killed, because the wounded monkeys escaped into the forest canopy and died unseen. They rotted in the trees and on the forest floor, because the ancestor couldn't find them.

When U Yum Maax, the Lord of the Monkeys, heard what had happened, he called together every monkey in the forest so they could decide what to do about the wicked hunter. And this is what they did: The next time the ancestor went into the forest, the monkeys followed him, leaping from tree to tree until they were gathered above his head. Then, all at once, they climbed down the trees and surrounded him. They grabbed the man's arms and legs and carried him through the forest, passing him from branch to branch, all the way to the home of the Lord of the Monkeys. And there, the Lord of the Monkeys declared the man their prisoner.

The Lord of the Monkeys told the ancestor that he would have to replace the spider monkeys he had killed so cruelly. He told the man to choose which of the female monkeys he wanted to marry—and he must marry one of them—because from now on he would live in the forest as a monkey and produce monkey children.

The ancestor was hardly happy. But, left with no choice, he began his new life with the monkeys. It wasn't easy. Quickly he learned that the resentful monkeys were free to pinch and bite him. They peeled skin from his palms and from the soles of his feet to make them look like theirs. When the man got a thorn in his skin, the monkeys bit it out, just as they do to themselves and to each other.

"Ouch, that hurts," the man would yell. And the monkeys would tell him, "That doesn't hurt. It's just a spine in your skin. The way you killed our brothers and sisters—that's what hurts."

The man was several years into living with the spider monkeys when he looked down one day and realized he was exactly above the place where he had been captured. He was within yelling distance of his family home. The Lord of the Monkeys saw the longing in the man's eyes and took pity on him. He told the man to climb down from the trees and run to his house.

When the ancestor stumbled into his house, exhausted but excited, he was so happy! He told his surprised family what had happened—that the monkeys had carried him away and bitten him and peeled the skin from his hands and feet. "It was horrible!" he told them.

"But the monkeys taught you a lesson," the man's wife said. The man hung his head in shame and agreed that from that day forward he would hunt monkeys in the proper fashion. He would never torture them with barbless arrows, and he would kill only monkeys that he intended to eat. Never again would he leave monkeys to rot in the forest.

And the man was happy again.

But not for long. After only a month at home with his family, he died.

The story doesn't tell us whether the man's soul went to be with the gods or if it went back to pay more debt to the Lord of the Monkeys. Nothing is known of that.

But at this point, the Lacandón children listening to the story glance nervously at one another in the glow of the fire, eyes wide, and grimace. Lesson learned.

14

The Snake in the Lake

Rafael Tárano López was the first person to see the giant snake. "It's gray-colored, 10 meters long, and as big around as an electricity pole," he said. "It has two tiny eyes that peek out of the water when it swims across the lake."

By contrast, Rafael is a five-foot-tall, fifty-five-year-old Lacandón Maya who wears a white cotton tunic and a beige, zippered vest with a patch that marks him as one of Mensäbäk's CONANP guards, an official of Mexico's National Council for Protected Natural Areas, paid to protect his community's forest and wildlife.

Recognize that Rafael is a man who knows his snakes. His ancestors have lived in this rainforest for centuries, and he's come across boa constrictors, fer-de-lances (*terciopelos*), coral snakes, eyelash pit vipers, green parrot snakes, speckled racers, and common garden snakes all his life (Campbell 1998; Lee 2000). He is also Mensäbäk's resident snakebite healer. On seven occasions, community members bitten by a poisonous snake have rushed to Rafael for treatment. Each time, he has hiked into the forest to find the leaves of the **mäk ulan che'** tree (*Piper schippianum*), boiled six leaves into a stringent tea, and convinced the victim to drink the bitter substance for fifteen to twenty days—until the person is cured to walk and work again.[1] The one time the treatment didn't work, Rafael said, was when the victim drank the tea, but also fled to a medical clinic in a neighboring Tzeltal Maya community, where a nurse injected him with pharmaceutical antivenom. The man promptly died.

"He would have lived if he had just drunk the tea," Rafael said. "You can't mix the two treatments."

Given Rafael's status as the resident expert on snakes and snakebites, if he tells me there's a giant snake in Lake Ts'ibanaj, I'm inclined to believe him. Plus, four other Lacandones have seen it—three men and one woman, all since 2009.

Minchu Valenzuela has seen the snake twice, the first time while fishing for catfish at night.

"I was with my brother-in-law, Lázaro [Castellano Gavino]," he said. "We were in a canoe near the land bridge where Lake Ts'ibanaj and Lake Mensäbäk connect, and we saw the snake swim by just beneath the water with its small eyes poking up. It was as big as the corner posts that hold up my house. And ten meters long."

"Some time later," Minchu went on, "Lázaro saw it again while he was paddling his canoe near Chäk Aktun," the red, half-dome mountain on the western shore of Lake Ts'ibanaj.

Four years later Minchu saw the snake again. "I was standing on top of Chäk Aktun and the snake was swimming through the water near K'uri Nabaj cliff on the northern shore."

Lázaro saw the snake again in February 2018. "It was 5 p.m., and Nuk and I were fishing in the lake near the old trail to Damasco," he said.

Nuk, Lázaro's wife, chimed in to verify the story. "I thought it was a log floating," she said, "but when we got closer, it moved. It swam away. It was as big and as long as a utility pole. It's not easy to see. It hides itself. It's not a boa. I call it anaconda."

The snake has other names as well. Minchu asked his father about it, and his father told him he probably had seen **u winki ja'**, which would translate as "its body, water," or more poetically, "the spirit of the lake." When I repeated the story to my buddy Chip Morris in San Cristóbal de Las Casas, he said, "You mean, 'The Shape of Water.'"

In the mind of some Lacandones, the snake merges with tales of Subín, a mythological creature in Lacandón oral tradition. Subín was a multilegged monster who lived at the bottom of the Lacandón lakes during long periods of low water.

In one version of the story, "It didn't rain, and all the water evaporated. There were no lakes, no rivers, only Subín. The only water to be found was where Subín lived. The animals and the people would go there to drink, and Subín would devour them when they got close to the water" (Boremanse 2006: 186).

Understandably, the Maya were reluctant to go near the water, but one day a Lacandón ancestor encountered a Rain God in the forest and told him about their dilemma. The Rain God went down to the water and brought the man a drink, which he gulped down quickly, because he was dying of thirst. Then the Rain God told the man, "Go drink your water a little farther away from here," and the man turned away to do so, but he was immediately thrown to the ground by an exploding flash of light.

He looked up to see that the Rain God was attacking Subín by throwing green axes into the water. (When Rain Gods throw green jadeite axes, they create lightning bolts and blasts of energy.) The Rain God threw axes at Subín until the water began to boil and burned Subín's many legs. Then, the Rain God hurled green axes to force Subín to flee all the way to the ocean. And there he ended him.

The Rain God came back to the forest and told the Lacandón ancestor that from now on, the Lacandones could drink as much water as they wanted without danger. Subín was dead (Boremanse 2006: 356).

We can only hope.

Add to this mix of oral tradition and field sightings the fact that when the water level of Lake Ts'ibanaj falls to its lowest point in especially dry years, a seven-meter-long carving of some kind of serpentine creature emerges from the water at the base of the limestone cliff on the lake's northern shore, precisely the place where people keep seeing the snake. Some Lacandones say the carving represents Subín; others say it's a depiction of the same giant snake that swims in the lake today.

From a scientific point of view, the creature Lacandones are sighting is too long and too large to be one of the known reptiles of the Mexican rainforest. An email conversation with Dr. Jonathan A. Campbell of The University of Texas at Arlington, the world's expert on the reptiles and amphibians of the Maya lowlands, confirmed that. "Few snakes in the region reach anywhere near these dimensions," Campbell wrote (Jonathan A. Campbell, email to the author, May 26, 2018).

Snakes from the area that approach or exceed three meters are the tiger rat snake (*Spilotes pullatus*), which is slender and mostly a tree snake, the boa constrictor (*Boa constrictor*), "which I would think is well known by locals and not likely to be confused with anything else," and the indigo snake (*Drymarchon melanurus*), which does sometimes reach 3 meters. "The indigo snake is black, but appears gray while shedding," Campbell said. "They prefer to forage along river and stream banks and will enter water, but I wouldn't consider it aquatic."

Campbell continued: "I think the locality is remote enough that no Mexican collector released an anaconda; nevertheless, this species has been sold in Mexican pet shops and almost every species imaginable has come through Mexico at one time or another."

"It would be unlikely, but indeed be spectacular, if it turned out to be an unknown species. These things sometimes happen."

Campbell knows this because, during the 1980s, he found a population of an almost 1-meter-long beaded lizard, now recognized as a distinct species (*Heloderma charlesbogerti*), in the Motagua Valley of neighboring Guatemala (Campbell and Vannini 1988). "This area has been a focus of collectors since the 1860s," he said, "and how such a large lizard could be overlooked defies credulity."

Still, the Lacandones began to see the snake in the lake only in 2009. Could it be an introduced species—even an anaconda? The snakes we call anacondas are actually four species of aquatic boas from tropical South America, the largest and most widespread of which is the green anaconda (*Eunectes murinus*), which is, "without doubt, the widest, bulkiest, and heaviest snake in the world" (O'Shea 2011: 53). Their natural habitat is the Amazon River system and the llanos grassland of Venezuela. They eat capybaras (a larger version of Mexico's tepesquintles), wading birds, other snakes, an occasional fish, and spectacled caiman, which are somewhat like the Morelet's crocodile of tropical Mexico. Where food is abundant, anacondas can grow to a length of 11.5 meters and reach 250 kilos. Large anacondas are almost entirely aquatic. Like the snake in Lake Ts'ibanaj, an anaconda's eyes are set high on its head, allowing it to watch its surroundings while it swims just beneath the surface (O'Shea 2011: 55).

But in the Mexican rainforest?

Not out of the question. Reptile collectors buy and sell animals in countries around the world. Melissa Morgan (2015) points out in the *Duke Law Journal*, "With an annual profit between $10 and $20 billion, animal smuggling has become the third-largest illegal trade in the world, behind only drugs and firearms." Collectors purchase, keep, and breed thousands of turtles, iguanas, geckos, rat snakes, pythons, and, yes, anacondas.

On the website *Reptiles,* Jordan Russell (2018) writes, "Captive-bred anacondas can make calm, tractable pets when raised properly, but they do get large, and their strength should be respected." He warns that, "This is not a species for anyone under the age of 18 or for anyone who does not have a reasonable amount of experience working with large constrictors." Finally, he notes that an anaconda's diet of mice and rat pups must be changed to larger prey as the snake gets larger. "Females thrive on a diet of medium to large rabbits every 10 to 14 days," he writes.

The *Costa Rica Star* reported the 2013 escape of an anaconda—originally from Brazil—being kept by a US expatriate living in Guanacaste Province,

Costa Rica. The wayward reptile was reported to be "12 meters long." Neighbors living along the Tempisque River saw it "feasting on small caimans," and Costa Rica's Ministry of Environment launched a search. So far, the snake has eluded capture. The newspaper noted that, "Exotic pet keeping is a phenomenon that tends to increase along with prosperity and the prevalence of drug trafficking" (Lopez 2013). In the 1980s, drug kingpin Pedro Escobar smuggled four African hippos—three females and one male—onto his private country estate in Colombia. After Escobar's death in 1993, authorities placed most of his collection of exotic animals with zoos, but they released the hippos into the wild, writes journalist Sarah Kaplan: "Now dozens of their wild spawn roam the wetlands north of Bogotá, the largest invasive species on the planet." Biologists expect their number to reach 1,500 individuals within 20 years (Kaplan 2021).

Collectors sometimes end up with snakes that grow too large for their enclosures, so they set them loose. Foiled collectors have released so many Burmese pythons in Florida's Everglades National Park that the snakes, native to Southeast Asia, are breeding and multiplying and feasting on park wildlife. They eat the park's wading birds and midsized mammals and occasionally try to eat an American alligator. Just outside the park, in January 2018, a Florida golfer came upon a python constricted around an alligator, trying to kill it, while the alligator simultaneously attempted to eat the python tail-first, creating an interspecies uroboros, the mythological dragon that eats its own tail (CBS News).

Unfortunately, Mexican drug lords have picked up the fashion of collecting exotic pets from their Colombian counterparts, focusing on rare birds, tigers, and reptiles (Arsenault 2011). Every year during Easter Week, Latin America's popular Semana Santa, several hundred Mexican vacationers drive down the dirt roads of the Selva Lacandona to picnic on the shore of Lake Ts'ibanaj and take lake tours with Lacandón guides in paddled canoes. It's not impossible that someone surreptitiously brought along an unwanted anaconda and released it "into the wild."

[Note to the hapless collector: Your snake is still out there, swimming across the lake in both moonlight and day.]

In 2019, a yearlong drought struck the Selva Lacandona, and Lakes Ts'ibanaj, Mensäbäk, and Joton K'ak' failed to fill as they normally do, leaving wide sandy beaches along their shores. The drought continued into mid-2020. Simultaneously, the COVID-19 pandemic kept me from visiting the Lacandón communities, so I followed the news through WhatsApp phone calls. When the rains finally began to fill the lakes again during summer 2020, I asked Rafael Tárano whether the giant snake had survived the drought.

Rafael first made a joke about having caught the snake and skinned it to sew into purses, but when I pressed him, he said, "When the lakes were low, the snake went into a cave in the limestone cliff near Lake Ts'ibanaj, next to the carving of Subín. I saw the impression of its body in the mud where it slithered along the shore and went down into the rocks. When the rains came and the lakes filled up again, the snake came back out. He's out there now, swimming just beneath the surface."

V

The Will of the Gods

15

Creating the World

Any Lacandón grandfather worth his salt can recount how the Earth and the rainforest came into existence. But the keeper of the knowledge, the grandfather who knew all the details, and the man to whom all others turned when they forgot their lines was Chan K'in Viejo of Naja', the last spiritual leader of the Northern Lacandón Maya. Until his death at the age of ninety-five in 1996, he would sit in the light of his wives' kitchen fires and fascinate listeners with an origin story dressed in the very conversations of the gods who made it happen.

This is how it went:

In the beginning was K'akoch, the Supreme Creator, who made the Earth. K'akoch was not the god of everything. The True People did not know him. K'akoch created water and made the sun, and he made the moon to keep the sun company. Most importantly, he made the Earth (Bruce 1974; McGee 1990: 65).

But there was a problem with the Earth. The surface of the Earth was soft. There was no stone. K'akoch was not pleased. While he considered the situation, K'akoch made the **bäk nikte'**, the plumeria tree, with colorful, fragrant flowers, each one with five petals.[1] After the creation of the plumeria, things began to look up. Because the flowers of the tree suddenly began to birth new gods.

The first god to emerge from the flowers was Sukunkyum, Elder Brother of our Lord. Then came Äkyanto', the God of Foreigners,[2] and Jachäkyum, Our True Lord.

The new gods looked down from the plumeria tree and quickly realized that something was amiss. There was no soil on the Earth, no stones, and no rainforest. And Jachäkyum said, "This is really not good."

While Sukunkyum and Äkyanto' still clung to their birth flowers, Jachäkyum decided to do something. He stretched out his legs and dropped down to Earth. Then he looked back up and called out to his brothers, Sukunkyum and Äkyanto', "Come with me so we can see whether the Earth is good." So, the two gods dropped from their flowers and followed their younger brother.

As they walked on the Earth, the three gods came upon the ruins of the ancient Maya city of Xok'ol Ja', "Near the Water," which today is called Palenque. Jachäkyum said to his older brother, Sukunkyum, "This will be our home."

At that very moment, the creator god, K'akoch, appeared to the three brothers and said, "Yes, this is your home." Then, he faded away in a cloud, and no human being has seen him since.

The three brother gods stood in front of Palenque and began to talk among themselves. "The Earth is not firm. How can we fix it?" they asked.

"Hmm, wait for me while I think about it," Jachäkyum said, and his brothers stood there, waiting, for about half an hour.

"I'm going to figure out what to do," Jachäkyum suddenly said. "Let's go."

"Yes, let's go," answered Sukunkyum. They walked until they came to a small hill. Jachäkyum looked at the hill and said, "That's it: Sand! I'm going to put sand all over the Earth!"

And he began to throw sand across the face of the Earth. When he finished, he planted a rainforest, and the rainforest began to grow.

And he saw that it was good. He saw that stones were emerging from the sand. There were now stones in the rainforest. The three gods looked around and agreed that the Earth was now very good.

After five days passed, other gods began to appear among the flowers of the plumeria tree. As they emerged, each of them acknowledged their duties to Jachäkyum, Our True Lord. Itsanal, Säkäpuk, and K'ulel would serve as Jachäkyum's assistants; Bol would become the lord of the ceremonial **balche'** drink; K'ayum would be the Master of Singing and Music; K'in, the Lord of the Sun; and K'ak', the Lord of Fire and War (and smallpox and measles). Mensäbäk would make the black powder that brings rain[3]; Ts'ibanaj would serve as Lord of Writing and Art; Itsanojk'uj would be Guardian of the Lakes and would control the number of crocodiles; U Jachil Jachäkyum would be the Master of Snakes.

Then a new god, K'anank'ax, emerged from the plumeria flower and said to Our True Lord: "I am K'anank'ax. I will guard the rainforest. I will guard all the rainforest." And Our True Lord replied, "Thank you, K'anank'ax, go and guard the forest."

At the same time, Sukunkyum, the older brother of Jachäkyum, became the Lord of the Underworld and the judge of souls after death. Äk'inchob emerged from another flower to become the Lord of Maize and the Milpa. Finally, one last deity emerged from the plumeria flowers: Säkapuk, the White Jaguar and Destroyer of Light.

In a final touch, a series of minor gods emerged to help the major gods sweep their houses, play the flute, mold offerings of copal incense, and prepare tamales from the meat of forest animals. There came a god of bees, of turtles, of thunder, and of lightning, and a series of lesser deities called Yum K'ax, Lords of the Forest.

The gods divided naturally into two types: the celestial gods, who live in stone houses (which humans refer to as Maya ruins), and the earthly gods, who live in caves hidden in the cliffs around the lakes. But there also appeared a deity who is neither celestial nor earthly, but who lives in the Underworld. It fell to Jachäkyum, Our True Lord, to create this god, but he took pains to create him not among the flowers of the sacred plumeria tree but from the flower of the plant that True People call **aak'älyoom**, "night foam," the plant that outsiders call poisonous night-blooming jasmine, which has an overpoweringly sweet smell.[4] The god that Jachäkyum created from the "night foam" flower was Kisin, the Smelly One, the Lord of Death.

To form Kisin, Jachäkyum mashed together soil and rotting wood and molded them into a mass that he placed on top of the "night foam" bush. Five days later, under the cover of darkness, Kisin came to life, stretched out his legs, and dropped from the plant to the Earth.

"It is I," Kisin called out to Our True Lord, Jachäkyum.

"Yes, it is you," Jachäkyum replied. "You are Kisin, the Smelly One, the Bringer of Death."

At that point, using a second flower from the poisonous jasmine, Jachäkyum created the wife of Kisin.

"Here is your wife, Kisin," said Jachäkyum.

"Eeh, that's delightfully good," Kisin replied. "Now I have a wife. I am very happy."

Jachäkyum gave clear directions to Kisin and his wife: "You will eat the fungus that grows on trees," he told them. "You will eat green blow flies. You'll think that they are beans. That will be your food."

"Very delicious," said Kisin, who was dressed in pants and a shirt instead of a white cotton tunic like the other gods. To top off his costume, Kisin grabbed a cone-shaped flower of the vine called "smelly ears" and popped it on his head as a hat.

Kisin was very happy.

But there remained one final problem. All the other gods were male, so things were still not perfect. At that moment, though, a miracle happened. Female gods began to emerge from the plumeria flowers. As they appeared, each of the female gods selected a male god as a mate and declared their purpose. Xkalejox, Goddess of the Breadnut Tree Leaves, took Jachäkyum as her husband and with him became the cocreator of human beings. In time they would have a son named T'uup, the Little One, and a daughter, Ixchel, who would marry Äk'inchob and become the Goddess of Childbirth, Medicine, Weaving, and the Moon.

Once the selections were completed, all the gods and goddesses saw that, finally, everything was very good.

And that is the story of how the gods and the Earth came to exist.

There were many gods, but no one knows them all, and when the gods move among the True People, no one sees them, because they move at night while everyone is asleep.

16

Paying the Gods

If horses and lions had gods, they would look like horses and lions.
—Xenophanes 540 BC.

In the rainforest world of the Lacandón Maya, mysterious spirits dance through the swirling ashes of newly burned milpas, shape-shifters roam forest trails, and inhuman voices warble from the depths of sacred caves. Numerous gods and goddesses watch over the True People as they go about their daily lives. With a host of minor spirits to assist them, the gods have the power to impose sickness and snakebites on human beings who offend them. They send fevers and accidents to punish people who fail to do things the proper way.

Fortunately, people can make amends by appeasing the gods with chants and prayers, with the pungent smoke of incense, with meals of monkey meat and corn gruel, and with small rubber figurines of human beings. Faith in this god/human agreement gave spiritual comfort to Lacandones for centuries.

In the view of modern anthropologists, spiritual beliefs—religions, if you will—are mental projections invented by every culture. A society's social and physical environment shapes these projections. As anthropologist Zora Neal Hurston pointed out, "Gods always behave like the people who make them" (King 2019: 289). The spirits that people fear and worship reflect the world that brought those spirits to life.

The Lacandones have gods of rain, childbirth, and fire—among others—because rain, childbirth, and fire are key elements in the world the families inhabit. Mensäbäk creates rain by making black powder, and his assistants seed the clouds using macaw feathers. K'ak', the God of Fire, Hunting, and Arrow-Making, can infect you with measles or smallpox. Ixchel watches over mothers in childbirth. K'anank'ax, Guardian of the Forest, is crucial in a society whose material culture came entirely from the tropical forest. Although the gods created the Earth and human beings, even they emerged from nature. The gods were born, after all, in the flowers of a tree that grows in the forest.

Not surprisingly, the deities of the Lacandón Maya look and dress like Lacandones. Male gods have long, black hair and wear white cotton tunics that reach to their knees. Lacandón goddesses tie their hair in braids and wear a colorful skirt beneath a white tunic, adorning themselves with necklaces made of jungle seeds. Much as the True People live in family compounds in the forest, the gods and goddesses live in family compounds in the sky.

As the code of conduct for life in the tropical forest, Lacandón religion echoes Lacandón social structure and ecological conditions. Until the final quarter of the twentieth century, Lacandón society had no overarching leaders who spoke for all other Lacandones. Respected spiritual leaders called **t'o'ojil** emerged within networks of families, based partly on heredity, but mostly on moral authority and knowledge of oral history. They were usually older, definitely wiser, men who could be counted on to answer questions, but they had no power of compulsion (Boremanse 1996: 75).

For the most part, Lacandón families lived in semi-isolated compounds of extended families, at least from the 1790s until the 1970s—for more than 180 years, in other words. Little wonder that their religious practices reflect this dispersed settlement pattern. In historical Lacandón religion, each married Lacandón man was independently charged with the survival and spiritual well-being of his immediate family. He might chant and pray alone much of the time, but he knew that his relatives, somewhere, were chanting similar words to the same gods beneath the same forest canopy.

All married men had a family god house or shared one with close relatives. Each god house had its own array of god pot censers, homemade ceramic vessels that represent the gods on Earth. Though each family had its own place of worship, networks of interrelated families periodically gathered for religious ceremonies that helped the people maintain social relations and cultural cohesion. The networks of isolated family clusters were held together across the forest by kinship, language, and commonly shared beliefs.

Men periodically took long pilgrimages to the earthly homes of the gods, hiking for days to chant and burn incense in the ruins of ancient cities and in sacred caves around rainforest lakes. More frequently, though, men enticed the gods to come to their god house, a palm thatch and pole structure built in the family compound for just that purpose.

Inside the god house, a shelf suspended under one of the eaves displays a row of handmade ceramic pots, each with a stylized head molded onto the outside rim. Painted white and decorated in patterns of red and black vertical stripes, cross hatches, and dots, the god pots are receptacles for visits from the deities.

Within each god pot is a small stone or artifact found in the ruins of the gods' forest home—in the case of Jachäkyum, Our True Lord, among the ancient temples of Yaxchilán. These artifacts are crucial elements of the god pots because they become the benches on which the gods sit when a man asks the gods to listen to his prayers (McGee 1990: 52).

To facilitate beneficial answers, a man pays the gods by burning copal incense, small rubber figures, and long strips of paper that he cuts from ficus bark and colors blood-red with a paste of crushed annatto seeds and water. The offerings come as payment for good harvests, for removing illnesses and pains from family members, and for protection from snake bites and accidents.

The payments are vital. When Lacandón gods are angered or feel neglected, they let the True People know (rather dramatically) by sending sickness, bad harvests, even snakes, to afflict the offending person or his family members. The gods can be convinced to remove the affliction through prayer and special gifts.

On a hand-carved mahogany paddle, a man and his sons arrange small pellets of sticky incense made from copal resin or pine tree sap. They ritually purify themselves by washing their hands and mouth with water from a gourd, then enter the god house and arrange specifically selected god pots on a mahogany board set on the floor and covered with palm leaves.

The man lights a fire in each selected god pot and begins to chant as he places pellets of incense, one by one, into the sputtering fires.

While the god pots blaze, the man chants in a rhythmic, sonorous voice, sometimes softly, sometimes loudly, demanding, then repeatedly beseeching, cajoling, accusing, challenging the gods to keep their end of the bargain. Invisible, the gods sit on their stones inside the god pots and ponder the poor human's requests: "Accept this burning incense," the man chants. "It carries my prayers in its smoke. My wife has no blame. My children have no blame. Remove their illnesses. Accept these gifts and make them well."

The incense turns into a dark stream of smoke with a heavenly aroma, carrying the man's prayers into the Sky of the Gods. As he chants, the man periodically bathes himself in sacred, cleansing smoke from the flaming god pot. He holds finger-sized fronds of palm leaves over the fire to smoke them black and capture the magical power of the gods. When he completes his prayers, the man takes the blackened leaves back to his house and transfers their healing energy to his wives and children by touching them with the leaves and placing the fronds next to their bed (McGee 1990: 47).

Although each married man serves as his own family's priest, women sometimes ask to be included in the prayers. Women enter the god house only occasionally—to froth ceremonial drinks of cacao that the men spoon onto the lips of the god pots or to accept a gourd filled with **balche'**, a sacred drink of fermented sugarcane juice and tree bark (Cook 2016: 360).[1] Sons watch and listen to their father, memorizing the words of the prayers and chants, knowing that when they are old enough they will be responsible for their own family's spiritual needs.

Men usually pray alone or with their sons or sons-in-law, but groups of men address the gods during larger ceremonies that bring their families together. Blowing on a conch shell, a man calls others to his god house to join him. Even in these social settings, each man usually performs his prayers individually while other men sit nearby, talking, joking, and laughing. The prayer is between the man and the gods, and others don't interfere.

In a field note entry of 1904–1905, anthropologist Alfred Tozzer described a rare case of group chanting during a corn gruel ceremony, and he noted the peculiar manner in which Lacandones performed it. The leader, he said, "takes his place, together with his son, at the western side of the line of blazing *braseros* [ceramic incense burners]. The other participants in the rite also gather round and all begin their individual chanting, waving at the same time the leaves in the smoke of the burning copal. Everyone seems to repeat the same chant, but it is not done in unison. The result is quite unintelligible and confusing" (Tozzer 1907: 121).

Anthropologist Jon McGee described a similar scene among Lacandones of Naja' in the 1980s while they performed a symbolic human sacrificial rite called a nahwah ceremony (**najwaj**, a type of black bean tamale covered in red sauce).

"In groups of two and three," McGee wrote, "every one of the ritual participants then picks up a pot of beans in each hand and stands for a moment in front of the god pots in prayer. This is the only rite during which I witnessed groups of Lacandón men praying in concert. In other rituals, men simply recited their own independent prayers at the same time" (McGee 1990: 96).

At harvest time, the god pots become the medium for showing thanks. Before the human family can eat the food they've grown, they first must offer a taste to the gods. In a ceremonial kitchen dedicated specifically to ritual foods, the wives of the household prepare the harvested crops, and the husband and sons carry the food to the god house in gourds and bowls. The father lowers the god pots from their shelf and aligns them on a palm-covered wooden plank placed on the dirt floor. He chants as he spoons corn gruel, corn dough, or chayote squash onto the protruding lips of each god pot. Later in the year, after the tobacco harvest, he will roll cigars, light them, and place their tips into the gods' mouth for a post-dinner smoke.

The first harvest ceremony concludes when the men take the food outside the god house and flick bits of corn gruel or squash in the cardinal directions, offering a taste to the lords of the forest. The human part of the celebration begins at that point, and the men share the remaining ceremonial foods with one another and with their wives and children.

Like humans, Lacandón gods like to eat. And, like humans, they have their favorite foods. The gods are known to be especially fond of tamales made from monkey meat. In the old days, when a man bagged a monkey in the forest canopy, women of the family compound would scorch the gutted carcass over the hearth fire to remove the hair, then cut up and cook it to make monkey meat tamales. When the meal was ready, chanting men would feed bite-sized pieces of the tamales into the open mouths of the god pots while the rest of the family waited to enjoy the leftovers.

The gods also crave **balche'**, said to be their favorite offering. Lacandones make **balche'** in canoes carved expressly for that purpose. They fill the hollow of the canoe with sugarcane juice and water, or (in the very old days) wild bee honey and water, and allow it to ferment, covered with palm leaves, for several days. Special chants accompany each step of the process.

Lacandones flavor the fermenting liquid with strips of bark from the **jach balche'** tree (*Lonchocarpus longistylus*), a native tree species they also cultivate in forest gardens or house gardens for this reason alone.

The resulting slightly alcoholic beverage, as Alfred Tozzer described it in 1907, "is milky white, sour to the smell, and at first very disagreeable to the taste. Drunkenness, the desired result," he continued, "is obtained by drinking large quantities" (Tozzer 1907: 123–124).

The bark of *Lonchocarpus* contains rotenone, a substance highly toxic to insects, fish, and most aquatic life. Once widely used as a garden and agricultural pesticide, its use today is mainly as a piscicide designed to kill entire populations of fish; for example, undesirable, exotic fish that have invaded a favorite fishing lake.

Rotenone is mildly toxic to humans, and its irritating actions cause vomiting. Lacandones not infrequently drink **balche'** until they throw up—

at which point they drink more. Men report that after a day or more of steady drinking, the buzz effected by **balche'** begins to express itself in new ways. Taken in sufficient quantities (a full day of drinking usually does it, they say), **balche'** produces a slightly hallucinogenic haze that is said to make the gods happy (humans too, according to some Lacandones). While Lacandón men (and women) drink **balche'** from ceremonial gourds, the gods have to make do with spoonfuls the men ladle onto the god pots' protruding lips.

Anthropologist Alfred Tozzer wrote in 1907 that some Lacandón men pierced their earlobes with a stone arrow point during **balche'** ceremonies and dripped their blood onto the god pots. "This custom seems to be dying out," he admitted, "as it is only the oldest men who carry it out" (Tozzer 1907: 136). More recently, Lacandones settled for feeding the gods small bites of bean tamales dripping with a bloodlike red sauce made from the ground seeds of annatto (*Bixa orellana*; achiote).

A **balche'** ceremony is more than an occasion for communing with the gods. It also brings together networks of Lacandón families, renewing kinship ties and reinforcing shared beliefs. Men sing songs and tell stories; young people learn rituals and absorb etiquette for religious and social occasions; women teach their daughters how to prepare ceremonial foods and joke and banter in the ritual kitchen as they drink the gourds of **balche'** the men carry to them (McGee 1990: 82–83).

Drinking **balche'** can serve as a social as well as physical purgative. Men accused of lying may be invited to a **balche'** ceremony in which they're challenged to drink gourdful after gourdful of **balche'** until they vomit ("Have another gourd, cousin!"). Special terms in the Lacandón language describe the act—to **chunluchtik** or **chumuchtik**—"to show the base of the drinking gourd" (Boremanse 1998: 72; McGee 1990: 73, 82).

Once the accused liar is drunk and silly, the other men make fun of him, reminding him of his falsehood in playful rather than bullying or angry ways. When the liar finally vomits, he purges himself of the lie, spiritually cleansing himself in front of his peers and allowing friendships to be rekindled with offended parties. There is an accompanying rule, however: if a man accuses another of lying and challenges him to drink **balche'**, the accuser must quaff an equal quantity, gourd for gourd, along with the accused. And the accuser cannot be the first to vomit. If he throws up before the liar does, the accused man is declared blameless.

McGee points out that the **balche'** ceremony delivers several vital functions in Lacandón society. The **balche'** ceremony "can serve alternately as a form of ritual payment, a vehicle for requesting a favor of the gods, or a form of ritualized punishment for deviant behavior." It is also "a forum for the performance of traditional songs and stories that reinforce the continuation and acceptance of traditional Lacandón lore" (McGee 1990: 82–83).

How Much Do I Owe You?

In historical Lacandón belief, illness or misfortune (breaking a bone, being bit by a snake) is punishment from a god for a human transgression. Someone in the family has offended a god and the god is castigating them. It falls to the father of the family to determine which god is angry, what made him angry, and what payment the god demands to halt the punishment.

The father may not know what offense has been committed. He knows only that someone has done something wrong (or failed to do something necessary). Did he fail to make an offering? Improperly say a prayer? Which god or gods did he offend? Who and what does he have to pay? Once the man has answered these questions, he can petition the gods for relief.

To answer the questions the man must depend on mystical means—divination (**k'inyaj**). Through **k'inyaj**, a man communicates with the gods and "sees" which of them has been angered, why they became angry, what payment they demand in recompense, and which gods are willing to serve as intermediaries in approaching the offended god. Lacandones have three techniques for doing this. Each revolves around ritually reciting the names of the major gods until the offended deity reveals himself/herself through physical manifestation—literally a sign from god (Tozzer 1907: 99–101; Boremanse 1978: 280–281; McGee 1990: 74).

The first form of **k'inyaj** divination involves self-inflicted pain. The petitioner recites the names of the gods while he vigorously scratches the flesh of his inner arm. When he gets to the name of the offended god, welts suddenly appear on his skin. Question answered.

A second (less painful) method requires pulling a single leaflet from the frond of the palm known as **boi** (*Chamaedorea oblongata*) and wrapping it tightly around its stem until it looks like a thin, closed umbrella. The petitioner holds the stem of the coiled palm leaf between his thumb and index finger and recites the list of gods. When he reaches the name of the offended god, the palm leaf unfurls, revealing the identity of the god who must be compensated.

In the third method of **k'inyaj** divination, a man who is both patient and sufficiently skilled brings his palms together and bends his fingers to match up the tip ends of his fingernails (omitting the thumbs). Keeping his nails perfectly aligned, he begins to chant the names of the gods. When a fingernail slips, breaking the connection, the name of the god on the man's lips at that moment is the god who's been offended.

All three divination techniques must be accompanied by prayers, among them this one transcribed by Tozzer around 1905:

My hand, my hand comes to say his name to the sky,
to say his name to my hand.
Don't let the name in my hand be false.
Take possession of me to receive his name.
Don't let the name be false as he says his name in the sky, in the
    home of the gods.
Tell his name to my hand, tell his name in the sky.
He will not lie to my hand
in the home of the gods.
He will say his words
in the home of the gods.
They are received in the wind.
Take possession of me.
Inside is the stem.
He will say it to my hand.
He will not hide it from my hand.
He will correctly tell the truth.
He ends his words to my hand.
He is rising up here, he is coming here.
He ends his words to my hand.

Once the chanter knows the identity of the offended god, he repeats the process to determine what the sin was, then again to divine what payment is required (Tozzer 1907: 170–171).

Even with all that done, the man does not communicate directly with the offended god. Such an act would be confrontational and potentially dangerous. Instead, the man turns to other gods with whom he is on good terms and asks them to inquire what payment the offended god requires. He chants a list of potential payments to the intermediary gods, waiting for a sign that he has hit on the proper gift.

Mats corn gruel if he wants it, Lord.
Corn gruel if he lets me pay it, Lord.

What payment does he want, Lord?
What does he desire? Corn gruel?
What does he want in payment? Corn gruel?
Here he is rising up.
Here he is animated.
Now I will pay you with my corn gruel[2]
  (Tozzer 1907: 171)

The seeming "randomness" of the **k'inyaj** divination process (not un-like throwing the I Ching or reading Tarot cards) introduces the possibility that the supplicant already subconsciously "knows" what offense has been committed and which god has been offended. Divination produces an "objective" action that allows the man to confirm his suspicion. (Or perhaps magic is happening—who's to say?)

A warning, though: the gods can be wrathful if the offense was seriously egregious. They may decide to go mum and refuse to be divined. In that case, the man must ask a relative or spiritual leader to step in for him. If the person he asks is on good terms with the gods, they'll respond to him and answer the questions.

Even then, "Sometimes the magic works, and sometimes it doesn't."[3] Celestín, a Northern Lacandón man who lived many years on the northern shore of Lake Mensäbäk, was afflicted with a large, bulbous tumor that hung like a grapefruit from his right upper arm. Celestín explained that his father had once promised a small ceramic bowl as a payment to Mensäbäk, the God of Rain, but Celestín's father had no canoe to row to Mensäbäk's cave to deliver it. Thus slighted, Mensäbäk punished the father by sewing the missing bowl beneath the skin of his son's arm, making physical work uncomfortable for him. Though Celestín was inconvenienced by the affliction, he knew that the revenge was aimed at his father, and that he himself had no blame (Boremanse 1978: 295; Boremanse 1998: 73).

Incantations

Lacandones must be wary not only of afflictions sent by the gods, but also of conditions produced by daily life in the tropical forest. An example: Like many new parents, Lacandón couples are sometimes frustrated by the discomfort of a newborn baby who cries incessantly for no apparent reason. If normal causes don't apply—if the baby's not hungry, wet, or sleepy—there may be a more exotic explanation.

One possibility is that the baby's father unknowingly crossed the path of a coatimundi and brought home "the growling disease." The animal in question, the coatimundi (*Nasua narica; pisote*), looks like an elongated red raccoon. They roam the rainforest in groups of ten to twenty, searching for edible tree fruit and invertebrates that live in rotting logs. Lacandones say that when coatis prowl the forest—their heads to the ground and their ringed tails held upright in the air—their feet and noses secrete a sticky substance that contaminates the ground where they walk. Humans who cross this trail get the secretion on their bare feet and may bring it into their home, where it can infect a newborn child. The child develops sticky skin, sleeplessness, and a lack of interest in suckling—"the growling disease."

To cure the baby, the child's father (or a trusted male relative) must perform a healing chant, called a **kunyaj**, that counters the condition. The man takes the child in his lap and, leaning over the baby's head, whispers a soft, rhythmic incantation that entices the coatimundi's spirit to cease tormenting the baby and return to the forest.

How do you entice a coatimundi to return to the forest? By promising the animal its favorite foods: wild figs, mameys, wild black persimmons, wild avocados.

Here, in a condensed version, is what the father whispers:

Truly wash it
on the deep road.
There all bunched together
there on the road,
where they move on the road
with tails raised in the air they move.
They are growling on the road,
moving through the trees.
That is their food:
monkey apple.
That is their food,
there on the road:
mamey.
That is their food.
From the top of hills,
through the valleys,
they come on the road,
brushing their disease on the road.

Squeeze its calcium.
It must be rubbed
with virgin spring water.
It must be truly well paid,
there on the road,
with godly words.
Excretions of the soles of their feet,
secretions of their tails,
there on the road.
Their growling must be cured.
True child
must come home,
must be cured,
must be truly paid.
That is their food:
wild figs
there on the road;
wild annona,
that is their food,
there on the road.
True child,
it must be cured.
Its disease,
it must be truly well paid.
The growling disease must be cured.
It must be chanted.
They must be truly well paid.
The disease must be cured,
true child on the road.

The man repeats the chant, exactly as he learned it, for ten minutes or so, by which time the crying child has usually been lulled to sleep by the rhythmic whisper. Patient relieved, case closed.

Lacandones also have a series of magical chants that cure diseases and disorders caused by forest animals; the chants cite the symptoms of the illness and call forth the creature that created the problem, thus encapsulating the information required to solve the problem, at least symbolically (Boremanse 1978: 87; Boremanse 1998: 67). To cure the pain of wasp stings, for example, the chanter calls on the **k'än kux** (black-headed trogon and/

or violaceous trogon, *Trogon melanocephalus* and *T. violaceus braccatus*) to find the wasps' nest and eat the larvae inside (Boremanse 1991). The prescription coincides with empirical knowledge gained from observing nature. Trogons, in fact, do perch on wasp nests and ravenously devour the larvae developing inside them.

Lacandones say that Jachäkyum created these physical ailments [**yaj**, "pains,"] and spread them through the forest, but that he also created the healing chants that counter the pains. He taught the healing chants to Ak'inchob, the Lord of Maize, who in turn taught them to the True People. Young men learn the chants from their father or another close male relative, and they in turn are expected to teach the words—perfectly—to their own sons at the appropriate time. At each level, individuals must learn the chants to the letter, because deviations can cause the malady to worsen.

Lacandón men seeking to learn a **kunyaj** chant meet in the god house with their father or another knowledgeable relative who is willing to share the knowledge. By meeting in sacred space, they prevent children from overhearing (and possibly garbling) the words, because this could lead to the children's death. For the same reason, a **kunyaj** healing chant is usually performed away from the ears of anyone who might try to repeat it and fail to do so properly (Boremanse 1978: 281).

The young men who learn the chants are absorbing more than magical words. They're also learning lessons in ecology and animal behavior. Among Lacandones, incantations are a way to transfer traditional ecological knowledge about creatures that inhabit the forest.

Changes

For as long as they were guided by their Indigenous religion, Lacandones lived in an orderly spiritual world that accorded with the ecosystems that surrounded them. Religious beliefs and oral tradition reflected the actions and reactions they saw taking place in their natural environment. These same beliefs helped guide them through daily life and through the stages of human life—birth, childhood, adolescence, courtship, marriage, parenthood, old age, death—always in keeping with the ecological processes they observed taking place around them. As they do in other cultures, spiritual beliefs helped Lacandón families create a shared identity and accepted rules of conduct. In the parlance of anthropology, Lacandón religion promoted tribalism—the good kind that we also know as "a sense of community" or "community identity."

On an individual level, spiritual beliefs provided explanations for why things happened the way they did—accidents, untimely death, the occasional earthquake. Religious beliefs helped explain the unexplainable. "It is the will of the gods."

Lacandón religious beliefs have always been adaptable. Families added new elements when social or environmental factors demanded accommodation to novel actors or drastic change. For example, Äkyanto', who created foreigners, metal, and money, also created contagious diseases such as measles, yellow fever, and smallpox, which were brought to the Maya world by outsiders. Lacandones believed that these diseases were spread by tiny, invisible Ladinos who shot the diseases into victims with arrows. Those diseases can be cured, but only by the medicines that were also created by Äkyanto'.

Lacandón beliefs have been impacted by outside religions since Colonial-era missionaries first combed the rainforest for families to Christianize. Elements of Christianity bled into Lacandón cosmology, but the central core of the Indigenous religion held firm as long as the Lacandones remained relatively isolated and the rainforest remained intact. Lacandón spiritual beliefs dovetailed neatly with the social and physical environment of the Lacandón people, helping preserve their society and the rainforest.

From the 1960s forward, Lacandones were forced to adapt to the invasion of their forest by loggers, cattle ranchers, and tens of thousands of farm families seeking land. Communities of Tzeltal and Ch'ol farmers pushed the agricultural frontier through the rainforest of eastern Chiapas, putting all but the most reticent Lacandones in at least periodic contact with the outside world.

Changes to the physical and social environment produced changes in Lacandón society as well. As more outsiders moved into the Selva Lacandona, as wildlife became scarcer, as disease affected the families more often, Lacandones began to question whether the gods were keeping their end of the metaphysical bargain. The old clothes no longer seemed to fit.[4]

17

A Special Place in Hell

The faint notes of a Christian hymn crawl through the forest regrowth to tell the world that Sunday services have begun in the Iglesia Viña del Señor on the edge of the Lacandón Maya community of Mensäbäk. A middle-aged Ladino woman from a neighboring village is crooning a plaintive, off-key song in Spanish. The phrases waft out the open door of the blue cement building with a corrugated tin roof, inviting all lost souls to enter and be relieved of their burdens.

A Lacandón woman in her mid-thirties and her fifty-something-year-old mother walk slowly up the hill, leading four small children by the hand. The women are wearing traditional Northern Lacandón dress—a white cotton tunic over a colored red-striped skirt and plastic shoes. But no beads, no earrings like those their mothers and grandmothers would have worn. The two young girls wear secondhand, commercially made dresses; the two boys are in traditional white tunics, their long, black hair brushing their shoulders as they walk. When the group reaches the open door of the church, they walk in and sit down on backless benches that face a low wooden platform where the singing woman stands, dressed in a long skirt and high-necked blouse. She welcomes the arriving group, one of two families she has convinced to worship her god since she began visiting Mensäbäk four years ago.

"*Gloria a Dios*," she says in Spanish, and with heightened vigor, she begins a new song about a long-haired Jewish man who wore a long white tunic and lived in the desert 2,000 years ago. The two women murmur along, off-key and out of sync, struggling with the foreign words. The children giggle and punch each other in the ribs.

The female pastor is a missionary from one of five Christian denominations that have fished for souls in the community since Lacandón religious tradition began to disintegrate during the late 1970s and 1980s. The cause? A mix of factors, really, but fueled by the arrival of loggers, immigrant colonists, cattlemen, government officials, and missionaries—in that specific order.

The loggers bulldozed roads into Lacandón tribal territory and hauled away a fortune in mahogany and tropical cedar trees. Colonizing farm families, most of them poor and landless Tzeltal and Ch'ol Maya, followed the logging roads and burned rainforest to plant corn and chili peppers. Cattlemen followed behind them, buying up land the colonists had cleared and seeding African grasses to raise beef cattle. The farmers pushed farther inward to clear more forest. Government officials arrived in single-engine bush planes and passed out bolts of cloth in exchange for thumbprints on logging contracts that would justify their extraction of the timber that was already being hauled away in trucks.

Families in all three of the major Lacandón settlements eagerly accepted the bolts of cloth and pressed inked fingers (men only) on documents no one in the communities could read. Each male head of household etched an X on the lines the officials pointed to at the bottom of the page. Among the stipulations in the unread fine print: The Lacandones would concentrate their dispersed households, some still scattered in the forest, into permanently defined communities and—one other thing—allow the timber companies open access to their legal forest territory.

Only one man, Chan K'in Viejo, the spiritual leader of Naja', waved away the request to sign. When government officials asked him why he wouldn't put his mark on the paper to sell his trees, he told them, "I didn't plant the trees. Jachäkyum did. Go ask him."[1]

The missionaries arrived around the same time. Their small planes bounced onto the mud and grass airstrip, off-loading vials of medicine and books with pictures of the god, Jesuklistu. Much as the loggers traded bolts of cloth for timber, the missionaries traded medicine for souls.

Attempts to convert the Lacandón Maya to Christianity had begun centuries earlier. During the 1780s, Spanish priests sought out isolated families living in the forest to convert to Christianity and tuck into Colonial society. Lacandones listened to the Spaniards' prayers, eagerly traded wild honey and copal incense for the foreigners' metal tools, then filtered back into the forest to pray to the traditional gods. Over the following 175 years, foreigners' attempts to change the Lacandones' religion would prompt families to move deeper into the forest to escape the infectious diseases the missionaries inevitably brought along with the word of god.

Hand it to the missionaries: they were relentless. Franciscan priests from Tenosique were still hiking the Lacandón forest as late as 1956, an effort that paid off when they came upon two extended families living on the shore of Lake Ts'ibanaj, near today's community of Mensäbäk. An additional half dozen families lived four hours south on Lake Naja'.

"Not long ago, I had the opportunity to baptize five of these Indians," wrote Father Juan Ibarra in his quarterly report to the Misiones de Tabasco y Chiapas, part of the Provincia Franciscana del Santo Evangélio de México. His Yucatec-speaking assistant, Adriano Cu, served as interpreter, Ibarra said, "since the people speak only Maya" (Ibarra 1956: 13, 14).

One of the two families Ibarra visited on Lake Ts'ibanaj included a ninety-year-old man, whom the Franciscans baptized with the Christian name of Domingo. A related "30-to-40-year-old" received the name Antonio.

"Before baptizing them I showed them the image of the Sacred Heart of Jesus," Ibarra wrote, "and they were very interested to see that Jesus had long hair just as they did. Before receiving baptism, the old man sang the praises that—before their conversion—they used to sing to their gods."

The religious beliefs the priest described to the Lacandón families didn't seem that outlandish. The priest insisted that there is only one god, but the god did have a son—just like Jachäkyum and his son, T'uup—and the saints and sacred hearts that floated around them in the framed images created a spiritual tableau that any forest god would be proud of. Like the traditional Lacandón gods, Catholicism was "a grand polytheistic bazaar, each deity bearing a specific celestial rank along with unique magical powers" (King 2019: 281).

The Lacandones in the second family he baptized, Ibarra went on, "are more or less young, and I baptized them with the names Alfonso, Anacleto, and Luís, names they already had before being baptized, because they have the custom of adopting whatever name they hear that they like, indifferent to whether it is for a man or a woman. For example, there are women named Atenacio."

Ibarra's report included three photographs of Alfonso, Luís, and Anacleto. The three men's purported baptisms apparently didn't take, because eighteen years later I found the same three men and their families living on the northern shore of Lake Mensäbäk, where they went by the names Celestín, José López, and the unrepentant Anacleto Echeverría Luís. All three had reverted to chanting vigorously to the ancient Lacandón gods.

The half dozen Lacandón families of Naja', a four-hour hike to the south, endured a more intense missionizing experience. Phillip and Mary Baer, Presbyterian emissaries of the Wycliff Bible Translators (Summer Institute of Linguistics), arrived in Chiapas in 1948 with the goal of translating the New Testament into Lacandón and converting the families to the Protestant faith (Brunhouse 1976: 178–179). Baer was a kind and affable man, and he gradually earned the Lacandones' permission to establish a household on a hill above Lake Naja'.

The Baers offered life-saving medicines and emergency plane flights for any Lacandón family that needed help. They administered the medicines using skills received at a missionary training camp at Yaxoquintelá, Chiapas. The emergency plane flights came courtesy of a sister organization, Mission Aviation Fellowship, known in Spanish as Alas de Socorro, "Wings of Mercy" (Motto: "Sharing the love of Jesus Christ through aviation and technology so that isolated people may be physically and spiritually transformed"). Baer called in the flights on a radio powered by a sputtering gasoline generator.

Gradually, the families of Naja' came to understand that, in exchange for the Baers' support, they were expected to step away from their traditional religion, give up liquor and cigars, and lift their souls to Jesuklistu. Once he realized the scope of the transaction, Chan K'in Viejo, the community's spiritual leader, moved his home and god house across the lake and away from the missionary family. The majority of families in Naja' followed him, and as long as Chan K'in lived (until December 1996), the men of Naja' continued to offer copal incense and prayers to the traditional gods their ancestors had communed with for more than 100 years. Only two men agreed to follow Jesus instead of their traditional leader.

From his base in Naja', Baer also reached out to the Lacandones who lived on the shore of Lake Ts'ibanaj. Celestín, one of the three lapsed Catholic converts (who suffered from a large, bulbous growth on his upper arm) reluctantly accepted Baer's offer of medical care and agreed to become a Christian. He loaded his god pots and prayer boards into his canoe and rowed across the lake to retire them in the cave of Mensäbäk, the deity who brings the rain. Celestín told linguist Roberto Bruce that afterward, as he rowed home in the empty canoe, he was overwhelmed with a loud humming sound in his head and "a heavy, oppressive presence bearing down on him, like the foot of an angry god."

Celestín swirled the canoe around and raced back to the cave to retrieve his god pots and prayer boards. He loaded the items into his canoe and rowed home, where he re-installed them in his god house, fired up an offering of copal incense, and began to pray. His fear subsided as he chanted, he said, and he determined that, "When the day comes, I will die, like everyone else. But until then, I will keep my gods like a True Person" (Perera and Bruce 1982: 23).

In Naja', the Baers came to grips with their lack of success and decided to go elsewhere. In 1957, they moved south to Lacanja' Chan Sayab, a community of Southern Lacandones, whose spiritual leader, Cerón, had died of yellow fever a few years before. Cerón's designated successor had failed to step forward, leaving a spiritual vacuum in place of an orderly universe.

The Baers' medicines and words of hope filled the synaptic cleft. Stories of Christian witness followed. Within a few years of the Baers' arrival, the Lacandones of Lacanja' had built a church and begun singing Christian hymns in their native tongue. Phillip Baer preached from the altar and prayed with the congregation in fluent Southern Lacandón. A draft translation of the New Testament appeared a few years later.

In the meantime, the Northern Lacandón families of Mensäbäk were wavering as well. The settlement's leader, Chan K'in Pepe Castillo, was suffering the long-term effects of sugarcane liquor, "medicine" he called it, and in 1974 turned over leadership to his twenty-nine-year-old son, Juakin Trujillo. But Trujillo was grieving a young son who had died from a respiratory infection, and he was angry that the Lacandón gods had allowed the boy to expire despite his prayers, his gifts of incense, and his pilgrimages to the sacred caves to ask that his son be spared.

Into this sad situation hiked Satuliño Chan, a squat thirty-year-old Maya missionary from Tzutzal, a small town in the Yucatán Peninsula. Chan was a recent convert to Seventh-Day Adventism, and he appeared in Mensäbäk in 1973 promising vaccinations, medicines, and a god who loved little children. Chan's wife and brother-in-law accompanied him during the first few months, but his wife soured on the idea of remaining when she discovered she was pregnant. Whereupon she returned to Yucatán, leaving her husband with Miro, her younger brother.

"Accept Jesus into your soul, and I will give you medicine," Chan told the Lacandón families. "Give your life to Jesuklistu and he won't let your children die."

Chan described a new religion, the "Real Religion" he told them, with a god who appeared in human form after being born from a virgin mother. This god, Jesuklistu, is so powerful that he will live forever. He can heal the sick, make blind men see, and walk on water. He is so powerful, Chan said, that when evil people killed his body, he resurrected himself and rose into the sky in a foaming white cloud. And, he's due to return any day. Those who believe in him will live forever. Those who don't will burn in a place called Hell. The process of accepting Jesuklistu into your soul, he added, included periodically drinking the new god's blood and eating pieces of his body. (All in all, a strange religion, but nothing the Lacandones hadn't heard of before.)

Still grieving his son's death, Trujillo decided to give the missionary, his medicines, and his new god a try. He retired his blackened god pots to the caves above the lakes and, as leader of the newly concentrated settlement, told the other men to do the same. Trujillo sent word to the families still dispersed in the forest that only those who moved into his settlement and accepted Jesus would be eligible for free medicine.

Most of the families swallowed the hook. Of the twenty-one families at Mensäbäk in 1976, twelve built houses in the concentrated settlement and ceased praying to the Lacandón gods. The remaining nine families, led by Juakin's older brother, shook their heads and voted with their feet. They moved their homes and god houses to a nearby lake, Joton K'ak', home of the Lacandón God of Fire. On the far side of Lake Mensäbäk, an hour away by canoe, Celestín, Anacleto, and José López also continued their chants to the Maya gods.

The families who converted to Adventism took their new religion seriously. When an unconverted Lacandón man, Amado Seis—following long-established custom—hiked into the Adventist settlement in June 1976 and asked to marry the daughter of a couple who had converted, the couple rebuffed him, saying that unless he "listened to the words of Jesus," he was not a human being, but "an animal living in the forest." They said they would not let their daughter marry an animal.

The newly Christianized community needed a place of worship, so Satuliño Chan had the men of the Adventist settlement build a pole and palm-thatch church that doubled during the day as a schoolhouse, where he began teaching their children to read and write in Spanish. José Valenzuela, leader of the unconverted settlement at Joton K'ak', bought a small notebook and approached the missionary to ask permission to send his oldest son, Chan K'in Pepe Ramos, to learn alongside them. Chan turned Valenzuela away, saying he would not teach the boy unless both he and Valenzuela came to hear the word of Jesus. Valenzuela declined the offer, but kept the notebook. From that day forward, anytime he got tipsy from drinking sugarcane liquor, he would pull the blank notebook down from the rafters of his house and tell the story of how his son almost learned to read.

Juakin Trujillo, the Mensäbäk leader, leveraged the timing of the missionary's arrival with the arrival of cash payments from government timber contracts. Timber company officials distributed the first round of royalty payments to all families in the communities—Adventist or not—but in Mensäbäk, Trujillo spread word that the money came not from the timber company, but from José Pepe Chan Bor, a Southern Lacandón Protestant, who Chiapas state officials had appointed president of all Lacandones, no matter where they lived. Trujillo told the unconverted families at Joton K'ak' that if they didn't move into the Adventist settlement, quit drinking liquor, and start listening to the words of Jesus, José Pepe Chan Bor would come and take back his money.

In the midst of the cultural chaos, the Adventist families gathered nightly in the pole and palm-thatch hut that served as a church by night and as a school by day. Using a battery-powered slide projector, Satuliño Chan flashed color photographs onto a sheet on the wall, dazzling the families with images of a bearded, long-haired man in a white tunic holding out his hands in supplication.

"This is the Son of God, the only God," the missionary told them. "He will not let your children die."

A young man near the back whispered to his cousin, "That's T'uup, the son of Jachäkyum, Our True Lord. He changed his name to Jesus."

When Chan traveled to Yucatán to visit his pregnant wife, the converted Lacandones were left alone to practice their new religion. At dusk on Saturday, they filed into the palm-thatch church, all but a few of the women and children on the dirt floor in front—allowed to participate in religious services for the first time—and the men and a few wives on board benches in the back. With no pastor there to initiate the services, the men talked, joked, and laughed, lighting up their faces with flashlights.

Mauricio, at twenty-two years an eager acolyte of the new faith, finally stood up and walked to the front of the room. His cousin, Hidalgo, walked forward and stood at his side. The families fell silent as Mauricio led a prayer. Then Hidalgo began to sing an Adventist hymn in a low, almost inaudible voice. The others joined in, each with their own beginning, singing the song in their own key and at their own pace. When the final stragglers finished the first verse, Hidaldo began the second, and everyone began to sing again, starting three or four seconds apart. The result was unsyncopated pandemonium—a murmured waterfall of multipatterned, off-key melodies that tapered down to the words of the final singer, then silence.

Mauricio stood up and prayed again. Hidalgo appeared with the bottom of a cardboard shoebox and handed it to Juakin Trujillo, who pointed his flashlight into the box and jabbed it in front of each man and woman. A few people dropped coins into the box as he made the rounds. After everyone had been offered the box, Juakin sat down and counted the take out loud. "Ten pesos," he announced, despite the fact that Satuliño Chan had told everyone to tithe 10 percent of their money to the Seventh-Day Adventist Church. Earlier in the month, each adult man in the community had received 5,000 pesos (US$402 at the time) as their share of the timber rights for the community's mahogany and cedar trees.

Mauricio flicked on the battery-powered projector and began the slide-show. A drawing of the Earth surrounded by rays of light jumped onto the sheet on the wall.

"Here you see the creation of the world by Jesus," Mauricio told the families. The next slide showed a semiclothed couple walking through a land of rivers and tall trees—Adam and Eve in Eden.

"This is the village of Jesus," Mauricio said. "When we die we will make our houses there. There are fish in the rivers, large fish, and all kinds of animals—elephants and horses, but we won't eat them."

The next slide showed the Earth as a round, blue ball with the moon in the distance.

"This is the Earth," Mauricio explained. "Jesus made it for us."

Enrique, the son of José Guerro, pointed to the smaller, yellow sphere next to the Earth and asked his wife sitting next to him, "What's that other one?"

"The other Earth," his wife whispered.

When a slide of praying hands appeared on the sheet, everyone stood up, and another young man led the final prayer. With that, the service ended. The women lit their kerosene lanterns and the families followed the yellow flames down the trail to their houses. Once at home, they ate dinner and listened to music on battery-powered radios. Some of the radios blasted Mexican dance music from the city of Tenosique, Tabasco. Others broadcast Christian hymns from radio stations on the Guatemalan side of the Río Usumacinta.

One man stood in the dark outside his house and searched the sky as if expecting that any minute, Jesus Christ would touch down in a single-engine Cessna.

Several weeks later, after returning from a visit to Yucatán, Satuliño Chan began to introduce new rules for the families of the Adventist settlement.

"No eating animals with cloven hooves—unless they chew their cud," he said, citing an Old Testament proscription against eating pork, but allowing beef.[2] "No rock-dwelling, rodent-like animals. No eagles, vultures, kites, ravens, owls, storks, herons, bats, or snakes. Nothing in the water that doesn't have fins and scales. Locusts, beetles, and grasshoppers are okay."

The families had no problem with not eating eagles, vultures, bats, or snakes. But the new rules meant that freshwater snails, a not-uncommon Lacandón meal, were taboo. There was no problem with the pigs. Lacandones didn't raise pigs. Their only domesticated animals were dogs, cats, chickens, and turkeys. But the first time a Lacandón hunter gifted the missionary a portion of meat from a tepesquintle, a tasty rainforest rodent, Chan decided that the animal's feet looked suspiciously piglike. And it was clear the little rodent had no cud to chew.

"You will no longer eat this animal," Chan told the families. "And no more crawfish or crabs. They are all unclean. You can eat fish and deer and beef."

And one more rule: "No smoking cigars or any kind of tobacco."

"And no drinking." Definitely no drinking.

This latter edict was eagerly embraced by many Lacandón women, because they had witnessed the effects of heavy alcohol use among their husbands. The women said they were happy to see their husbands give up sugarcane liquor and **balche'** and no longer come stumbling home in the dark. If the family had to give up the gods to achieve that, so be it.

"The old gods are bad!" one woman yelled at her drunk husband.

Other new rules followed: "No more multiple wives," the missionary announced during Saturday morning service. Several people audibly caught their breath. Polygamy is a centuries-old Lacandón tradition. At the time, eight of the twenty-one nuclear families in Mensäbäk included multiple wives. Six men had two wives, and two men—the eldest—had three. Chan told the men they would have to select one wife—and only one—and distribute the others among the unmarried men of the community. Over the following months, wives who had lived with their husband for decades began to move their possessions into the house of another man, some of whom were just turning seventeen.

All but one of the converted men bowed to the missionary's new rule and gave up their second and third wives. That man—Juakin Trujillo, the settlement leader—selected his wife, María, the twenty-five-year-old mother of the son who had died, but said that Chavera, the thirteen-year-old girl who had recently joined their household, should stay to help care for his two other children. Though Chavera had been Trujillo's child bride, he explained that she was now household help. The missionary relented and looked the other way.

Satuliño Chan made one other exception. The youngest of the three wives of Pepe Castillo, Luisa Hernández, age eighteen, had been reassigned as the wife of a teenage Lacandón who had no wife, but she also became a frequent visitor to Chan's own house (Boremanse 1998: 38). Chan explained that the young woman sometimes fixed meals for him while his wife was away in Yucatán.

The families who had rejected Adventism and moved to Joton K'ak' noted the contradictions. "She just makes tortillas," someone would say. And the others would burst into laughter.

They were even more amazed by Miro, the nineteen-year-old brother of Chan's absent wife. Miro had come to Mensäbäk in 1976 to visit his sister and brother-in-law and to be an example of Christian values to the Lacandones. But the boy had trouble adapting.

"At first Miro tried to convince the boys to go with him into the cornfield," one unconverted Lacandón told me, "but the boys wouldn't go."

He had better luck with Luisa Hernández, the young ex-wife of Pepe Castillo who sometimes made tortillas for the missionary. Luisa and Miro were caught *in flagrant delicto,* much to the young woman's embarrassment.

When Satuliño Chan learned of the tryst, he angrily confronted the boy. Lacandones who overheard the exchange said that, in semicontrolled Christian outrage, Chan demanded to know why Miro would do such a thing.

The boy's reply was simple, the Lacandones said.

"Why did I do it? Because I like it."

Anthropologist Margaret Mead once said, "You can't just change one thing."[3] The conversion of the Mensäbäk Lacandones to Adventism is a case in point. As in all cultural change, there were unintended consequences of the Adventists' religious conquest, some minor, some not. By the summer of 1975, the converted women of the Adventist community had ceased wearing the earrings, red bead necklaces, and feather hair adornments that had been key elements of their traditional dress for centuries. Another of the pastor's rules.

Elements of enjoyment appeared to melt into religious doctrine. No one—man, woman, or child—was permitted to work, swim, or bathe on Saturday, the seventh day, and therefore the day of rest and worship. Saturdays became an exercise in boredom, almost mourning. Women, men, and children stood outside their houses, waiting for dark and the nighttime slideshow, when Jesus would again appear on the white sheet on the wall. One Saturday afternoon, when I tried to engage several of the children in a game of Frisbee—an activity they normally relished, calling the flying disc **sek**, "bat"—one of the boys pointed at the disc on the ground and said, "Not today. Tomorrow."

On both a regional and local scale, the conversion of Maya families—not just Lacandones but Tzeltal and Ch'ol Maya, as well—had impacts on the rainforest environment. During the 1960s and 1970s, both Protestant and Catholic missionaries in Chiapas coordinated with government officials to promote colonization of the Selva Lacandona by Indigenous families from other regions of the state and other regions of Mexico. Operating under the ideological tenet that Indigenous migration to the Selva "was an act of liberation and would offer the opportunity to build a new life in 'a promised land,'" missionaries and government functionaries urged poor farmers in the Chiapas highlands and foothills to claim land in the perceived wilderness of Lacandón territory and clear the forest for farmland and pasture. Some religious groups provided legal and logistical support to encourage the movement. Tens of thousands of families moved into the rainforest to take their chances (O'Brien 1998: 117; Paladino 2005: 279).

Local environmental impacts also rippled through Mensäbäk. Satuliño Chan had grown up in a Yucatec town modeled on a Spanish urban design that dated to the Conquest 500 years ago. Civilized villages, Chan told the Lacandones, should be built around a central plaza with a church on one side and shade trees and benches in the middle—a marked departure from the traditional settlement pattern of the Lacandón Maya, who dispersed their houses beneath the forest canopy.

Chan insisted that the families cut down the tall trees around their houses. "In a big wind, they will fall on your home," he told them. "Cut them down."

The community's young men obeyed the request, moving methodically between the houses, using axes to fell a dozen 35-meter-tall trees. Chan stood in his doorway and smiled.

There were impacts on wildlife as well. Tamales made from monkey meat are one of the Lacandón gods' favorite food, and Lacandón families formerly hunted monkeys to feed their god pots. (Humans were allowed to eat the leftovers.)

Lacandón tradition required that hunters kill only what they and their families could eat. (A few predators, mainly cougars and poisonous snakes, were excepted.) Centuries of this Lacandón conservation ethic guaranteed that when a hunter went searching for a monkey, he would almost certainly find one. However, the Adventist missionary determined that monkey meat was taboo—decidedly not on the list of edible animals. To demonstrate his fealty to the new doctrine, one Lacandón convert chased down a troop of five howler monkeys in the forest and killed each of them with his .22-caliber rifle, then left them to rot in the forest.

That same year, a gaggle of Adventist church officials from the state capital flew into Mensäbäk, met with the pastor, and deep-dunk baptized the Lacandón converts in the river that flows into Lake Ts'ibanaj. They gave everyone a baptism certificate and a Spanish-language songbook. Then they urged them to save the souls of the resisting families near Joton K'ak'.

Even in the zeal of their conversion, the Adventists held on to old beliefs. The leader of the Adventist settlement, Juakin Trujillo, told the others that his brother, Chan K'in José Valenzuela, had caused the death of his own second wife, María, by chanting against her to the traditional gods. (She had, in fact, died of infectious hepatitis.)

Valenzuela was distraught when a Lacandón visitor from Naja' related the story of his brother turning against him. He fidgeted as he explained to everyone around him that his wife's eyes had turned yellow and that she had died in three days. It was an antagonistic taunt by Trujillo against his older brother, but also a signal that the Adventist leader still believed that a True Person could harm another by chanting to the gods.

The public shaming apparently compounded Valenzuela's grief to the point that he decided to abandon his gods and move closer to the Adventist community. He retired his god pots in the caves, but he never accepted the Adventist belief system and would not attend their services.

In September 1975, Chan K'in Viejo in Naja' passed on a report that Trujillo and the Adventist pastor were planning to burn the forest on the cliff of K'uy Ak (the Lord of Turtles) to demonstrate that the cliffs around the lake were not sacred after all. Shortly afterward, fire spread through the rainforest that covered the cliff, leaving behind blackened trees and scorched limestone rocks. The unconverted Lacandones of both Naja' and Mensäbäk blamed Trujillo and the missionary for the fire, though no one would actually say they saw it happen. (Almost half a century later, the forest on the cliff has regrown, and it would take a botanist to tell that the vegetation had ever burned.)

When the logging roads finally reached Mensäbäk in 1979, the Adventist church in Tuxtla Gutiérrez trucked in cement blocks and metal roofing to build an Adventist temple on top of the highest hill in the community. But tensions within Mensäbäk were reaching a breaking point. Not long after the church was constructed, Satuliño Chan left the community after an internal dispute that may have involved his extramarital affair. With the flight of the missionary, Juakin Trujillo, the community leader, lost his prestige and migrated south to create the settlement of Bethel a few kilometers east of Lacanja' Chan Sayab. All but one of the Adventist families—fourteen families in all—packed their belongings and went with him (Boremanse 2020: 218).

In Lacanja' Chan Sayab itself, Phil Baer had never convinced the Southern Lacandón men to give up their multiple wives, and seven of the twenty Lacanja' families at the time were still polygynous (Boremanse 1998: 39). Southern men practiced sororal polygyny, meaning they married two or more sisters, so everyone was family from the get-go. The Adventist Northerners complained to one another about the sins of their southern neighbors, but most of them stood fast with the Adventist church as they moved into the twenty-first century.

When the Adventist converts abandoned Mensäbäk, most of the unconverted families living at Joton K'ak' moved back to the original settlement on Lake Ts'ibanaj, but only a few rebuilt their god houses. Because of the arrival of the road, their lives were now openly accessible to the outside world. A few families moved to Naja', where god houses and **balche'** ceremonies were still thriving under the leadership of Chan K'in Viejo. Several other families maintained their isolation in the forest around the lakes, hiding their god houses and rituals. In time, as migrating colonist communities edged closer and closer to their territory, the families one by one began to abandon their religious practices and drift into a spiritual void. One man fell under the influence of a Pentecostal Tzeltal from a neighboring community and built his own church building next to his house—much as if it were a god house—and he and his wife and children sing and pray there on Sunday mornings.

Of all the Adventist converts, one family remained in Mensäbäk to keep the lights on in the cement block temple on top of the hill. In the several decades since the community split in two, the Adventist services have attracted only one other individual, a Tzeltal woman who married a religionless Lacandón man. Periodically, Adventists from other communities visit on Saturday mornings in the hopes of sparking a revival.

Even the one Lacandón Adventist who stayed behind in Mensäbäk saw a split in his family. His father and mother moved to Naja' where they remained solid traditionalists. Until he died in 2020, the father still knew the spells and chants of the old ways, but he was unable to walk more than a few steps at a time, his knees shot from a lifetime in the milpa and from kneeling before the Lacandón gods.

In 1986, the families who lived across the lake under the cliff of Mensäbäk—those of José López, his brother Anacleto, and their stepfather Celestín—moved to be with family in Naja', leaving only one man, José Camino Viejo, still practicing the historical religion anywhere around the lakes. Ironically, every time I visited him, José would temporarily disappear into his house and reemerge wearing an aged, metal Christian cross on a fiber cord around his neck. I never determined what message he was trying to send: "I'm not a heathen? Don't try to convert me, I'm already covered? We're not so different?" No one mentioned the crucifix, because it was clear that José was still actively worshipping the gods in his nearby god house.

When José Camino Viejo died in the late 1990s, his god house was still intact, but he had no sons to continue the chants and traditions, and the structure slowly collapsed on itself and disappeared into the vines and re-growth. ("This is the way the world ends.")[4] His god pots gradually sank into the ground on the same spot where they once flamed with burning copal.

Traditional religion thrived for a few more years in Naja'. Families continued to resist missionizing attempts, deflecting their appeals gently and directly. I heard one Naja' man say to a visiting Protestant Lacandón from Lacanja' Chan Sayab, "You read your book, but you never look up to see Jachäkyum himself."

When Chan K'in Viejo, the last northern spiritual leader, died in 1996, the polestar that the Naja' families spiritually revolved around finally went dark, and even the old man's sons drifted away from the god house. Today, Naja' has six denominations of Christian churches. In 2013, of 184 families in the community, 43.5 percent declared "none" when asked about their religion. Twenty-two percent declared themselves Catholic, 8.2 percent Presbyterian, 7.6 percent traditionalists, 7 percent Evangelical, 5.4 percent Baptists, 3.3 percent Pentecostals, and 2.7 percent Adventists (Contreras and Mariaca 2016: 33–34).[5]

Only one man in Naja' is known to still light the flames of his god pots, though his son-in-law is learning the traditional prayers.

The Adventist leader of Mensäbäk, Juakin Trujillo, who led his fellow Adventists to move south to Bethel, died in the mid-1990s after relapsing into alcohol use. Lacandones in Bethel told anthropologist Didier Boremanse that Juakin became diabetic, but continued to drink and eventually had his legs amputated. He ended his life in a wheelchair, "knocked over by a truck when he was drunk on the road" (Didier Boremanse, personal communication, February 13, 2022). Juakin's two wives, María and Chavela, live today with Trujillo's surviving son in San Javier, near Lacanja' Chan Sayab.

Chan K'in José Valenzuela, who led the traditional families at Joton K'ak', died in 2017 at the age of eighty-three. Neither he nor his children ever converted to Christianity. His sons and daughters appear to live in spiritual limbo. They grow quiet if someone mentions the old religion.

Satuliño Chan long ago returned to his village in Yucatán to resume life with his wife and child. No one has seen him or young Miro since. Whether or not they continue as Seventh-Day Adventists is unknown.

"He lied," Chan K'in José Valenzuela told me before he died. "Satuliño Chan said when he came to Mensäbäk that those who listened to Jesuklistu wouldn't get sick. Their children wouldn't die. But everyone got sick anyway, and some of them died. I think the missionary brought the diseases with him when he came here."

The almost simultaneous arrival of missionaries, medicines, and roads—joined with the death or defection of Lacandón spiritual leaders—sounded the death knell for the old ways of religious belief. The insertion of new religions was made easier when the Mexican government convinced the Lacandones to concentrate their families into three main communities (Mensäbäk, Naja', and Lacanja' Chan Sayab/Bethel), now with legalized boundaries, roads, and electricity. The basic lesson of the Lacandón conversion follows a pattern seen in traditional cultures around the world: autochthonous religions dovetail with a people's culture and history and with the ecosystems they live in, but drastically altered physical and social environments can open the way for drastically altered systems of belief.

Or so it seems. The families of Lacanja' Chan Sayab seem to be content as Protestants. Many of the migrant Adventists of Bethel continue in their faith, but there is plenty of empty space on the wooden benches of the half dozen churches in Mensäbäk and Naja'.

Despite the existence of three churches in Mensäbäk, 80 percent of the families declare that they have no religion at all. The father of one family told me in 2015 that he doesn't know what to believe anymore. "Right now," he said, "I am without a religion."

He added, though, that he has a recurring dream about his seeming lack of faith. "Every time I have the dream," he said, "missionaries appear and tell me to give my soul to their god. But each time, the traditional gods—Jachäkyum, Ts'ibanaj, K'ak'—suddenly appear and say, 'Not him. He stays with us.'"

The dream always startles him awake with heart palpitations, he said. But in the following days, as the missionaries make the rounds to his house in the waking world, he simply tells them, "No, thanks."

"The old ways are gone now," Amado Seis told me in 2019. "There are no more god houses and **balche'** ceremonies. All the old ones are dead. We didn't learn from them like we should have. They knew how to talk to the gods. They washed themselves with copal smoke, and they cured diseases and snakebites with their prayers. We don't have that anymore. They're not with us anymore."

Still, on quiet evenings, when a deep orange sunset illuminates the limestone cliffs that surround the lakes, it's not difficult to imagine the Lacandón gods waiting patiently inside their caves, watching the rainforest grow.

VI

Conservation
The State of the Forest

18

What Happened to the Selva Lacandona?

In the Selva Lacandona, enormous mahogany trees (*Swietenia macrophylla*) with ribbonlike buttress roots grow to a height of 45 meters, popping their crowns through the rainforest canopy as if keeping a lookout for danger. Lacandón Maya prize mahogany for its straight-grained, rot-resistant wood, which is ideal for carving canoes, corn-grinding tables, tortilla-pressing tables, and sacred boards on which to place god pots flaming with copal. The mahogany tree's companion, tropical cedar (*Cedrela odorata*), called **k'uj che'**, "gods' tree," in Lacandón, is almost as tall and useful as mahogany. Lacandones use it to make ceremonial canoes for brewing the sacred **balche'** drink and for house walls and cooking utensils.

Mahogany and cedar trees have long been part of the Lacandón Maya toolkit, but the trees became "green gold" when discovered by outsiders in the mid-nineteenth century. Industrial countries prize mahogany and tropical cedar for making fine furniture, doors, office paneling, yachts and boats, guitars, violins, grand pianos, cigar boxes, and billiard and pool cues.[1]

Lacandón families used the wealth of mahogany and tropical cedar trees in the Selva Lacandona in a paced, sustainable manner measured in decades. Exploitation by outsiders occurred in voracious gulps, bringing financial wealth to a few individuals, but at great cost to the environment. Logging played a seminal role in converting much of the Selva Lacandona into an impoverished landscape of cornfields and cattle pastures.

The process began slowly, when companies backed by investors from Europe, the United States, and Mexico began to exploit mahogany and cedar in Chiapas during the 1850s. Traveling by boat and on foot, exploratory teams searched for trees near the banks of rivers and marked them for cutting teams that followed behind (González Pacheco 1983: 57–153).

The difficult work of chopping down the trees, peeling their bark, and hauling the trunks to the river with oxen fell to semi-enslaved Maya from Tabasco and the Chiapas highlands, many of whom were tricked into signing contracts to pay off drinking debts incurred during religious festivals. Once the men were delivered to the camps, company stores charged them exorbitant prices for food, clothing, and equipment, causing many to fall further into debt the longer they worked. Men who tried to escape by flee-ing into the forest were hunted down by attack dogs and Ladino foremen on horses, then punished with whipping, hanging in chains, and increased workloads (O'Brien 1998: 73; Brito Foucher 1931). Novelist B. Traven (real name Berick Traven Torsvan) wrote about these rainforest logging camps in his book, *Rebellion of the Hanged* (1936).

Workers rolled the peeled tree trunks to the river using teams of oxen, and for the next six weeks the logs floated down the rivers of the Selva Lacandona, funneling from one tributary into the next, past crocodiles on riverbanks and monkeys howling overhead. Crashing through sudden rap-ids where the mountains end, the trunks merged into the massive water highway that is the Río Usumacinta. Just before the logs reached the river-side town of Tenosique, log wranglers wrestled them out of the water and deciphered the initials carved into them to identify which company they belonged to. They tied the trunks together into giant rafts and—in one of the most dangerous steps in the process—rode them downriver, precari-ously unclogging logjams along the way. Once safely on the flat water of the Tabasco plains, the teams barged the logs out to ships waiting in the Gulf of Mexico to transport them to the United States, England, Germany, France, Spain, and Belgium (González Pacheco 1983: 95; de Vos 1988: 69).

Commerce was so lucrative that timber companies competed for forest ownership and logging concessions. Through good connections and sharp political skills, in the dozen years between 1883 and 1894, three business-men from Mexico City came to own half of the Lacandón forest. The rest became the property of five logging companies from the Mexican State of Tabasco—Bulnes, Romano, Sud-Oriental, Valenzuela, and Agua Azul. A sixth company was owned by a Spanish noble named Claudio López Bru, known colloquially as the Marqués de Comillas, "the Marquis with quota-tion marks," whose designated territory in the southeastern corner of the Selva Lacandona still bears his nickname today (de Vos 1996: 260).

Anthropologist Alfred Tozzer noted during his trips to visit Lacandones in 1902–1905, "The greater part of the country occupied by this people is under grant by the government to companies formed for the exploitation of mahogany. These companies have headquarters on the rivers and from these settlements as centers radiate temporary camps called *monterías,* which are found practically everywhere throughout the territory occupied by the Lacandones. The Indians thus have a limited contact with the Mexicans who live in these logging camps" (Tozzer 1907: 33).

But Lacandones did visit the camps, trading natural forest products and bows and arrows for metal tools and salt, and not infrequently picking up infectious diseases in the process.

When the Mexican Revolution reached the Selva Lacandona in 1913, soldiers led by General Luís Felipe Domínguez traveled through the forest to liberate the debt-enslaved workers they found in the logging camps, and they sometimes executed camp officials and overseers. The forays forced many companies to abandon the Selva for two or three years, but when the army left the region, the companies went back to felling trees and abusing their workers.

Lacandones eventually learned that the loggers—or someone who was paying them—claimed ownership of their traditional tribal lands. On her second horseback expedition to find the Southern Lacandones in 1948, Gertrude Duby Blom noted that the Lacandón families were bewildered by outsiders' concept of "property." They did not grasp the idea that the forest they had always lived in was not theirs, but belonged instead to people they had never seen.

Duby wrote: "The Lacandones told me one and a thousand times, all the time, like an obsession, 'The Lacandones have no land. The land is all for logging'" (Blom and Duby 1955–1957: 71).

Green Gold

The Lacandones and the forest enjoyed a brief respite in 1948, when Mexico changed its forestry law to prohibit the export of unprocessed logs in the round until national demands for timber, pulp, and paper had been met (O'Brien 1998: 74). The new law temporarily halted logging operations in the Chiapas rainforest. But what the halt anticipated—or perhaps precipitated—was a new strategy for extracting the "green gold" of the Selva Lacandona. The new strategy was industrial-scale logging focused on building roads, felling trees, and transporting the trunks to timber mills for processing in-country. This change required companies to bulldoze dirt and mud roads through the forest so cutting teams could access trees that previous loggers could not reach because they were too far from the rivers.

Despite the requirement that logging operations satisfy Mexican markets first, the opportunities presented by Mexico's rainforests attracted one of the largest American timber companies of the time, Vancouver Plywood Company of Vancouver, Washington. In 1949, the company sent an American forester named Thomas H. Mills to survey the tropical forests of Campeche, Tabasco, and Chiapas. After months of exploration, Mills reported back with two messages—one good, one bad. The good news was that the Selva Lacandona of eastern Chiapas had huge reserves of unexploited precious hardwoods—hundreds of thousands of valuable trees. The bad news was that Mexican law would not permit a foreign company or foreign citizens to own land within 100 kilometers of the nation's borders, thus prohibiting Vancouver Plywood, or any other foreign company, from buying the rainforest of the Selva Lacandona (de Vos 2011: 63).

To meet this challenge, in 1951 Vancouver Plywood teamed with eighty investors from Mexico City to create a new Mexican-owned company, which they named Maderera Maya. Although the new company's financing and management came from the United States, 51 percent of Maderera Maya was "owned" by Mexican citizens. In other words, the company employed an informal sidestep called *presta nombre*, "name loaning," in which blocks of rainforest land were purchased in the name of individual Mexican citizens who then became part of the company. The result was a "Mexican" company that technically was not "owned by" but was, in fact, controlled by Vancouver Plywood (de Vos 2011: 64).

In an important legal move, officers of the newly created Mexican company approached Mexico's Secretaría de Agricultura y Ganadería (SARH, Secretary of Agriculture and Ranching), seeking permission to create an "industrial forestry exploitation unit" that would allow logging operations on a massive scale over several decades. Operating as Maderera Maya, Vancouver Plywood planned to construct a sawmill and plywood factory in the Selva Lacandona, along with houses, schools, and medical clinics for the workers they intended to hire. In its appeal to the Mexican government, the company promised to supply Mexico's domestic market with timber, pulp, and paper before exporting lumber to the United States.

The up-front investment was expensive. To turn a profit, Vancouver Plywood and Maderera Maya needed a legal agreement guaranteeing them at least twenty-five years—ideally up to sixty years—of exclusive rights to harvest hardwood timber in the Selva Lacandona (González Pacheco 1983: 177). In their business proposal, the companies said the areas they had purchased held 999,871 mahogany trees and 117,630 tropical cedar trees, as well as 87 other species of hardwood trees that could be sold in national and international markets. The company mounted publicity campaigns and provided financial enhancements to government officials in anticipation of launching a major logging operation in the Selva Lacandona (de Vos 2011: 71).

The secretariat warned that such an agreement would require the signature of the president of Mexico. But Vancouver Plywood and Maderera Maya were so certain of success they continued to acquire forestland. By 1954 the company had purchased 288,000 hectares (1,112 square miles) of rainforest through *presta nombres* and acquired logging concessions for an additional 132,000 hectares (510 square miles) of land owned by others (González Pacheco 1983: 157–158; de Vos 2011: 69).

But in a sobering disappointment to the companies, word came back that the president of Mexico, Adolfo López Mateos, would not be signing the decree authorizing the companies' operations. The deal was a nonstarter. Years later, former president López Mateos would tell a colleague that he chose not to sign Maderera Maya's decree because "he did not want to be the president who terminated the Selva Lacandona" (González Pacheco 1983: 179).

New Settlers, New Vision, New Life

More bad news came on the heels of the president's announcement. Maderera Maya learned that Tzeltal Maya families from Bachajón, Tumbalá, and Tila were invading company lands and clearing and burning forest for milpas and cattle pasture. Government officials from Mexico's Departamento de Asuntos Agrarios y de Colonización (DAAC, Department of Agrarian Matters and Colonization), the forerunner of today's Secretaría de Reforma Agraria (Secretary of Agrarian Reform), had told the families that the lands were soon to become national territory open to colonization. The announcement was part of the agency's strategy to nullify the land ownership of logging companies and private individuals and declare the Selva Lacandona "national territory appropriate for agriculture" (de Vos 2011: 76; Paladino 2005: 69 ff.)

There was a background to this strategy. During the late 1930s, President Lázaro Cárdenas had declared the nationwide goal of taking back ownership of huge plots of land acquired by politically connected Mexican citizens during the presidency of Porfírio Diaz. Among the lands targeted for nationalization were those of Maderera Maya and of the private landowners who had signed contracts allowing the company to harvest their mahogany and cedar (de Vos 2011: 77).

Researcher Karen O'Brien points out that the large private estates in the

Chiapas highlands and Ocosingo Valley were facing increasing population pressure from land-poor farm families. Yet the estate owners "continued to be fortified against potential breakups or takeovers, both by national and state policies." Continuing confrontations prompted government officials to defuse the situation by promoting colonization of the Selva Lacandona. As O'Brien says, opening the Selva to colonization "was not so much in the interests of expanding agricultural production, but rather in diverting the focus of agrarian reforms away from the breakup of large estates" (O'Brien 1998: 144–145).

The colonizing families had specific goals: "to create a new life, free of the servitude to the regional elites; to create wealth for themselves and not just for someone else, and to leave the opportunity for a better and different life to their children" (Paladino 2005: 278).

Urged on by federal authorities, families from the Chiapas highlands and Ocosingo Valley began to migrate into the Selva Lacandona (Schumann 1982). "For the most part," wrote historian Jan de Vos, "the new occupants were indigenous families, pushed out of their original villages by misery provoked by the lack of cultivable land and by harsh working conditions on cattle ranches and coffee plantations in the Chiapas highlands" (de Vos 1988: 27).

Colonists were also prodded into the Selva by religious groups. Protestant missionaries of the Summer Institute of Linguistics and Catholic officials inspired by liberation theology saw migration to the Selva Lacandona as a modern exodus to the promised land. They pressed landless Indigenous families to liberate themselves from indentured servitude and establish Christian communities of God's Kingdom on Earth in the lowland rainforest of the Selva Lacandona (Paladino 2005: 105).

The migrating colonists brought a new vision to the Lacandón forest. Where loggers had sought the Selva Lacandona's valuable hardwoods, Indigenous farm families had their eyes on the land itself. Farmers looked at the land over the long term, as a substrate for growing corn, chilies, beans, and other food crops. To access the soil, the families had to fell the forest, burn the vegetation, and plant crops. Clearing the forest had a corollary benefit: The quickest and most definitive way to demonstrate ownership of land was to "improve" it by clearing the vegetation and burning it. At the least, if someone contested his land claim, the farmer could sell his *mejoras,* his "improvements," and move farther into the forest to try again.

Through the 1950s, more and more Indigenous families seized the opportunity to migrate into the Selva Lacandona. A Chiapas state forestry engineer conducting overflights of the Maderera Maya lands discovered that in nine years—1950 to 1959—farm families had colonized and deforested 75 percent of the company's northern holdings. In a further blow to the company, in 1961 the Mexican government declared almost 70 percent of Maderera Maya's purchased lands "national territories" destined to become new agricultural colonies and concentrated *Centros de Población,* "Population Centers" (de Vos 2011: 79–80).

Hearing of the Mexican government's intentions for his company's giant holdings, in 1962 Don Plummer, the head of Vancouver Plywood, appealed to his US senator, Henry "Scoop" Jackson (D-Washington), asking that he put the company's plight on the agenda of President John F. Kennedy's upcoming trip to Mexico. But nothing came from the company's appeal. There would be no US presidential intervention. So, after fourteen years of investment, planning, and lobbying, in 1964 Vancouver Plywood and its Mexican counterpart, Maderera Maya, changed their plans. Cutting their losses, Vancouver Plywood's owners offered a contract to the Weiss Fricker Mahogany Company of Pensacola, Florida, for a ten-year logging concession on the forested land that Vancouver Plywood still controlled. Simultaneously, Vancouver Plywood began to sell blocks of its land to cattle ranchers from the state of Tabasco and city of Palenque, the only individuals with ready cash and the ability to obtain bank loans.

The Florida-based Weiss Fricker Mahogany Company was no newcomer to tropical logging, having spent years harvesting trees in the rainforests of Central America. To open operations in the Selva Lacandona, the company—like its predecessor—created a 51 percent–owned Mexican counterpart, Aserraderos Bonampak, S.A., and began constructing a sawmill in the small town of Chancalá, south of Palenque. Working ahead of the wave of colonization sweeping into the Selva, Aserraderos Bonampak bulldozed roads to connect their new sawmill with Palenque in the north and with the archaeological site of Bonampak in the south. Then they built feeder roads and sent their logging teams into the forest to begin felling trees (de Vos 2011: 83).

The Tripartite Wave

Aserraderos Bonampak's initial results were lucrative. The company exploited one of the richest stands of mahogany and tropical cedar in Chiapas, reaching into the rainforest near Monte Líbano, southwest of Najá, an area that had never been logged. But there was one minor problem. As they bulldozed into the region, the logging teams encountered family compounds of Northern Lacandón Maya living quietly in the forest, farming small plots of land and hunting wildlife. In quick resolution of the issue, in 1964, the company sent a timber man with a long history in the Selva Lacandona, Pedro Vega, to advise the families that the land they were living on belonged to someone else—a politically connected woman named Fernanda del Villar, who had signed a logging contract allowing Aserraderos Bonampak to build roads and cut 15,000 mahogany and cedar trees on "her" land. Vega told the Lacandones they would have to leave (de Vos 2011: 59–92). Most of the Lacandón families picked up their possessions and moved north into the forest around Lake Ts'ibanaj and Lake Mensäbäk, forming the original nucleus of the families who still live on these lakes today (see chapter 7).

Throughout this time, Weiss Fricker Mahogany and Aserraderos Bonampak continued to face the dual threats of nationalization of their land and its spontaneous colonization by farmers and ranchers. Frustrated by the situation, Vancouver Plywood cut its ties to Chiapas and left its land and operations in the hands of its Mexican counterparts in 1966. But Weiss Fricker Mahogany Company and its Mexican counterpart, Aserraderos Bonampak, held on and continued to fell mahogany and cedar trees for its sawmill in Chancalá. Its ten-year logging concession would be valid until 1974.

Between 1966 and 1973, Weiss Fricker Mahogany Company—acting as Aserraderos Bonampak—built a network of capillary roads through the forest to high-grade mahogany and tropical cedar. The network grew to 135 kilometers of principal and secondary roads, including sections from the Chancalá sawmill to Palenque and from the sawmill to the railroad in the town of Pénjamo. The roads to Bonampak and Monte Líbano served as arteries for extracting the logs being harvested in deep rainforest (González Pacheco 1983: 185; Paladino 2005: 70; de Vos 2011: 89).

But as the logging teams radiated into increasingly distant parts of the forest, the costs of road construction and maintenance expanded. And wherever the roads penetrated, the forest was soon occupied by Maya farmers and ranchers. Tzeltal Maya moved into the Selva from Altamirano, Bachajón, and Yajalón and from smaller villages in the Ocosingo Valley. Tojolabal Maya migrated eastward from Comitán and Las Margaritas into the San Quintín region of rainforest near Lake Miramar (Marion 1997). Ch'oles came from villages near Palenque, Tila, Tumbalá, and Yajalón. In one of the grand ironies in the history of the Selva, some of the migrating

Ch'ol Maya were likely descendants of Ch'oles the Spaniards had removed from the area 300 years before (as described in chapter 1).

In an almost choreographed sequence, colonizing farmers began by clear-cutting the forest, then drying and burning the vegetation and planting corn and other crops. After several years of harvests, those who could afford to buy cattle planted their fields in African grasses and dedicated the land to pasture. Access to railroad lines and to bank loans for beef cattle (but not for food crops) prompted Indigenous families to emphasize beef cattle over corn production on the land they deforested (Paladino 2005: 72). Actually owning cattle was not a requirement for this transformation. A farmer who had no cows and calves could always rent the land to someone who did. But then, the farmer had to find new land on which to grow his corn. During the 1960s and 1970s, this tripartite wave of destruction—logging, colonization, and cattle ranching—devastated the northern half of the Selva Lacandona.

Not everyone was pleased with the results. As some agencies of the Mexican government urged on the wave of colonization, officials in other sectors were dismayed to see rainforest being cut and burned before its hardwood timber could be harvested. For some officials, the goal was to colonize the Selva, but in an organized fashion, and only after the mahogany and cedar had been cut and sold for profit (de Vos 2011: 89).

"Since Time Immemorial"

The world of loggers, colonists, cattlemen, and Lacandones was soon turned upside down. Over a period of two years—1972 to 1974—Mexican government officials nationalized most of the Selva Lacandona, declared the land the communal property of the Lacandón Maya, signed a logging agreement with the newly mandated Lacandón owners, and began to log the forest themselves.

The strategy was set into motion in November 1971, when the president of Mexico, Luís Echeverría Alvarez, nationalized most of the remaining privately owned lands in the Selva, including the parcels that Vancouver Plywood had turned over to the Mexican *presta nombres* who controlled Maderera Maya. The new law declared that 614,321 hectares (2,372 square miles) of the Selva Lacandona were henceforth to be known as the *Comunidad Zona Lacandona*, "the Lacandón Community Zone," and that the area was now *terreno comunal*, the communal property of the sixty-six known Lacandón Maya heads of families (eight of whom were women), because they had occupied the land "since time immemorial." The federal government established the Comunidad Zona Lacandona through a constitutional procedure called "recognition and titling of communal lands," which aimed to return land to its recognized Indigenous owners. The land was to be administered by the community as a whole, without the titling of individual parcels, unlike an *ejido,* which does allow individual plots to be divided among the community's population (Moretti-Sánchez and Cosío-Ruiz 2016).

The total Lacandón Maya population at the time, according to the decree, was 375. The area deeded to these individuals was—and continues to be—the largest Indigenous land reserve in Mexico (Calleros-Rodríguez 2014: 129; DOF 1972: 10–13). It was an enormous expanse of land—almost half of the Selva Lacandona—especially considering the small number of families who now became its legal owners. At first glance, the decree appeared to ignore the fact that many other Indigenous families were already established within the zone, clearing land, planting corn and pasture, harvesting crops, and selling pigs and cattle into commercial markets.

Importantly, though, the presidential decree left the door open for shared ownership with these non-Lacandón families when it stated that the communal land grant was also intended for "the indigenous groups of the region who do not have sufficient land for their sustenance and development." Government officials knew that Tzeltal and Ch'ol Maya families were already living in forty farming communities inside the boundaries of the newly declared communal lands. In fact, six of these communities had already secured legal title to the land they were occupying, and several more were in various stages of applying for *ejido* status. But, disturbingly, in deeding the Comunidad Zona Lacandona to sixty-six Lacandón Maya heads of household, the decree implied that the Tzeltal, Ch'ol, (and a few Tzotzil) Maya inside the land grant's boundaries were now illegal encroachers on Lacandón land (de Vos 2011: 99).

None of this strategy originated with the Lacandón Maya, who were not asked to help plan the Comunidad Zona Lacandona nor consulted in its design. Only after the deal was done did the Lacandones become aware they had become legal owners of a rainforest they thought was already theirs.

The presidential decree became federal law on March 6, 1972. Following the declaration, the Lacandón Maya convened in the community of Lacanja' Chan Sayab on September 24, 1972, to receive legal title to the Comunidad Zona Lacandona from the governor of Chiapas, Manuel Velasco

Suárez. Mexican authorities appointed José Pepe Chan Bor, the social and (Protestant) religious leader of Lacanja' Chan Sayab, to be the *comisariado* (commissioner) of the Comunidad, making him, a Southern Lacandón, the de facto leader of all Lacandones, north and south (de Vos 2011: 112).

Several months would pass before someone pointed out that the Northern Lacandón communities of Naja' and Mensäbäk were not actually inside the geographical boundaries of the Comunidad Zona Lacandona, although the families there were among the listed owners of the zone. The oversight was corrected in September 1975 through the addition of 3,847 hectares surrounding Naja' and 3,368 hectares surrounding Mensäbäk (de Vos 2011: 122; DOF 1975; CONANP 2006a, 2006b). These two Northern Lacandón communities, which were already recognized as *ejidos,* would become Áreas de Protección de Flora y Fauna under federal law in 1998—at the communities' request (Nations 2006: 147–148).

Government officials urged Lacandón Maya families who were still living dispersed in the forest to relocate into more concentrated settlements within the Comunidad Zona Lacandona. They promised cash payments and medical care to the Northern Lacandón families still in Monte Líbano and El Censo (S'am) if they would move to Naja' or Mensäbäk. They convinced the small group of Southern Lacandones living near San Quintín to move to Lacanja' Chan Sayab. But as subcultures, the Northern and Southern Lacandones continued to maintain geographical separation. By fall 1976, 84 percent of the entire population of Lacandón Maya lived inside one of the three designated communities of Naja', Mensäbäk, or Lacanja' Chan Sayab. Only seventy-five individuals remained isolated in the forest (Nations 1979).

Under New Management

Historian Jan de Vos hypothesized that the photographer-activist Gertrude Duby Blom inspired the incoming president of Mexico, Luís Echeverría Alvarez, and the incoming governor of Chiapas, Manuel Velasco Suárez, to create the Comunidad Zona Lacandona when the three met at Na Bolom, Blom's home in San Cristóbal de Las Casas in 1970 (de Vos 2011: 99). It is true that Blom had been a vociferous advocate for the Lacandones for almost three decades, and she supported protection of their rainforest lands, but it seems more likely that the two politicians met with Blom to gain her acquiescence to a strategy they had already conceived (Nations 1984). Because something else was afoot in the Comunidad Zona Lacandona.

A year after the declaration of the Lacandón land grant, in 1973, Mexican federal authorities informed Aserraderos Bonampak and its American owner, Weiss Fricker Mahogany Company, that the companies would have to stop cutting timber on the lands of the Comunidad Zona Lacandona. The ten-year timber concession that Vancouver Plywood (as Maderera Maya) had signed with Weiss Fricker (and its counterpart Aserraderos Bonampak) was about to expire, and at the end of the year, December 1973, the companies would be required to cease all operations. Government officials told the companies' owners that their sawmill at Chancalá would be allowed to process only the trees already felled and brought in from the forest. After that, they would have to abandon the enterprise completely (de Vos 2011: 91).

There was still a vast quantity of mahogany and tropical cedar in the Selva Lacandona at the time, and most of it was now legally owned by the Lacandón Maya. But government functionaries had a plan. In September 1974, a new, separate presidential decree created two parastatal companies under the control of the federal economic development agency Nacional Financiera, S.A. (NAFINSA). The first of the two companies was Compañía Industrial Forestal de la Lacandona (COFOLASA), which was charged by the government with harvesting the hardwoods of the Comunidad Zona Lacandona. The second company was Compañía Triplay de Palenque, S.A., which was assigned the task of processing the timber felled by COFOLASA. As one of its first actions, COFOLASA assumed control of the Chancalá sawmill being abandoned by Weiss Fricker and Aserraderos Bonampak (González Pacheco 1983: 185; Paladino 2005: 122; de Vos 2011: 91).

NAFINSA then signed a sixteen-month timber concession with the new owners of the unlogged rainforest, the sixty-six Lacandón Maya heads of household who had just become owners of the Comunidad. In sequence, company representatives flew into the three major Lacandón settlements in fall 1974 and asked the families to gather at the airstrip. The officials tore lengths of white and colored cotton from commercial bolts of cloth and passed them out to the excited Lacandón women. Amid the hubbub, the officials asked the Lacandón men to put their mark on a thick, printed contract they had brought with them. The few men who could sign their name did so; those who could not read or write smeared ink on their thumb and authorized the document with a thumbprint.

The document the Lacandones agreed to was a logging concession authorizing COFOLASA to cut 35,000 cubic meters of hardwood timber annually for ten years running—a quantity that represented 10,000 mahogany and cedar trees per year for a total of 100,000 trees (de Vos 2011: 113; Contreras Cortés and Mariaca Méndez 2016: 16). The contract guaranteed the Lacandones a portion of the international market price for their trees, but did not cite a price. The families were to receive 30 percent of their royalties in periodic cash payments, while 70 percent would go into a communal fund administered by a federal government agency called the Fondo Nacional de Fomento Ejidal (FONAFE). FONAFE would use the funds to carry out a series of ill-conceived and poorly executed development projects in the communities, including rustic supermarkets that offered Lacandones commercial foodstuffs such as refined wheat flour, refined sugar, packaged cornmeal, dried pasta, bottles of cooking oil, canned chilies, cookies, and flashlight batteries. The royalty funds also paid for the construction of cement block mini-clinics in each Lacandón community, though these would soon be abandoned for lack of medicine and medical personnel.

With the signing of the COFOLASA contract in 1974, the challenge of salvaging timber from the Comunidad Zona Lacandona was almost under control. The federal government itself was now felling, processing, and selling the mahogany and cedar trees of the Selva Lacandona with the help of interested businessmen and engaged politicians. The foreman of one logging team boasted that in a single work period of twenty days, his team wrenched $2 million worth of mahogany and cedar from the new concession (Nations 2006: 132).

Despite its apparent success in harvesting the hardwoods of the Selva Lacandona, the Mexican government faced another challenge: What to do about the Tzeltal and Ch'ol Maya colonists who were still clearing and burning trees before they could be harvested? There was a plan for them as well.

The Tzeltal and Ch'ol Maya families who lived inside the boundaries of the newly declared Comunidad Zona Lacandona were understandably angered when they learned that they were now interlopers on Lacandón land. They also were stunned to learn that sixty-six Lacandón heads of families were receiving cash payments for the sale of the Selva's trees while they were receiving nothing. In reaction, Tzeltal and Ch'ol families demanded that they be included in the timber payments. To emphasize their position, they blockaded COFOLASA trucks headed toward the sawmill (González Pacheco 1983: 190).

At the time, 1972–1973, more than a thousand Tzeltal and Ch'ol families were living in settlements and small villages inside the boundaries of the Comunidad Zona Lacandona, some of them with legal *ejido* status. The rest of the families had intended to apply to the government for *ejido* status to secure title to land as communal co-owners. But agents of the Secretaría de Reforma Agraria now told them that communal land grants were no longer an option, because the land they lived on had been absorbed into the Lacandones' Indigenous land grant. In fact, the government expected the Tzeltal and Ch'ol to abandon their farms and ranches and move elsewhere (Paladino 2005: 144).[2]

The families had other ideas. By 1974, they began to strategize ways to remain on the land they occupied. Most importantly, they lobbied the Secretaría de Reforma Agraria for inclusion as legal occupants of the Comunidad Zona Lacandona on the basis of language contained in the 1972 presidential decree that the Comunidad could include, "Indigenous groups of the region who do not have sufficient land for their sustenance and development."

In a crucial move, Tzeltal and Ch'ol representatives met with José Pepe Chan Bor, the Southern Lacandón leader of the Comunidad Zona Lacandona and convinced him to agree in front of an official from the Secretaría de Reforma Agraria that the families could remain within the Comunidad Zona Lacandona on the condition "that they fell as little forest as possible" (Paladino 2005: 147). Tzeltal and Ch'ol representatives were then chosen to participate in a cooperative council charged with working with the federal government and with the Comunidad Zona Lacandona.

A 1975 census of the inhabitants of the Comunidad revealed 1,340 heads of families living in twenty-three settlements who wished to be part of the agreement and remain within the Comunidad. But the families still were not legal members of the Comunidad Zona Lacandona. In exchange for abiding by the laws of the Comunidad, the Tzeltal, Ch'ol, and two settlements of Tzotzil Maya families would be allowed to remain within Comunidad boundaries, but with no financial benefits. The royalties the timber companies paid for trees would continue to go only to Lacandones.

The proposed agreement relieved the Tzeltal and Ch'ol of the threat of expulsion, but government officials made it clear that they expected them to leave their existing communities—which were scattered across the forest of the Comunidad Zona Lacandona—and concentrate instead into Nuevos Centros de Población, "New Population Centers," that the government would create. The families were told that living in concentrated communities would give them access to roads, electricity, schools, and health clinics that the government would provide and would allow the families to consolidate their milpas and cattle pastures into areas already cleared, thus preventing any chance that wildfires would destroy timber and forest resources (Paladino 2005: 150).

As negotiations proceeded between government officials and the families, some Tzeltal and Ch'ol households decided not to cooperate and not to relocate. A few returned to their original villages in highland Chiapas, but most of the resisting families said they would simply remain on the cleared rainforest land they were living on. To empower their position, they created a new organization, *Quiptic Ta Lecubtesal,* and vowed as a group not to move. Their decision would have ramifications into the twenty-first century, leaving many families with no legal title to land and with a solid resentment against the federal government (Paladino 2005: 147–148; Calleros-Rodríguez 2014: 139).

Building a New World

History went differently for the Tzeltal, Ch'ol, and Tzotzil families who agreed to relocate. In June 1975, each cooperating head of family was issued a photo identification card recognizing the family's right to live inside one of the two population centers that would be established within the Comunidad. Text on the back of the card recognized the bearer as a "guardian of the Comunidad Zona Lacandona," and stated that the goal of the population centers was "to preserve the forest's wealth and prevent spontaneous colonization by forming a containment barrier against future invasions" (Paladino 2005: 158).

The participating Tzeltal Maya families (and two communities of Tzotzil Maya) were assigned a block of land in the northeastern section of the Comunidad land grant, near an existing colony called Nuevo Palestina. Families from the disparate settlements left their homes, milpas, and pastures and in 1976 began to coalesce in their newly assigned population center. There, they readjusted from life in villages of 60–70 families to life in a planned community of 550 families condensed into an urban center on cleared rainforest land. Within a year, the number of families in the community had reached 650 (Paladino 2005: 171).

With the help of guides from the Southern Lacandón community of Lacanja' Chan Sayab, the Ch'ol Maya selected a forested site along the Río Usumacinta in the southeastern region of the Comunidad Zona Lacandona, a few kilometers upriver from the Classic Maya site of Yaxchilán. The new community took on the informal name of Frontera Corozal.

Using funds provided by programs of the United Nations, the Mexican government paid contractors to lay out urban plans, bulldoze tree trunks, and grade dirt streets in the two new urban centers, but the bulk of the work was left to the arriving colonists. During the dry season of 1976, officials paid families of both communities 25 pesos per day (US$2) for ninety days to clear vegetation from their town centers, build wood and palm leaf municipal buildings, and work in teams to construct houses for the arriving families. Each family received basic construction tools, tarpaper roofing, nails, wire, and some food, and the government opened and stocked a grocery store in the emerging urban center. Still, overall government support fell short of what the families had expected to receive. There were no medical clinics, no electricity, no water systems, no waste disposal systems, and no latrines. The families would be on their own to provide these amenities until the late 1980s (Paladino 2005: 160).

The Tzeltal Maya who built Nueva Palestina found that many of their abandoned settlements were within walking distance of their new urban center, so they hiked back to their milpas to harvest crops and carry them to their new location. They also benefited from a dirt spur road connecting their new community to the Chancalá-Bonampak logging road, providing them with access to the cities of Palenque and Tenosique (Paladino 2005: 157, 160).

The Ch'ol Maya who built Frontera Corozal were less fortunate. Their land spread along the Chiapas side of the Río Usumacinta, 40 kilometers from their original milpas and house gardens. They brought what crops they could as they rode in trucks to the new site, but when the rainy season hit in late spring, vehicle transport came to a halt. The families carried what they could on long walks through the forest and supplemented their diet by hunting wildlife in the forest (Paladino 2005: 162).

The Tzeltal and Ch'ol families were frustrated by the inadequacy of government support. Their resentment boiled over during early 1977. They could see COFOLASA trucks emerging from the forest loaded with mahogany and cedar logs, headed to the sawmill at Chancalá, but their requests for materials and services in their new urban centers went unheeded. In protest, some Tzeltal and Ch'ol blocked logging roads, sequestered company personnel, and set fire to machinery (Paladino 2005: 163).

To calm the situation, Chiapas Governor Manuel Velasco Suárez met with Tzeltal and Ch'ol representatives in March 1977 and signed an agreement (subject to presidential approval) that would recognize the residents of the two new population centers as legal occupants equal in status to the Lacandón Maya. The agreement granted the Tzeltal and Ch'ol families a portion of COFOLASA timber payments and outlined a plan that would assign each of the three ethnic groups a general subregion of the Comunidad's territory (Paladino 2005: 163).

The accord formalized the Comunidad's internal governance by establishing a three-member council consisting of one Tzeltal representative, one Ch'ol representative, and one Lacandón Maya representative, with the latter always designated as the commissioner of the Comunidad Zona Lacandona. None of the positions were paid. Also implicit in the agreement was assignment of the Lacandón commissioner as head of all Lacandones.

The new agreement defined the process for sharing timber royalties among the three ethnic groups. Thirty percent would be divided among the Tzeltal, Ch'ol, and Lacandón Maya families, though the sixty-six Lacandón families would receive a double portion because they were fewer in number than the Tzeltales and Ch'oles. Another 35 percent of the timber royalties would be held by the federal government to cover emergency assistance to the three Indigenous groups, and a final 35 percent would be held in a fund used for general development and infrastructure within the Comunidad Zona Lacandona (Nations 1979; Paladino 2005: 165). Some of the funds went to promote cattle ranching. In 1978, the fund provided the Lacandón Maya with 280 head of cattle as a communal resource, and families dedicated 40 hectares of land to raising them. But the Lacandones had no experience in raising beef cattle and little interest in doing so. Many of the animals died, and the families sold the rest (Trench 2002: 128).

When the law establishing the Comunidad Zona Lacandona was published in the federal government's *Diario Oficial* on March 8, 1979, it recognized 1,598 families as communal members of the Comunidad Zona Lacandona—931 Tzeltal Maya families, 601 Ch'ol Maya families, and 66 Lacandón Maya families—representing approximately 8,000 Indigenous women, men, and children (DOF 1979; Paladino 2005: 164; Contreras and Mariaca 2016: 17–18).

The Tzeltal Maya of Nueva Palestina, the Ch'ol Maya of Frontera Corozal, and the Lacandón Maya of Lacanja' Chan Sayab, Mensäbäk, and Naja' were now guaranteed some measure of land ownership security, communal though it be. In deeding communal lands to Indigenous people as a group rather than as individual landowners, Mexican government authorities were seeking to accommodate Indigenous traditions of communally held land. The Indigenous groups were expected to determine the rules for internal land rights and responsibilities.

By contrast, colonist communities who applied for *ejido* status elsewhere in the Selva Lacandona—outside the Comunidad Zona Lacandona—learned that the legal system required the involvement of federal officials in determining which family got which lands and where. The situation was even more challenging for the several dozen communities that had been denied *ejido* status or whose petitions were still under government review. Lack of land title limited their access to government loans, production credits, and technical assistance, miring them, "in spirals of increasingly impoverished soils and lowered production, and few options but to open up new forest lands," which of course then put them in conflict with the owners of that land (Paladino 2005: 157).

Within this mosaic of challenges, the federal government appears to have followed several motivations when they nationalized the Selva Lacandona and established the Comunidad Zona Lacandona. Protecting still unharvested hardwoods was a clear economic reason, especially after the government assumed ownership of the timber industry. Another motivation may have been preventing social unrest. Decades of unequal land distribution, student uprisings in urban areas, and perceived government repression had combined to foment guerrilla movements in Mexico during the late 1960s, and by the 1970s some of these groups had set up military training camps in the Selva Lacandona. The government sought to dampen unrest by building roads and reaching into Indigenous communities with projects that aided families and established government presence. On an international level, Mexico could justify its actions by pointing to the protection of Indigenous rights through creation of the large communal land grant.

The Maya families included in the Comunidad Zona Lacandona were aware that their agreement with the federal government included a role as "guardians of the forest." They were also aware of a valid need to protect their land from newly arriving colonists, because communities were still emerging along the outside border—and sometimes inside the border—of the Comunidad Zona Lacandona. The Tzeltal, Ch'ol, and Lacandón *comuneros* began to resist attempts by these newly arriving families to clear land. Agrarian archives record at least eighteen clashes—invasions, evictions, relocations, and jailing, including seven cases of violent evictions. Disputes have continued into the twenty-first century (Calleros-Rodríguez 2014: 130).

Montes Azules Biosphere Reserve

Land tenure challenges in the Selva Lacandona became even more complicated in January 1978, six years after the Comunidad Zona Lacandona was formed, when the Mexican government responded to national and international clamor for the protection of tropical rainforests by establishing the 331,200-hectare (1,280 square miles) Montes Azules Biosphere Reserve in the south-central region of the Selva Lacandona (DOF 1978; O'Brien 1998: 155; INE-SEMARNAP 2000). The area is a dense, high-biodiversity rainforest watered by forest tributaries that feed into the Río Jataté and Río Lacanjá, which in turn flow into the Río Usumacinta.

The declaration of Montes Azules laid a veneer of protection over forests, wetlands, and rivers that conservationists view as the biologically most important ecosystem in Mexico—itself a megadiversity country. A third of Mexico's bird species, half its butterfly species, a quarter of its mammals, and a fifth of Mexico's plants live within the boundaries of the reserve. Add to this biological wealth the region's history, especially that of the Classic Maya, and Montes Azules ranks as a globally important hotspot for the protection of both biological and cultural diversity (Nations 2006: 144).

Biosphere reserves are part of a 124-country global network organized by the United Nations Educational, Scientific, and Cultural Organization (UNESCO). Individual countries nominate sites within their boundaries, and UNESCO's Man and the Biosphere Program (MAB) determines which areas qualify for membership. By MAB standards, the area must have global or regional significance for biological conservation, one or more inviolate core zones, and one or more buffer zones and/or transition zones where human communities are allowed to use natural resources in ecologically sustainable ways (Nations 2001a: 1231; UNESCO 2020).

Reserves approved by MAB commit the host country to managing the area according to international standards, but on-the-ground ownership and management of biosphere reserves remain with the participating country according to their national laws. UNESCO's role is to provide guidance and technical assistance and facilitate financial support from international organizations. Like biosphere reserves around the world, Mexico's Montes Azules combines the goals of conservation, scientific investigation, and sustainable economic development.

In 1992, President Carlos Salinas de Gortari increased the amount of land under protection by declaring additional conservation areas along the northeastern border of the Montes Azules Biosphere Reserve. The new law established the 61,873-hectare Reserva de la Biósfera Lacantún as a national protected area (though it has not been submitted to UNESCO as part of MAB); the 12,184-hectare Refugio de Flora y Fauna Silvestre Chan K'in; the 4,357-hectare Monumento Natural Bonampak around the ruins of Bonampak; and the 2,621-hectare Monumento Natural Yaxchilán around the ruins of Yaxchilán. One year later, in 1993, the Comunidad Zona Lacandona established the 35,400-hectare Reserva Comunal Sierra la Cojolita, which serves as a biological corridor to connect Montes Azules, Bonampak, and Yaxchilán (Nations 2006: 145). Because these more recent protected areas adjoin Montes Azules Biosphere Reserve, they expand biodiversity protection in the Selva Lacandona and restrict the amount of deforestation legally permitted within the Comunidad Zona Lacandona.

The challenge presented by Montes Azules and its connected protected areas is this: 85 percent of their territory overlaps with land belonging to the Comunidad Zona Lacandona. Yet this situation violates neither the tenets of biosphere reserves nor Mexican law. Biosphere reserves permit occupation by communities as long as the families use the natural resources sustainably. Similarly, Mexican law allows communities to coexist with protected areas on the same territory. The residents maintain ownership of the land, but the government retains the right to regulate the use of vegetation and wildlife that live on it. In the case of Montes Azules and its adjoining protected areas, the Comunidad Zona Lacandona owns 85 percent of the land the reserves occupy, but Mexico's Secretaría del Medio Ambiente y Recursos Naturales (SEMARNAT, Secretariat of Environment and Natural Resources) legally protects the natural resources that grow there.

So far, the situation has benefited biocultural protection in Montes Azules, because the strictly protected core areas of Montes Azules Biosphere Reserve lie within the subregions of the Comunidad Zona Lacandona associated with the Lacandón Maya and Ch'ol Maya. The Ch'oles are essentially surrounded by protected forest on three sides, and the Lacandones' tradition of forest conservation and lack of interest in cattle ranching make them eager protectors of the region's ecosystems.

Satellite images of the reserve taken in 2022 showed that the core protection zones of Montes Azules Biosphere Reserve and its adjoining reserves were surviving but under threat. Deforestation was squeezing the panhandle of Montes Azules—the region surrounding the Lagos Ocotales west of Nueva Palestina—and colonists were clearing milpas and pastures in the valleys leading southeast from Ocosingo, pushing into the biosphere reserve along its southwestern border.

The most serious challenges for Montes Azules emerge in the 15 percent of the reserve that does not overlap with the Comunidad Zona Lacandona. This section of land, centered on Laguna Miramar in the southwest, has become an extension of the Las Cañadas agricultural frontier that follows valleys that are parallel to the Río Jataté. There, colonists are clearing land, planting corn and pasture, and raising beef cattle inside the biosphere reserve. Because this section of Montes Azules is not part of the Comunidad, it has few vocal defenders beyond the Mexican federal government and Mexican conservation groups.

Just beyond the southeastern border of Montes Azules Biosphere Reserve lies the Marqués de Comillas sector of the Selva Lacandona, an area still being deforested in a grid pattern similar to that impacting the Amazon Basin. Wherever roads penetrate, deforestation stretches out in parallel lines, transforming forest into pasture and monoculture plantations of African oil palm (*Elaeis guineensis*). Stands of forest remain where roads have not yet reached, and so far colonization has not jumped the Río Lacantún into Montes Azules, but inside the Marqués de Comillas, rainforest is mostly a memory.

By 2020, 64,000 hectares of the Marqués de Comillas region had been planted in African oil palm, and the State of Chiapas announced a goal of reaching 100,000 hectares by providing cash incentives and technical support to producers. According to government agriculturalists, the state government of Chiapas plans to establish four oil palm nurseries that are "the largest in Latin America." Oil palm is being planted on some lands that previously were pasture, but other plantations are being developed "on newly cleared rainforest land" (Mongabay Latam 2020).

Green Gold to Black Gold

Adding yet another threat to the ecosystems of the Selva Lacandona, the potential for oil exploitation hangs over the region like the sword of Damocles. During the 1970s, international petroleum companies discovered oil deposits in the northwestern corner of the Guatemalan Petén—just across the Río Usumacinta—in a wetland known as Laguna del Tigre (since 1990, part of Parque Nacional Laguna del Tigre). Guatemala was already pumping oil from the area and searching for additional deposits along the Río Chixoy, only a few kilometers from the international border, when Mexican officials realized that Guatemala was actively exploiting petroleum deposits that lay beneath the countries' dividing line (de Vos 2011: 53).

The competition prompted the Mexican government to initiate a search for oil in the Selva Lacandona during the same years that the Comunidad Zona Lacandona and Montes Azules Biosphere Reserve were being established. In 1976, the state-owned oil company, Petróleos Mexicanos (PEMEX), began cutting new roads through the forest to conduct seismic tests. Workers bulldozed a grid of testing lines through 250,000 hectares (965 square miles) of rainforest, cutting 4-meter strips and drilling 20-meter holes every 80 meters to plant and detonate dynamite. The process revealed three potentially promising deposits, and PEMEX continued to explore. The company paused during 1982 and 1983 while road crews constructed a highway along the international boundary with Guatemala. When completed, the road encircled the Selva Lacandona and pulled the region into the national fold (González Pacheco 1983: 191).

By the early 1990s, PEMEX had nineteen wells in various stages of planning and production, eleven of them in Marqués de Comillas and eight in Las Cañadas. Although a half dozen rigs were still actively drilling, in 1992, for unexplained reasons, the company loaded its equipment onto trucks and drove away (de Vos 2011: 54). They have not yet returned, though the roads they built remain.

Why PEMEX abruptly withdrew from the Selva Lacandona remains a mystery. Perhaps someone had a premonition of the Zapatista uprising that would shake the Selva only two years later, pitting armed Indigenous fighters against the Mexican army. More likely, economics lured the industry to more promising fields. Only 15 percent of Mexico's crude petroleum reserves lie beneath the states of Chiapas and Tabasco, and only a portion of those lie beneath the Selva Lacandona. During the past several decades, PEMEX has focused its operations on productive offshore deposits in the Gulf of Mexico, but the company may someday return to the Selva Lacandona. The basic ground work has already been completed (Paladino 2005: 71; Sandrea 2019; Library of Congress 2020).

Guatemalan Refugees

Social tensions increased further in the Selva Lacandona during the mid-1980s, when Guatemala's civil war spilled across the border into Chiapas. Tens of thousands of women, men, and children escaping the Guatemalan military and militarized Civil Defense Patrols crossed the river into Mexico. More than 90 percent of the refugees were Maya, mainly Kanjobal, Mam, Chuj, and Jacalteco, and 95 percent were farmers. The possibility that Guatemalan soldiers might pursue the families into Mexico threatened national sovereignty and prompted the Mexican government to relocate almost half the families into refugee camps in the states of Campeche and Quintana Roo. But more than 24,000 Guatemalan Maya remained within the Selva Lacandona in 119 camps scattered along the Río Lacantún and in the rainforest of Marqués de Comillas, a region pinched on three sides by Guatemalan territory (CARE/Conservation International 1995; O'Brien 1998: 136).

To guarantee control of the area, Mexican government officials increased the number of military troops and expanded the network of roads in the Selva Lacandona. Most of the Guatemalan refugees survived on food and medical aid supplied by international organizations, especially the United Nations, though a few found work with Mexican farmers. Despite their confinement to refugee camps, the families' diet and health care improved—so much so that their natural rate of increase rose to 4 percent per year, causing their population to double in 17.5 years. When the refugees began to repatriate to Guatemala in 1994, authorities discovered that 45 percent of them had been born in Chiapas and had never been to their home country (CARE/Conservation International 1995).

Most of the land the families had been forced to abandon in Guatemala had meanwhile been absorbed by other farmers, and the new lands the returnees were assigned were poor, isolated, ecologically fragile, and in some cases, inside Guatemalan protected areas, including Parque Nacional Sierra del Lacandón, which had been named for the Lacandón Maya who had lived there decades before. Refugees continued to return home through the signing of the 1996 peace accords that formally ended Guatemala's civil war (CARE/Conservation International 1995).

The Mexican government's focus on road construction during the Guatemalan refugee crisis benefited the Mexican families who lived in the Selva Lacandona, and these improvements attracted new colonists. Drawn by federal projects aimed at creating new *ejidos* in the border zone of Marqués de Comillas, non-Indigenous colonists came from as far away as the Mexican states of Veracruz, Sinaloa, Campeche, Guanajuato, Michoacán, Guerrero, and Querétero (Marion 1997). Highways built to monitor the region militarily increased the families' access to markets, and the extension of power lines brought light to communities that previously had been lit only by fire.

Logging Redux

During the late 1970s, the parastatal logging company COFOLASA was still paying timber royalties to the families of the Comunidad Zona Lacandona and to small landowners who had title to land along the edge of the Indigenous land grant, but the company's costs for timber rights, road maintenance, salaries, and operations had begun to exceed the pace of timber extraction, reportedly leaving no room for profits. By 1978, the company had experienced a 70 percent decline in production from its original years. Combined with the challenges of social unrest and forest destruction, these costs caused COFOLASA and Triplay de Palenque to go bust in May 1980.

Seizing the opportunity, the government of Chiapas created a new parastatal company, Corporación de Fomento de Chiapas (CORFO), which took over COFOLASA's logging operations for the next decade. But for that company too, high costs and increasing scarcity of hardwoods brought operations to a halt by 1989. Small-scale logging, both legal and illegal, meanwhile continued in the Marqués de Comillas. As farmers and ranchers acquired land there, they sold their mahogany and cedar to a Palenque-based enterprise called CARPICENTRO, which offered to reimburse anyone fined for illegal harvesting of wood. Eventually, even this last gasp of timber harvesting was overtaken by deforestation as the Marqués de Comillas was transformed into farms, cattle ranches, and African oil palm plantations (O'Brien 1998: 81; Paladino 2005: 187).

"No Longer a Possibility"

Then the rules governing land distribution in Mexico changed, and the world turned upside down. In 1992, the national legislature modified Article 27 of the Mexican constitution to end a policy of land redistribution that had been in place since the Mexican Revolution of 1910–1917. Federal agencies would no longer receive applications for *ejido* status on newly colonized lands. Negotiations already in process were allowed to continue, but as researcher Stephanie Paladino put it, "Expansion to new lands with the hope of gaining legal tenure was no longer a possibility." Within the Comunidad Zona Lacandona, the Tzeltal and Ch'ol *comuneros* negotiated internal regulations that recognized each member's right to 50 hectares of land, and—anticipating their own population growth—an additional 10 hectares for each of two sons (Paladino 2005: 139, 176).

Still, new colonists continued to flow into the Selva Lacandona, clearing land for farms and ranches. In 1992, 100 settlements, ranches, and *ejidos* of differing legal status occupied land inside the boundaries of the Comunidad Zona Lacandona (Calleros-Rodríguez 2014: 140). As new communities cleared forest near the unmarked boundary line of the Comunidad, tensions rose between *comuneros* and new arrivals. Some colonizing families occupied Comunidad lands that Tzeltal and Ch'ol families had abandoned when they moved to the government-mandated population centers. The situation led to disputes that began with harsh words and sometimes ratcheted into violence (Paladino 2005: 178–180).

The impact of the colonists' push for new land was magnified by the fact that more than half the land cleared in the Selva was dedicated to cattle pasture. Beef cattle ranching on thin tropical soils requires large amounts of land per animal and results in uninspiring yields—an average of 10 kilos of beef per hectare per year. Cattle ranching also forces people off the land, because less human labor is required per unit of land than raising food crops (Nations and Komer 1983a; Nations and Komer 1983b: 237; Muench 1997).

But if an aspiring rancher in the Selva Lacandona can get a single cow to market in a good year, he can make 8,000 to 12,000 pesos (US$444 to US$667 in 2021), more than he can earn from most other activities available to him. In the Selva Lacandona, monetary income per days of labor from raising cattle is exceeded only by growing marijuana or poaching endangered scarlet macaw chicks from their nests (Iñigo-Elías 1996). Though most small-scale farmers acquire only a few head of cattle, those few head are like a savings account—a guarantee against financial ruin and a sort of unemployment insurance. Like money in the bank, cattle can be held on the hoof until market prices improve, and they are self-ambulatory—they can move themselves toward market (Ford and Nigh 2016: 161).

The animals these small-scale cattlemen produce only infrequently become food for the family or community, because little of the beef produced in the Selva Lacandona remains there. Instead, like clockwork every year, eighteen-wheel cattle trucks pull into the larger communities of the Selva to purchase the cattle produced by small-scale Indigenous cattlemen, a few from this family, a few more from the neighbors. Cattle from the Selva Lacandona, as well as that produced in the states of Tabasco and Veracruz, are driven to cities in other parts of Mexico to be consumed in restaurants, institutions, and family dining rooms. In a giant shuffle of live animals, beef cattle produced in the drier states of northern Mexico are simultaneously exported to the United States for fattening and slaughter

(Gonzáles-Pacheco 1983; Nations 1994; Peel 2005; Ríos Flores and Castillo Arce 2014). In short, small-scale Indigenous farmers and ranchers in the Selva Lacandona are being used as cheap, off-site labor by the national and international livestock industry at the expense of local food production and at the expense of the natural environment (Ford and Nigh 2016: 164, 173).

Zapatistas

As if things weren't complicated enough: On New Year's Day 1994, Mexican officials who expected to wake up to celebrate Mexico's entry into the North American Free Trade Agreement (NAFTA) instead woke up to an armed rebellion in Chiapas. Indigenous groups carrying rifles, machetes, and wooden sticks attacked and seized public squares in several regions of the state, including villages in the Selva Lacandona and medium-sized cities such as Ocosingo, Altamirano, and San Cristóbal de Las Casas. The sudden violence threw the country into an initial confusion that increased when insurgents hacked into the government's website and began broadcasting revolutionary messages (Beckett 2001: 249).

The insurgents called themselves the Ejército Zapatista de Liberación Nacional, the "Zapatista Army of National Liberation" (EZLN), soon to be known around the world as Zapatistas, having adopted their name from Emiliano Zapata, a hero of the 1910–1917 Mexican Revolution who fought for "Land and Liberty." The Zapatistas were (and remain) a movement populated by Tzeltal, Tzotzil, Ch'ol, and Tojolabal Maya, along with a sprinkling of Ladino auxiliaries. When they burst forth in 1994, spokespeople for the group (women and men) declared that they fought for land and freedom for the Indigenous people of the Selva Lacandona. Firefights between Zapatistas and the Mexican army continued through the first weeks of 1994, resulting in at least 300 deaths. When the Mexican army counterattacked in force, the Zapatistas faded back into the valleys of central and eastern Chiapas as guerrilla fighters, eventually to emerge as a political force. But almost thirty years later, some still have not disarmed (Vidal 2018).

Many of the core Zapatista fighters came from Tzeltal Maya families in Las Cañadas, a region of river valleys and mountain crests that begins south of Ocosingo and spreads southeastward into the rainforest of the Selva Lacandona. Most of these families migrated into Las Cañadas from other regions of Chiapas during the second half of the twentieth century, escaping population growth and lives of hardscrabble farming on depleted farmlands. Once in place in Las Cañadas, their population expanded due to additional in-migration, high birth rates, and improved childhood survival (Legorreta Díaz 2015).

It is not surprising that the increasing number of families played a fundamental role in the Zapatista rebellion. In the thirty-four years between 1960 and the 1994 uprising, the population of the Selva Lacandona grew from 6,000 to 300,000, with 52 percent of the population still under the age of fifteen years (World Bank 1994; Nations 1994). The emerging *ejidos* and ranches of Las Cañadas represented 10 percent of the families in the Selva Lacandona, making it the most densely populated region in the Selva (SEMARNAP 2000: 50). As the number of families grew, disputes over land tenure also increased. With an economy focused on producing corn, beef cattle, chilies, coffee, and pigs on cleared rainforest land, the inhabitants faced a constant need for additional territory. Between 1979 and 1993, farmers and cattle ranchers in the Selva Lacandona cleared an average of 33,500 hectares (129 square miles) of rainforest every year.

The 1994 NAFTA complicated the situation even further, because it facilitated the export of agribusiness-produced corn from the United States to Mexico, threatening the livelihood of thousands of Indigenous farmers. Corn produces modest gains when sold locally, but it is the major food staple in the Selva Lacandona, the basis for every family's diet. It is not so much a commodity as the key to feeding the family. As Ford and Nigh state, "Maize [corn] offers reliable yields, high nutritional value, and simplicity of cultivation" (Ford and Nigh 2016: 162). Almost every family in the Selva Lacandona raises corn. But in reaction to the threat presented by NAFTA's treatment of corn as an international agribusiness commodity, the Zapatistas made the trade pact one of their primary targets for political attack. Sub-Comandante Marcos, a former university professor and an early Zapatista spokesman, declared NAFTA, "a death certificate for the indigenous people of Mexico" (Nations 1994).

But NAFTA was only part of the problem. Five years before the Zapatista uprising, Mexico had dismantled coffee price controls, thinking global coffee prices were secure. Almost simultaneously—though for unrelated reasons—world coffee prices plummeted, threatening financial ruin for small-scale coffee producers in Las Cañadas and the rest of the Selva Lacandona. Three years later, another hit came when the Mexican government altered Article 27 of the national constitution, privatizing *ejido* lands and allowing communal farmers—for the first time in history—to sell their share of their community's land. The stated intent of the Mexican government was to increase agricultural production through "more efficient" production on larger land holdings. But the change threatened to leave thousands of small farmers with no land at all.

It is not difficult to imagine an Indigenous farmer sizing up his alternatives: He could migrate to a nearby city and sell Popsicles from a pushcart, he could become a farm laborer for someone else, or he could rebel against the situation and demand the land he needed to survive. That so many farmers chose to rebel comes as no surprise.

Although Zapatistas declared in press releases and interviews that they were fighting for land and freedom for the Indigenous families of the Selva Lacandona, they conflated the rebelling families of Las Cañadas with the Tzeltal, Ch'ol, and Lacandón Maya of the Comunidad Zona Lacandona. In reality, the Maya of the Comunidad wanted nothing to do with the rebellion. A Lacandón Maya political leader reported that Zapatista representatives invited the *comuneros* of the Comunidad to join them, but they declined (Calleros-Rodrígez 2014: 137).

Instead, after the fighting began in 1994, the Comunidad's elected officials—one each from the Tzeltal, Ch'ol, and Lacandón Maya populations—issued a public letter, disavowing involvement in the insurgency and declaring support for the Mexican government. The Lacandón, Tzeltal, and Ch'ol Maya of the Comunidad Zona Lacandona said they shared the Zapatistas' desire to be treated with respect and justice by the dominant, Spanish-speaking society that surrounds them, but they feared the Zapatistas' goal of expanding their land holdings would threaten their own Indigenous territories.

Since then, Lacandones have been exceedingly clear and direct about their attitudes toward the Zapatistas. As José Pepe Chan Bor, commissioner of the Comunidad Zona Lacandona, told a visiting group of government officials and conservationists in the mid-1990s (I was part of the group), "The land the Zapatistas are demanding is the rainforest we are trying to protect. It is our land. Any new land for colonists should come from the large cattle ranches and *fincas* (estates) of the Mexican families in the Ocosingo Valley." [The historical record makes clear that unnamed government officials protected those large land holdings from redistribution when the Comunidad Zona Lacandona was established in the 1970s (O'Brien 1998: 144–145).]

The *comuneros* of the Comunidad Zona Lacandona knew that the Zapatista rebellion was, in fact, about land—who controls it and how they use it—and they also knew that the land in question was theirs. They viewed the Montes Azules Biosphere Reserve as a buffer between their territory and the expanding agricultural frontier of Las Cañadas. In a meeting with Mexican government officials, Carmelo Chan Bor, a former commissioner of the Comunidad Zona Lacandona, stated his opinion precisely: "The colonists have turned all their forest into pasture," he said, "and now they want to clear the forest we've kept alive for our families."[3]

Ironically, the Zapatistas' public statements cited one of their goals as "respect for natural resources," and the sixteen laws for EZLN-liberated territory, most of them focused on expropriation and redistribution of land, included this as number thirteen: "Virgin jungle zones and forests will be preserved, and there will be reforestation campaigns in the principal zones" (Womack 1999: 254).

Despite these reassurances, some Zapatistas took advantage of the unrest to seize land that belonged to other Maya families. Tzeltal farmers from the *ejido* of El Jardín cleared 100 hectares of rainforest belonging to the community of Naja' and began planting grass for beef cattle (Palacio Peralta and Moguel Viveros 2008: 87). An hour's drive to the north, Tzeltal farmers from the *ejido* of El Tumbo jumped their boundary with Mensäbäk and began chain-sawing forest for cornfields and pasture.

In both cases, Lacandón community leaders sped to the Chiapas state capitol to protest the invasions. When Mexican authorities appeared in the two communities several days later, the invading Tzeltales retreated to their villages. One of the would-be occupiers later reported to his Tzeltal comrades, "These Lacandones are no fools."[4]

A Tzeltal Maya representative of the Comunidad Zona Lacandona told Mexican researcher Héctor Calleros-Rodríguez that the Zapatistas "don't want to negotiate with the Lacandón Community, what they want is to take possession of the land without the interference of the government; that's how it is with the Zapatistas" (Calleros-Rodríguez 2014: 137).

The fires of the Zapatista rebellion began to cool only months after fighting began, but the movement had long-lasting impacts on the Selva Lacandona. One result was increased military presence. Some of the military camps established in the Selva in reaction to the rebellion remain active today. The Mexican military occupied ecotourism camps that belonged to Indigenous communities, including a research station staffed by families from Nueva Palestina on Laguna Ocotal Grande. Near Laguna Miramar in Montes Azules, the army built a permanent camp in the *ejido* of San Quintín, creating a daily face-off with Zapatista families living on the other side of the fence.

Establishing federal control over the Selva Lacandona also expanded the region's infrastructure. To appease disaffected families, government agencies stretched power lines into rural areas of the Selva that had never before had electricity. In 1996, the government asphalted the 422-kilometer Frontier Highway that parallels the Río Usumacinta and the Mexico-Guatemala border, making it possible to circumnavigate the Selva Lacandona by vehicle. The highway also makes it easier to move troops into the region in case trouble flares again.

Domestic support for the Zapatistas weakened after Mexican voters elected presidents from parties opposed to the entrenched Partido Revolucionario Independiente (PRI), in 2000, 2006, and again in 2018, but the persistent vision of masked, mounted Zapatistas fighting for Indigenous land rights continues to earn the group financial support among international sympathizers (Gollnick 2008: 155).

Conflicts Inside and Out

Ripples from the Zapatista rebellion continue to complicate efforts to relocate illegal settlements from the Comunidad Zona Lacandona and Montes Azules Biosphere Reserve. Federal authorities have resettled several irregular settlements by buying land for them elsewhere. But in other cases, attempts to negotiate have prompted protests and resistance from pro-Zapatista communities, causing government officials to back away. The continuing presence of irregular colonies inside the boundaries of the Comunidad Zona Lacandona prompt Tzeltal and Ch'ol Maya comuneros to complain that protesting colonists are allowed to clear and plant land they've colonized illegally, but the comuneros are denied permission to increase the amount of agricultural land inside their own legal boundaries (Calleros-Rodríguez 2014: 146–147; Paladino 2005: 135).

The comuneros have also had to cede large bites of their communal land to colonists who resisted being incorporated into the Comunidad Zona Lacandona but also fought to keep land inside its boundaries. Ten years into the struggle, in 1989, recalcitrance paid off for some of the resisting communities when President Carlos Salinas de Gortari delivered legal titles to twenty-six "irregular" communities, at least one of which had colonized the Selva Lacandona as far back as 1959. For the excision of land from their Indigenous land grant, the Lacandón, Tzeltal, and Ch'ol comuneros of the Comunidad Lacandona received monetary compensation from the Secretaría de Reforma Agraria. Between 2004 and 2006, comuneros ceded 44,006 hectares to internal communities and were compensated 265 million pesos.

Since 2006, the government has paid them 109 million pesos for another 58,259 hectares of land turned over to resisting communities (Calleros-Rodríguez 2014: 147).

Overall, ceding communal land to other communities has diminished the original extent of the Comunidad Zona Lacandona from 614,321 hectares to 501,106 hectares, a loss of 18 percent of the original Indigenous land grant. Making the issue even stickier is the fact that more than half of the Comunidad's remaining land is inside the Montes Azules Biosphere Reserve (de Vos 2011: 122).

The challenge of land disputes is not disappearing. When they received title to their land, the *comuneros* of the Comunidad Zona Lacandona—Lacandones, Tzeltales, and Ch'oles—agreed to abide by specific governmental policies, but they also requested two things: (1) that government authorities physically demarcate the Comunidad's boundaries to prevent illegal encroachments, and (2) that the government remove the illegal settlements already there.

The two requests are related. Colonists in some irregular communities fervently resist government attempts to demarcate the Comunidad's boundaries, because defining the boundary might reveal they are occupying land within the Comunidad Zona Lacandona or Montes Azules Biosphere Reserve. When engineering teams attempt to mark the boundaries on the ground, the colonists push back, sometimes through the courts, but sometimes by blocking roads and kidnapping teams trying to survey the land. The land disputes put the Mexican government in a tight spot. Officials are hard pressed to balance the land rights of the Comunidad Zona Lacandona and protection of the Montes Azules Biosphere Reserve with threats of social upheaval. The situation is complicated (Paladino 2005: 180; Calleros-Rodríguez 2014: 129, 137, 147–148).

Internal Conflicts

By mid-2020, the Comunidad Zona Lacandona was home to 22,000 legal residents, plus several thousand colonists living in contested settlements within the *Comunidad's* boundaries. While conflicts continue to exist between *comuneros* and colonists, an inexorable increase in population density is also creating tensions among the *comuneros* themselves. The three Maya groups who control the Comunidad Zona Lacandona operate under a government-recognized "traditional" form of governance—communal Indigenous lands—by which they're obligated to make decisions among themselves through negotiation and cooperation. The democratic nature of the arrangement has decreased forest clearing inside the boundaries of the Comunidad, because the three ethnic groups view land-use decisions differently and are forced to move cautiously.

Different economic livelihoods among the Tzeltal, Ch'ol, and Lacandón produce different impacts on the land. The Tzeltales of Nueva Palestina are the most numerous of the three groups and, as cattlemen, corn farmers, and coffee and chili producers, they require large expanses of land. The Ch'ol Maya of Frontera Corozal are fewer in number, raise food crops, pigs, and some beef cattle, and supplement their income by gathering xate palm leaves in the rainforest. Ch'oles also benefit from living in the gateway community for the Classic Maya site of Yaxchilán. Archaeological and ecological tourism generate income from the outside world, and proximity to the border brings opportunities for international trade with Guatemala.

Lacandón Maya, even fewer in number, benefit from ecotourism income because of their proximity to picturesque tropical lakes in the north and to the rainforest ruins of Bonampak and Lacanja' in the south. Lacandones raise no beef cattle or pigs and actively promote forest protection. In the Northern community of Naja', for example, each head of household has rights to 20 hectares of communal land, but on average uses only 3.64 hectares. Of those few hectares, an average of only 1.2 are actively used for agriculture, leaving the rest for house gardens, yard animals, and regenerating forest gardens. This turns out to be sufficient space to produce staple foods for a family of six for a year. As a result, the bulk of each household's communal "holdings" are left in natural forest, useful as a source for building materials, wildlife, and edible forest products, not to mention the environmental benefits (Contreras and Mariaca 2016: 40).

The economic livelihoods of the three ethnic groups of the Comunidad Zona Lacandona express themselves differently on the terrain. Satellite images reveal heavy deforestation in the northern sector of the zone around Nuevo Palestina. The Ch'ol area of influence shows less impact, and the Lacandón areas—Naja', Mensäbäk, and Lacanja' Chan Sayab/Bethel—are barely touched, the only signs being dirt roads and scattered houses accompanied by milpas and garden plots surrounded by forest.

When differences in attitude and economic use of the land lead to disputes among the *comuneros* of the Comunidad Zona Lacandona, the three groups sometimes approach Mexico's Procuraduría Agraria, which provides advice and legal representation to farming communities throughout Mexico. In 2019, the three representatives of the Comunidad, led by the

Southern Lacandón commissioner, Pepe Chambor Yuk, met with officials of the Procuraduría Agraria in Mexico City to seek their counsel on land problems that had vexed the Comunidad for years (Procuraduría Agraria 2019).

The main problem, Chambor Yuk told the officials, was definition of the boundaries of the Comunidad Zona Lacandona so that neighboring communities would know where to halt their agricultural expansion. But he acknowledged that the three ethnic groups of the Comunidad also had disagreements, primarily about deforestation.

At a follow-up meeting in Palenque a few months later, Procuraduría Agraria officials recommended the division of the Comunidad's land among the three different groups. They proposed to end the decades-long management of the Comunidad Zona Lacandona as common lands, in which the three ethnic groups hold equal ownership, and instead to assign each group a specific territory for which they alone would be responsible. Each ethnic group—Lacandón Maya, Tzeltal Maya, and Ch'ol Maya—would receive one-third of the communal territory, including the forest of the Montes Azules Biosphere Reserve and its adjoining protected areas and wildlife reserves. The officials proposed that the Lacandón Maya take possession of the 99,350-hectare core protection zone of Montes Azules, and that another 232,000 hectares be made available for farming and ranching by the Tzeltal and Ch'ol (Ramos Ortiz 2019).

Understandably, the proposal led to increased tension. According to Sergio Montes Quintero, director of the Montes Azules Biosphere Reserve, Lacandón Maya representatives indicated that, "Palestina and Frontera Corozal were soliciting land to increase beef cattle production by increasing deforestation in the Áreas Naturales Protegidas."[5]

Researcher Arturo Ramos Ortiz provided a terse report on the situation: "The problem," he wrote, is that "division of the Bienes Comunales [communally held land] would leave the Lacandones with only the nucleus of the Reserve, while the south (theoretically the Ch'ol area) would be left without defense against the invasion attempts that have multiplied there" (Ramos Ortiz 2019). The southern area that Ramos Ortiz refers to includes the Refugio de Flora y Fauna Silvestre Chan K'in, the Reserva de la Biósfera Lacantún, and the Reserva Comunal Sierra la Cojolita.

"The northeastern zone, the Tzeltal area," he continued, "is very devastated, and it is probable that the division of the Comunidad lands will lead to the dissolution of these lands from legal protection and their final deforestation."

According to Ramos Ortiz, "The past system of governing the region has strongly eroded because of internal conflicts and pressure from popular rural organizations in the zone (the EZLN being only one of them), which has led to the idea that each community receive land rights over the land they occupy instead of forming part of a generalized common group."

The Procuraduría Agraria's proposal, Ramos Ortiz said, would leave the Lacandones and their traditional conservation ethic "with a little more than 30 percent of the still-forested land, the last in Mexico." As Ramos Ortiz implies, the expansion of farming and cattle ranching in the Comunidad Zona Lacandona, Montes Azules Biosphere Reserve, and the adjoining natural protected areas would threaten the survival of biocultural diversity in Mexico's highest priority conservation area (Ramos Ortiz 2019).

Director Montes Quintero of the Montes Azules Biosphere Reserve said that when Andrés Manuel López Obrador, president of Mexico, learned of the proposal presented by the Procuraduría Agraria, "He stated in one of his morning conferences that not a single hectare of forest in Lacandona would be felled, and that the agency responsible for attending to the social conflict was not the Procuraduría Agraria, but the Secretaría de Gobernación," Mexico's Office for Governance of Domestic Affairs.

The president's statement calmed things down for now, Montes Quintero said, and reaffirmed peaceful coexistence among the three ethnic groups of the Comunidad Zona Lacandona.

Montes Quintero added another positive note. "The expansion of cattle ranching and deforestation is not infinite," he said. "Between 1980 and 2015 there were high levels of deforestation due to pasture expansion, but cattle require water and flat land, both of which are becoming scarce in the Selva Lacandona."[6]

During the last few years (2015–2020), Montes Quintero noted, far fewer areas have been incorporated into cattle ranching. Still, he acknowledged, while cattlemen in some locations are working to intensify cattle production on lands they've already cleared, "others have opted to invade lands inside the Selva Lacandona's protected areas. I believe we should promote intensification of cattle ranching," he concluded, "to prevent lands inside the Protected Areas from being colonized."

How Will This End?

At the beginning of the twentieth century, the rainforest of the Selva Lacandona had covered 1.8 million hectares (6,950 square miles). But by the beginning of the twenty-first century, the forest had been reduced to only 500,000 hectares (1,931 square miles) (de Jong et al. 2009; SEMARNAP 2000; de Vos 2011: 45–46). More than half the deforested land is now cattle pasture, with another 23 percent in milpa and food production (Muench 1997: 95). African oil palm, introduced into the Selva in 2005, already occupies 64,000 hectares of land, mainly in Marqués de Comillas, accounting for a small but growing percentage of forest loss (Castellanos-Navarret and Jansen 2015: 4; Hernández-Rojas et al. 2018; Mongabay Latam 2020).

And forest clearing persists. The Mexican conservation nonprofit organization Natura Mexicana reports that 142,000 hectares (548 square miles) of the Selva Lacandona were converted from rainforest to farmland and pasture in the dozen years between 2000 and 2012, a deforestation rate that researchers at Mexico's UNAM called "untenable." The rainforest that remains, they state, is home to the highest density of biological diversity in Mexico, including scores of species that appear nowhere else in the world. This same forest also recycles and regulates massive amounts of Mexico's freshwater, including a vital network of major rivers. Clearing rainforest diminishes rainfall and water flow, meaning less rain and less freshwater (Soberanes 2018). Globally, the Selva Lacandona is part of a vital carbon sequestration process that impacts the world's climate.

As Anabel Ford and Ronald Nigh have pointed out, "Satellite views of the region demonstrate all too clearly the trajectory of increasing population growth with the expansion of pastures and plowed fields. Expanding Western systems of pasture and plow are eliminating the biodiversity of the forest" (Ford and Nigh 2016: 174).

The human population of the Selva Lacandona, currently estimated at 500,000, continues to increase at 3.75 percent per year, a rate that would double the number of people in just under nineteen years (Hacienda Chiapas 2020). How will these individuals support themselves in the future? Will we see massive outmigration to cities, to other regions of Chiapas, to other states of Mexico, to other countries? Or will most people remain in the Selva and try to make a go of it in agriculture and cattle ranching?

In 2023, the majority of families in the Selva Lacandona, including the *comuneros* of the Comunidad Zona Lacandona, continue to depend on the production of beef cattle, pigs, corn, coffee, and chilies for their livelihood. Many of these families hold secure title to their land but face challenges as human population expands around them. Other families live on land claimed by others or on land nominally protected as archaeological monuments, biosphere reserves, or wildlife reserves.

Thus, the dilemma: If the number of families in the Selva Lacandona continues to grow, and if those families continue to depend on corn farming, cattle ranching, and export crop production for their livelihood, the region's population will eventually run out of land. If the Selva's legally protected ecosystems continue to be protected, the looming deadline for running out of land comes even sooner.

And the protected areas should, in fact, be protected. Despite protests from a few shortsighted organizations, the scenario is not a choice between environmental conservation or land rights for Indigenous people. Biological resources are crucially important to the families of the Selva Lacandona. They are the basis for their survival. To eradicate the natural foundation their livelihoods depend on—biological diversity, naturally functioning ecosystems, rainfall-absorbing forest—would be more than counterproductive. It would sacrifice a productive, potentially sustainable future for destructive, short-term benefits.

A half dozen government agencies and nonprofit organizations have tried (and are trying) to spark economic enterprises such as orchid cultivation, vanilla production, rubber trees, macadamia nuts, and beekeeping. But without sufficient technical and marketing follow-up, most attempts flounder, leaving families to depend for survival on the tried and true activities of farming and ranching (Paladino 2005: 187). Alternative projects tend to fail because they're designed by outside engineers and politicians who have little knowledge or appreciation for traditional Maya food production systems (O'Brien 1998: 167–168).

Better options exist: More precisely, the region requires a new focus on food production that uses the Mayas' traditional technological knowledge, with emphasis on agroecology and agroforestry "within the context of the natural setting." The key action is to relieve the Indigenous farmers and ranchers of the Selva Lacandona of their role as small-time players in a destructive pattern of Mexico's national livestock industry. Emphasizing food and crop systems that build forest rather than replacing it with pastureland would re-create a positive human-environment relationship in Mexico's last, large rainforest (Ford and Nigh 2016: 155–156).

An example: A few kilometers from Naja' and Mensäbäk, Tzeltal Maya of the *ejidos* of Zaragoza and El Tumbo have established fields of shade-grown, organic coffee at the base of the forested crests of mountains that border their milpas and pastures. The forest is part of the communities' communal lands, but, "You can't plant anything there," said Diego Sánchez of El Tumbo. "The land is too steep to plant so the *ejido* keeps the forest in reserve."

Francisco Hernández Luís of Zaragosa noted, "Our cooperative benefits because the forest generates water for the coffee trees." He went on to explain that the forest crowning the mountains releases absorbed rainwater over the course of the year, creating good conditions for the coffee trees they've planted downslope.

"So, we don't need fertilizers or chemicals," Hernández Luís said. "And the forest protects the birds so we can call our product organic, shade-grown, bird-friendly coffee. Last year, we sold it all to Holland."[7]

Conservationists cite the Selva Lacandona as the most important biological region in Mexico. It is also important to the world at large for its global contributions to biological and cultural diversity. Finally, as a note of basic logic, eradicating the biological foundation that supports human life on Earth is not a successful strategy for survival. Continuing deforestation in the Selva Lacandona will not benefit local Indigenous families, and it will not benefit the human future.

If there is to be a future for the Selva Lacandona, it lies in helping—more than that, *allowing*—families to identify ways to produce income on the land they live on without eradicating the resources of that land. Promise for some families comes in the form of ecological tourism, archaeological tourism, organic coffee, a dozen varieties of agroforestry, and intensified production of crops on land that has already been cleared. Intensified beef cattle production—higher yields produced on smaller units of land—will likely have a role in that future.

But as long as the Indigenous farmers of the Selva are used as incidental producers of cows and calves for the national and international beef cattle industry, the forest outside protected areas—perhaps inside, as well—doesn't stand a chance.

This quote from Ford and Nigh captures the solution: "The potential for the contemporary Maya to influence the conservation of the forest into the future rests on, first recognizing their contribution to restoration agriculture and, second, including them in the process before it is too late" (Ford and Nigh 2016: 156).

With the active involvement of the region's Indigenous families, Mexico's last large tropical rainforest may yet have a positive future.

19

Saving a Rainforest

A century ago, when the entire Lacandón rainforest was still a world filled with wildlife and folklore, Lacandón Maya took weeklong pilgrimages to visit the ruins of Classic Maya cities, burn copal incense before stone carvings of ancient rulers, and search among temple debris for finger-sized ceramic figures to take home to their god houses as talismans from the places they called **Xok'ol Ja'** ("Close to the Water," Palenque), **K'anank'ax** ("Guardian of the Forest," Sibal), and **Chi' Xokla'** ("Mouth of the Río Usumacinta," Yaxchilán).

Returning home, they hiked trails that tunneled through the rainforest, watching for wildlife and asking questions: How high are the rivers and lakes? Any fish breeding? Are there snails and crawfish in the shallows? Which trees and vines are flowering? Any fruit that can be foraged? What animal tracks are visible?

Today, Lacandones still take long patrols through the forest, but in the twenty-first-century, they're focused on protecting the forest itself. Lacandones patrol their territory to prevent outsiders from killing wildlife and stealing resources. They walk the trails, observing the birds, the fish, the levels of the lake, vigilant for signs of change, blending what they see with knowledge they gained while hunting with their fathers and from folktales told around nighttime fires. Today's Lacandones blend centuries-old oral history with data from topographical maps and digital cameras, and they carry walkie-talkies instead of bows and arrows.

Conservation Patrol, May 2019

Hiking through the logwood forest toward Lake Ts'ibanaj, all I could think of were the huge lakes of cool water waiting at the end of the trail. Enrique Valenzuela had invited me to join a team of Lacandón park guards headed out on conservation patrol of Mensäbäk's territory, and I was looking forward to a canoe trip across the community's large, tropical lakes.

"The Tzeltales who live in the adjoining *ejidos*—Cristóbal Colón, Damasco, and El Tumbo—have cut down the forest on their own lands," Enrique told me. "They burned it to plant pasture for cattle. If there's no forest, there are no animals, and no xate palm leaves to sell, no palm for a thatch roof or poles for a new house. So, when they need something that comes from the forest, they come and take it from ours. We have to patrol the forest to protect it."

By patrolling their territory, Lacandones seek to prevent wildlife poaching, resource theft, and territorial encroachments through direct intervention and by "establishing presence"—making themselves visible to would-be hunters and fishermen. Doing so is no easy task. The Lacandón families of Mensäbäk own 3,368 hectares (13 square miles) of rainforest and wetlands, including twenty-one lakes, three of them among the largest in the Selva Lacandona.

The lake closest to the community, Lake Ts'ibanaj, spreads over 179 hectares and stretches more than a kilometer from one side to the other. In most years, heavy rain fills the lake to the point that the forest on the opposite shore looks like a distant strip of green between water and sky. Waves sparkle, and long-legged aquatic birds stand motionless in the shadows, waiting for breakfast to swim within a beak's strike. On the western shore of the lake, the mountain called Chäk Aktun rises as a half-dome, its face scraped away millennia ago (Lacandones say) by a **ba'al kaan**, "a thing that came from the sky." An ancient Maya temple at the top of the mountain served as a pilgrimage site for Maya communities of previous eras and today offers a bird's eye view of the surrounding territory.

Where Did All the Water Go?

The trail through the logwood forest ended at what was supposed to be a narrow sandy beach at the edge of the lake, where I had expected to see gnarled logwood trees stretching over a surface of turquoise water. But Lake Ts'ibanaj was so low this day, there was as much beach as water. The past year had been exceptionally dry, and the lake was the lowest I'd seen it in forty-five years of visiting the Northern Lacandones. A diminished Lake Ts'ibanaj simmered in the sun, its beach a cascade of muddy concentric circles descending toward the water like rings of dried coffee in an unwashed cup.[1]

Where did all the water go?

Knowing where the water comes from is easy. The Río Naja' flows out of Lake Naja' (in the Lacandón community of the same name) and serves as the primary water source for a series of Tzeltal *ejidos* as it flows north toward Lake Ts'ibanaj 13 kilometers away. When it releases its water into the lake, the river also fills two adjoining bodies of water, Lake Mensäbäk and Lake Joton K'ak', which connect to Lake Ts'ibanaj like neighboring bowls in a Chinese water clock. Another eighteen small lakes, fed by local rainfall and small streams, punctuate the surrounding forest, providing drinking holes for mammals and lairs for crocodiles.

Lacandón elders say the three largest lakes fill and empty according to two natural cycles. One cycle is annual: The lakes' water levels fluctuate according to the amount of rain that falls in their watershed during the rainy season. The other cycle is much longer, measured in decades.

"My father said the lakes fill up a little more every year for 20 years," the late Chan K'in José Valenzuela told me in 1976. "Then, during the next twenty years, they get a little lower every year." He used the Lacandón term for twenty, **jun tul winik**, "one person," meaning twenty fingers and toes, the base for the ancient Maya numerical system. Given that Maya families have lived on the shores of these lakes for a thousand years, they probably have a solid fix on the local hydrology.

"During the first twenty years, the lakes fill so much they flood the forest," Chan K'in José said. "Then they begin to shrink."

But, again, where does the water go? The lakes have no obvious exit, no escape valve, no outflow. No rivers or streams lead away from them. Water flowing into the lakes appears to have arrived at its ultimate destination. So it would seem.

But the lakes are part of a much larger ecosystem. The rainforest of the Selva Lacandona—and of the Guatemalan Petén just across the Río Usumacinta—grows on a thin layer of soil spread over an enormous limestone shelf. The limestone shelf is made of compressed calcium carbonate from billions of ancient marine organisms that died and drifted to the bottom of the ocean that once flooded this section of the planet. Pressed by time and pressure into stone, the shelf was lifted from the sea millions of years ago to form the bedrock of the Yucatán Peninsula, southeastern Mexico, and northern Central America. In some places the limestone is 3,500 meters thick and everywhere is as porous as a block of swiss cheese. Known topographically as karst, its eroded surface is pocked with sinkholes, *cenotes,* and subterranean rivers that capture and carry away surface water like a sponge. Following the force of gravity, the water swirls into the ground and travels unseen beneath the landscape until it breaks to the surface kilometers from where it disappeared.

Chan K'in José Valenzuela told me he knew where the water from the lakes goes every year. "The water drains out holes in the bottom of the lakes and comes out of the ground again as a river—the Río Tulijá." He was certain about this.

And he was as right as rain. The water from Lakes Ts'ibanaj, Mensäbäk, and Joton K'ak drains into meters-wide sinkholes in the lake bottoms, then travels through karst bedrock for 8 kilometers to magically emerge as a gushing spring near the Tzeltal Maya *ejido* of Jo' Tulijá, northwest of the community of Mensäbäk. The water bursts out with force because the lakes lie at 680 meters above sea level, while the *ejido* of Jo' Tulijá lies 190 meters below—as much difference as the height of a sixty-story building. Filtered through millions of tons of limestone, the water rushes to the surface as cold, clear water at the base of a mountain 1 kilometer east of Jo' Tulijá's community center (Nuestro-México 2020a; Nuestro-México 2020b).

The place where the water emerges from the ground is known to Lacandón families as **u jo' t'uli ja'**, "the source of the rabbits' water," and the Tzeltal Maya farmers who colonized the area adopted that name for the community they built near the water's edge.

"There among trees, stones, and silence," says the tourism website, *México Desconocido*, "the mountain opens its small mouth to release water from the depths below."

"Just above the mouth of the spring is a shrine with a cross where people carry out ceremonies," the website continues, "giving a magical, religious touch to such a humble place. It is surprising to see such a modest opening for such a grand river, the Río Tulijá."

Local families have wisely protected the trees that surround the spring, and they maintain strips of vegetation on both banks of the river that flows from the site to the town. The water that collects there in a series of small lakes is so clear, the website says, "that you can see the bottom from any angle, no matter how deep it is" (*México Desconocido* 2020).

"Not Enough Enforcement of the Law"

Walking down the 200-meter-wide beach exposed by the low water levels, I could see a group of Lacandones gathered around a boat tied up on the lake shore. Enrique Valenzuela and his son, Freddy, were standing with José

Angel Salórzano near a 5-meter-long fiberglass boat, strapping on back-packs and sliding machetes into long scabbards. Rafael Tárano was using a long-handled mahogany paddle to scoop pools of water from the stern of the boat, and José Angel's son, Humberto, was mopping up the inside of the bow with an old cotton tunic. Gustavo López walked up carrying another mahogany paddle he had retrieved from its hiding place in the shoreline vegetation.

Rafael sat on a bench at the stern of the boat and began to adjust the out-board motor that would power our trip across Lake Ts'ibanaj. The fifteen-horsepower "ecological" motor is the only one permitted on any of the lakes. To prevent oil and gasoline contamination, no other motors are allowed.

Rafael was wearing traditional Lacandón clothing—a white cotton tunic hanging to his knees, but also a tan canvas vest. He tossed his long hair over his shoulders as he worked. The other men climbing into the boat had crew cuts and Western clothes—navy blue uniform pants, a long-sleeved uniform shirt or T-shirt, and leather boots. As did Rafael's vest, each of the shirts displayed the logo of either the Consejo Nacional de Areas Natural Protegidas (CONANP, National Council for Protected Natural Areas) or the Policía Estatal Chiapas (Chiapas State Police), the two government en-tities that authorize and pay the Lacandones to protect their community forest.

Lacandones gained the authority to patrol their territory in 1998 when Mexican federal law allowed communally owned settlements (*ejidos*) to designate their lands Áreas de Protección de Flora y Fauna (Flora and Fauna Protection Areas). The Southern Lacandón communities (Lacanja' Chan Sayab and its satellite settlements of Bethel and San Javier) were al-ready protected by existing conservation areas—the 354-square-kilometer Reserva Comunal Sierra la Cojolita and the adjoining Montes Azules Bio-sphere Reserve—so threats to the territory have been rare there. But the Northern Lacandón communities of Naja' and Mensäbäk are encircled by Tzeltal and Ch'ol Maya communities that have converted their own forest into pasture and secondary regrowth. As Enrique had told me, neighbors from these communities sometimes sneak into the Lacandones' rainforest to kill wildlife and steal xate palm leaves, which they sell into the interna-tional floral industry.

When Lacandones from Naja' and Mensäbäk learned of the opportu-nity to legally protect their tropical forest, they seized it. Working with CONANP and the nonprofit Conservación Internacional México, families in the two communities gathered in a series of meetings and mapping sessions to establish their own zoning and land-use rules. They agreed to grow crops only in specific areas of their territory and determined they would no longer clear primary forest. Instead, they cleared and cultivated milpas used in previous years and allowed to regenerate in tree crops and natural vegetation.

The management plans produced by the Naja' and Mensäbäk families designated 90 percent of their territories for rainforest preservation and sustainably managed resource use. The rules allow families to fish and raise chickens and turkeys, but not to kill forest animals unless they threaten human life or food crops. As a result, wildlife populations in the Northern Lacandón territories are the healthiest they have been since the 1970s, and Naja' and Mensäbäk have the largest remaining blocks of tropical rainforest in the northern Selva Lacandona.

Outside the Lacandón reserves, the northern Selva Lacandona is essentially deforested and devoid of its original wildlife. When asked about the missing animals, many Lacandones deflect the obvious answer. "They went far away," several Lacandón friends told me.

Others blame the missing animals on "too many people." Still others say, "Tzeltales ate them all." Which is probably close to the truth. Because families in the surrounding Tzeltal communities have converted their forest to pastureland, little of the original habitat remains, and wildlife has become increasingly scarce. One result is that Tzeltales not infrequently poach animals on Lacandón conservation lands.

The most piercing answer to my question about the missing wildlife came from José Camino Viejo, an aged Lacandón farmer who lived near Mensäbäk. When I asked him where all the animals had gone, he simply answered, "They aren't here anymore. They went away. Their souls hurt."

In any given year, each of the major Lacandón communities has three to eight CONANP guards and another six to eight state police, all of them Lacandón Maya and a half dozen of them women, who are charged with patrolling and protecting their respective community territories. The number of salaried positions fluctuates according to state and federal budgets. CONANP's national budget has never been adequate for the agency's tasks, and it was further cut by one-third in fall 2018 and again in May 2020. Overall, Mexico's federal environmental protection budget dropped by half in the five years between 2015 and 2020 (Fisher and Malkin 2019). But Lacandones continue to carry out their assigned jobs, dividing the funds the community receives among as many positions as possible, working to keep the teams paid and together. Members of the community volunteer for the teams as unpaid Vigilantes Comunitarios, "Community Guards," and don caps marked with the logo of CONANP and an embroidered image of the rainforest parrot called **k'acho** (*Amazona farinosa*).

As they headed out on patrol this particular day, the team members carried no firearms, although the Policía Estatal are trained and authorized to do so. Mensäbäk's CONANP guards stopped carrying weapons eight years ago, after a dicey confrontation in the forest. Rafael and Minchu Valenzuela were on conservation patrol when they came upon a Tzeltal Maya man illegally cutting xate palms in their community forest. When he saw the Lacandones coming toward him, the Tzeltal lifted his .22-caliber rifle and aimed the weapon directly at Rafael's face. Rafael was also carrying a .22, and he aimed it at the Tzeltal intruder. The two men were looking at each other down the barrel of their rifles.

Minchu Valenzuela calmly stepped in between the men, speaking the fluent Tzeltal he had learned from his Tzeltal wife, Adela. Recounting the event several years later, he said, "I started talking to the Tzeltal in his own language and to Rafael in **Jach T'an**, telling them to lower their rifles. Both of them eventually did, but it was a scary moment."

Minchu said the poacher looked down at the burlap sack he had filled with stolen xate leaves, then spun around and took off running down the trail.

Since that close encounter, Mensäbäk's CONANP guards have carried no firearms—only their trusty machetes.

The Policía Estatal are a different story. Within Ocosingo, the large county in which both the Northern and Southern Lacandones live, the Policía Estatal are the law, and they are authorized to carry pistols and rifles. Most of the time, however, they stick to defensive, side-handle batons and handcuffs.

Watching the men load into the patrol boat reminded me of what one of the Lacandón state policewomen had told me back in the community.

"When we come up on someone stealing xate or hunting animals, they usually drop everything and run the other way," she said. "If we recognize them, we go to their community and denounce them. Nothing violent. Their community arrests them, but a couple of months later, they're out of jail, back in the community, and sneaking back into our forest to fish and steal palms and kill wildlife."

"The challenge comes from lax law enforcement," a CONANP guard added. "There's not enough enforcement of the law after people are arrested."

"Changed, the Weather"

As we pushed the boat off from shore and began to move across the lake, we watched for wildlife and talked about all things Mensäbäk. We saw a dozen small kingfishers (*Chloroceryle amazona*) darting back and forth over the water, searching for unsuspecting minnows, then watched a white hawk (*Leucopternis albicollis*) pass silently overhead. In the mud along the shore we could see smears of webbed footprints where crocodiles had slipped from the bank into the water, and in the shallows we could see 12-centimeter-deep basins where fish had cratered out nests for laying and fertilizing their eggs.

The Lacandones talked mostly about changes in the weather, the rain (or lack thereof), and plans for the years' crops. Most families in the community had already cut and burned the vegetation on the plots they would cultivate this year, but the year had brought little rainfall so far, and several of the men were worried that the corn they had planted wouldn't germinate.

Enrique pointed to the lakeshore. "There's not enough rain, so the lakes didn't fill up this year, and water is still draining out. But I think they'll fill up in a few months," he said. He looked at the sky without smiling.

As it turned out, 2019 ended up being one of the driest years many of the younger Lacandones had seen. Of the twenty-one bodies of water within Mensäbäk's territory, several of the smallest dried up completely. Joton K'ak', third largest of the lakes (after Ts'ibanaj and Mensäbäk), was reduced to a series of unconnected ponds, leaving crocodiles and fish to compete for reduced concentrations of water and mud.

Even the younger adults talked about how the timing of the rainy season seemed to have changed. Lacandón farmers can still determine the appropriate days to plant their crops by watching the flowering of specific "indicator" trees and vines in the forest, but they say the beginning of the rainy season has pushed later into the year.

"The rains used to begin earlier," Amado Seis told me. "We used to plant during March or April, but now we plant in May or June."

"The temperature is warmer," he said, "and there's less rain."

Vocabulary for climate change has already emerged in Lacandones' native language: **k'axbä u chäkbil**, "changed, its heat," or **k'axa'an u chäkalbil**, "changed, the weather," the former among farmers in Mensäbäk, the latter in Naja' (Cook 2016: 355).

Lacandones point to a specific reason for this change. "Outsiders cut down all the forest," one farmer told me. "If there's no forest, there's no rain."

The Lacandón farmers, of course, are onto something. Vegetation in unperturbed rainforests absorbs rainfall and releases it slowly by sweating water vapor back into the atmosphere to seed more rain. When forests are fragmented or cleared, the amount of regional rainforest declines. Studies in the Amazon indicate that deforestation can disrupt regional climate to the point of extending the dry season by a full month (Fisher 2019).

Declining precipitation brings another worry as well: the potential for wildfires. Rampant forest fires are increasingly threatening the tropical forests of southern Mexico and Central America due to rising temperatures and altered patterns of rainfall. In the Selva Lacandona, many farmers and ranchers burn their fields and pastures every year to clear the land of weeds and add nutrients from the ash to the soil. The increasing number of farmers and ranchers heightens the chances that fire will escape into neighboring fields and forest.

In both their traditional agroforestry system and in their less diversified twenty-first-century farming system, Lacandones actively control their agricultural fires. Many Lacandón farmers simply gather and burn crop residue from last year's harvest, then spread the ash over the field for another year's planting. They can harvest the same field two or three years running before they need to clear another milpa to begin the cycle anew. By burning the dried weeds and crop waste in small, separate piles, Lacandón farmers reduce the chances that a fire will get out of control.

When a farmer intends to cultivate a new area by clearing regrowth from a fallowed milpa, he seeks the aid of other families by notifying the community president, who puts out a call for all farmers to meet on a specific day to assist in controlling the fire. At the indicated time, the men of the community gather at the designated milpa, scrape firebreaks around the perimeter, and carefully monitor the fire as the farmer initiates a controlled, slow burn. The other farmers benefit from this cooperative process when it becomes their turn.

The larger threat from wildfires comes from neighboring communities. Milpa and pasture fires have jumped community boundaries in the past and spread into Lacandón forest reserves. In 1998, an escaped fire torched 30 percent of Naja's territory. Later that year, when the community declared itself a Flora and Fauna Protection Area, the burned area was classified as a recuperation and restoration zone, and it is gradually regenerating as mature rainforest (CONANP 2006b: 32).

"Poor Crocodile"

When Lakes Ts'ibanaj and Mensäbäk are full, a narrow peninsula of land that separates them is inundated and their waters merge, making it possible to row from one lake to the other through flooded vegetation. On the day of our patrol, though, the lakes were at low ebb, and we were looking at 100 meters of dry land between the lakes. When we reached the northern shore of Ts'ibanaj, we climbed out of the motorized canoe and tied it to a tree branch, then walked across the peninsula to the southern shore of Lake Mensäbäk. When we got there, we could see a steep beach reaching down to the water and a second, smaller canoe tied to a tall pole stabbed into the mud of the shore. There was no motor on this craft, so Rafael retrieved two long mahogany paddles stowed in the nearby forest and slid them into the canoe while the men divided into two groups.

Freddy, Humberto, José Angel, and Gustavo adjusted their gear and took off single file down a trail along the eastern shore of the lake. They would spend the next hour searching the forest for signs of poachers or illegal fishermen while Rafael, Enrique, and I used the canoe to patrol the northern shore of Lake Mensäbäk.

Rafael and Enrique grabbed the paddles and began to row, one man in front, the other in back, both standing up Lacandón style, straining the long-handled paddles through the water while remaining on their feet and perfectly balanced. They've paddled this way all their lives, just as their ancestors did, previously in mahogany dugouts, nowadays in manufactured boats. Sitting on a built-in bench in the middle of the canoe, taking photos like a tourist, I could feel the canoe roll slightly beneath us as we navigated toward the limestone cliff of Mensäbäk.

The scene surrounding us was magnificent. Intensely blue water stretched 360 degrees toward white limestone cliffs dressed in vivid green forest. In a bird's eye view, we would have been tiny figures in a small canoe sketching a diagonal line across a water-filled basin surrounded by mountains. In no direction were there visible signs of human impact—just water, white cliffs, and rainforest.

Rafael pointed to a comma-shaped island with its own mini-stand of forest just off the southern shore. "Her name is **U Muul Äk Nä**," Rafael said, "Her mound, our Lady."[2]

"She's the daughter of Mensäbäk, who lives in the cliff over there, and her mother, Xtabej, lives in a cave in that cliff." He pointed to a wall of white limestone on the southwestern side of the lake.

"Mensäbäk makes rain, but he's also the god who takes revenge on your soul if you committed sins during your lifetime, so it's best not to make him or his wife or daughter angry."

We skirted the island cautiously.

As we neared the lake's northern shore, a colony of cormorants burst from the branches of a tree, filling the sky with wheeling birds (neotropic cormorant, *Phalacrocorax brasilianus mexicanus*). In the distance, we could see other cormorants diving into the water to chase small fish.

When we reached the shore, we began to paddle parallel to it, searching for footprints. Every few hundred meters, we stopped to pick up trash left by intruders. Rafael and Enrique spotted several sets of footprints just below a Mensäbäk cliff, a clear sign that poachers had walked there during the past week. Where the ground was too muddy to climb out of the canoe, we used the paddles to scoop up plastic bags, soda bottles, and empty cans and collected them in the bottom of the boat.

"Tzeltales from the *ejidos* of Cristóbal Colón and Damasco walk an hour through the forest to get here," Enrique said. "No one lives on this lake, so unless our patrol shows up when the people are here, no one sees them. They catch fish and take them home. They leave their trash on the lake-shore, and sometimes they kill animals."

In fact, Minchu Valenzuela had told me several days earlier about coming upon the putrefying body of a crocodile washed up on the beach (Morelet's crocodile, *Crocodylus moreletii*).

"A poacher killed it," Minchu said, "but he didn't take the skin or even the tail for the meat. I think he shot it and couldn't reach it, and the crocodile died after the man left."

"Poor crocodile," he said.

The wanton killing of wildlife seems to especially offend Lacandones. When they declared their territories conservation areas in 1998, Lacandón families stopped hunting wildlife and began to study it instead. During the last decade, they've worked with Mexican conservationists to deploy motion-sensitive wildlife cameras (camera traps) along trails through the forest. The work has produced images that include the expected assemblage of regional animals—brocket deer, great tinamou, coatimundi, tepesquintle (paca), agouti, collared peccary, and curassow—but also some that surprised everyone: ocelots, tamandua, jaguars, a harpy eagle, and at least one coyote that even the Lacandones hadn't known still lived in their forest.

Missing from the images captured by the camera traps were tapirs and white-lipped peccaries, which are adapted to living in large territories with minimal disturbance from human beings. Cougars are also absent from the forest of the Northern Lacandones, but the families admit that they helped extirpate them from the area.

"Cougars will kill people," Chan K'in José Valenzuela told me in 2009. "I killed three of them myself when we first moved to Mensäbäk [in the 1960s]."

Conservation biologists sometimes describe what they call empty forests—natural areas that have been "defaunated" of their original community of animals—in other words, forests that still have trees, but little to no wildlife because of poaching and over-hunting (Bogoni et al. 2020). This is not the case in the Lacandón communities of the Selva Lacandona. The two Northern Lacandón conservation areas of Mensäbäk and Naja' are missing some keystone species—scarlet macaws, cougars, tapirs, and white-lipped peccaries—but the areas around Lacanja' Chan Sayab, Bethel, and San Javier in the southern Selva still have complete assemblages of regional wildlife, including these rarer species, primarily because of the large size of Montes Azules Biosphere Reserve and its adjoining wildlife reserves. Regulations that limit hunting also keep wildlife populations healthy there.

In the Northern Lacandón settlements, decreased pressure from hunting and poaching has allowed some species to recoup their numbers. Lacandones in Mensäbäk even managed to reintroduce one species that had been locally wiped out—the white-tailed deer (*Odocoileus virginianus*), one of the prized food animals of the forest. In the early 2000s, officials from the Miguel Álvarez del Toro Zoo in Tuxtla Gutiérrez, Chiapas, offered a breeding pair of deer to Enrique Valenzuela, who was president of Mensäbäk at the time. Enrique and his wife, María, installed the deer behind a tall wire fence around their house and fed them corn. The deer soon began to multiply.

"Very quickly, there were a half dozen deer living inside the fence," Enrique said. "But one day something frightened the original male. He bolted cleanly over the fence and disappeared into the forest. I looked at the other deer and decided to open the fence for them. I yelled, 'Go! Go with your father,' and all the deer ran into the forest after him."

"Now, they're thick here. Sometimes in the evening we see five or six deer at a time grazing in our milpas."

A Hole in the Lake

We had almost completed our survey of the northern shore when Enrique's walkie-talkie came alive with a squawk and the voice of José Angel on the other end. After a brief conversation, Enrique turned to us and said, "Let's go," and we began to paddle back to rejoin the other team. They had finished their patrol of the eastern shore and were waiting for us at the southern edge of the lake. When we reached them, we tied up the canoe, secured the paddles, and walked across the peninsula toward Lake Ts'ibanaj. José Angel said they hadn't come across any interlopers, but they had seen footprints indicating that people had recently been in the area.

We arrived at the boat we'd left at Lake Ts'ibanaj and climbed in, and Rafael brought the motor to life and pointed us toward home. Halfway across the lake, though, as we neared a spit of land called La Punta, he eased the whine of the motor and said, "I'm going to show you something," as he veered the boat toward land.

Rafael maneuvered the bow of the boat onto the mud bank, and everyone climbed out and cautiously approached a 3-meter-wide gap in the shore—a large divot that looked like a mega-crocodile had taken a bite out of the beach. A section of the bank had collapsed into a sinkhole, and water was swirling into it like bathwater going down a drain.

"There are more sinkholes like this beneath the water in other places in the lake," Rafael said. "But we don't see those. This one is close to the shore, and we can see it when the lakes are low."

Wary of being sucked into the underworld of the god Mensäbäk, we kept our distance from the opening.

Walking back toward the boat, we stepped around a scattered collection of potsherds sticking out of the mud. Freddy picked up the thick, earlike handle of a centuries-old pot, and I turned over a hand-sized slab of pottery with an incised groove encircling its top. When they're at their low points, the lakes reveal evidence of Maya villages from centuries past. Most of the pieces looked to be from broken household water jugs and cooking pots dropped here hundreds of years ago and transformed now into data for archaeologists. Enrique pointed to a rounded depression in the mud that was perfectly lined with broken pieces of pottery, forming the bottom of what must have been a half-meter-wide clay pot. He declared it a **pak**, the large, round jug Lacandones use to transport and serve the ritual drink, **balche'**.

Lacandones (and archaeologists) also find unexpected artifacts protruding from the mud, including ceramic stamps used to decorate bark cloth or clay vessels, perfect half spheres of hard stone used perhaps to smooth the surface of an unfired ceramic pot, an occasional jade bead, and in one case the curved bowl of a marine conch shell carved into a graceful human hand.

I took photos of the ceramics we found, but we left them where they were and climbed back into the boat to head for home. When we reached the southern shore of Lake Ts'ibanaj, we put the boat and gear away and walked through the logwood forest toward home. As they neared their houses, the men called out to one other, "Okay, see you tomorrow."

Lessons

Back in the community, I sat down at my makeshift desk in one of the visitor cabins and began to take notes about the Lacandones' work to protect their rainforest/wetland environment. They've been fortunate compared to Indigenous groups in many places. Lacandones have legal title to their lands, vital assistance from Mexico's National Council of Natural Protected Areas (CONANP), and positive alliances with university researchers and nonprofit organizations that support their communities and conservation work. Still, because their territories are encircled by an increasing number of colonists and ranchers, they've had to adapt to the threats of encroachment, poaching, and wildfires. As long as the population of farmers and ranchers around them continues to grow, the Lacandón communities will need to maintain constant vigilance. Until their neighbors develop alternatives to milpa farming and cattle ranching, pressure will be heavy on the remaining rainforest of the Selva Lacandona.

Lacandones are not alone in this situation. Around the world, Indigenous people and their environments are threatened by exploitation. With a population of 1,700 individuals, Lacandón Maya represent 0.00009999 percent of the estimated 1.6 billion people on the planet who are "forest-dependent," meaning that forests form the basis for their agriculture, energy, water supply, building materials, and economic activities, including artisanry and ecotourism (Newton et al. 2016, 2020).

But Lacandón Maya are a successful example of how Indigenous people and tropical forests can coexist in the twenty-first century. They also demonstrate how partnerships with Indigenous families can improve the management of protected areas.

Biodiversity conservation in the twenty-first century increasingly depends on comanagement of protected territories with the people who live on the land. Protected areas based on partnerships among Indigenous groups, governments, and the conservation community achieve two important goals simultaneously: They effectively conserve biological resources and they support Indigenous sovereignty, land rights, and self-determination, allowing for corollary conservation of cultural traditions (Nations 2001b; Lennon 2006; Kothari 2006b; Reid and Lovejoy 2022).

Indigenous people can bring enormous benefit to protected areas, starting with the fact that many Indigenous groups live in homelands that are rich in biological and cultural diversity. They are living archives of knowledge about local geography and ecology, and left to their own devices they utilize resource management practices that are carefully adapted to local ecosystems. Indigenous people with a homeland continuously monitor changes in land use and environmental conditions, and they are deeply committed to defending their land and resources against outside threats.

In turn, protected areas benefit Indigenous people by providing greater recognition of their legal status and distinct group identity and, in some countries, legal ownership of their traditional lands and sacred places. Protected areas enhance Indigenous groups' national and international visibility, draw attention to human rights and welfare, and help defend against encroachment and threats from commercial interests. Protected areas also can provide Indigenous families with income from entrance and licensing fees, financial support from national and international organizations, and political and moral support for traditional conservation values.

One key element in the Lacandones' conservation success is property rights. The Lacandón Maya of Mensäbäk and Naja' are fortunate to legally own the defined territories they have chosen to manage as protected areas. Lacandón communities in the southern Selva Lacandona—Lacanja' Chan Sayab, Bethel, and San Javier—benefit from owning defined community territories that are embraced by a corridor of protected lands that belong to the Comunidad Zona Lacandona, in which they are major players.

Around the globe, relationships between Indigenous groups and protected areas range from top-down imposition of conservation regulations on traditional tribal territories to complete local management of land and resources by Indigenous people themselves. In top-down management, Indigenous groups participate in the conservation of the land they live on, but important decisions are still made by outsiders. In comanaged areas, Indigenous families have equal say in the management of their territory, but their decision-making power is diluted by the influence of outside officials.

The most effective situation, both for Indigenous families and the protected areas they live in, comes with full Indigenous management, in which Indigenous peoples are the key players in declaring their legally defined territory a protected area and where they have legal authority to manage their natural resources (Kothari 2006a). Full Indigenous management means government agencies recognize the sovereignty, self-determination, and decision-making authority of the land's Indigenous owners. It is a highly effective way to achieve conservation. Researchers at the University of California San Diego compared satellite images of forest cover with government records of property rights in the Brazilian Amazon and found that territories owned fully and collectively by Indigenous tribes had 66 percent less deforestation from the outside world than lands that were only partially—or not at all—the legal property of Indigenous tribes.

The researchers concluded that, "Full property rights give Indigenous groups official territorial recognition, enabling them not only to demarcate their territories, but also to access the support of monitoring and enforcement agencies."

From a national viewpoint, the researchers said, "Not only do Indigenous territories serve a human rights role, but they are a cost-effective way for governments to preserve their forested areas and attain climate goals" (Baragwanath and Bayi 2020).

The Lacandón Maya communities have been fortunate to have active, cooperative partners in the creation and management of their Áreas de Protección de Flora y Fauna and in the management of the Montes Azules Biosphere Reserve and its connected protected areas. Officials of CONANP, the federal agency charged with conserving Mexico's natural heritage, have allowed Lacandón families to make their own decisions about land use, forest management, and wildlife protection on their own territory. Supported by a strong tradition of ecological knowledge and a rich oral history, Lacandones have maintained a through-line of conservation ethics that allows them, and prompts them, to keep their forest alive. The end result is an Indigenous, forest-dependent people who are in charge of their own future and who are actively protecting the largest remaining rainforest in Mexico.

VII

Resilience

The Forest and the Future

20

A Question of How We Will Live

The question is no longer whether we will survive but how we will live.

—Paul Chaat Smith (Comanche) [1]

For centuries, Lacandón Maya kept their families and rainforest alive by teaching rising generations time-tested techniques for survival in a tropical rainforest environment. Information flowed from parent to child through an interlocking mosaic of fables, myths, and religious beliefs that emphasized the sustainable use of natural resources. Oral tradition bolstered Lacandones' daily efforts to grow food and harvest wildlife and plants from the ecosystems that surrounded them.

Lacandones lived in geographical retreat from the outside world from the 1700s until the latter decades of the twentieth century, but through adaptation and resilience, they maintained their culture of sustainability. When "civilization" finally surrounded them, forcing them to confront competing uses of land and resources, Lacandón families adapted their survival practices and moved into defined communities in much reduced territories. As the friction from this cultural collision cooled, the families learned that they were the legal owners and guardians of the largest block of rainforest in the modern Republic of Mexico.

In the twenty-first century, enveloped by a globalized world, Lacandones have learned to read and write Spanish, drive pickup trucks, and do work that dovetails with Mexico's national economy. Although Lacandones still grow the bulk of their own food, they also serve as forest guards, ecotourism guides, minibus drivers, handicraft producers, chili and coffee growers, and harvesters of forest palms for the international floral industry. An increasing number of individuals employ their ecological knowledge as consultants to Mexican, U.S., Canadian, European, and Japanese researchers, providing insight into rainforest ecology, agroforestry, and archaeology.

Lacandón women and men also earn income by selling handicrafts made from natural materials: bow and arrow sets, bags and tunics of pounded bark cloth, wooden spoons, corn-washing baskets, and ceramic figures of crocodiles, armadillos, and jaguars. Lacandón women have long crafted beads and necklaces from rainforest seeds and nuts—Southern men also wore them during the nineteenth century—and they continue to make them today to sell to visitors entering the ruins of Palenque and Bonampak. To these traditional crafts, Lacandones have added nontraditional, but nonetheless natural, products such as seed earrings and fired-clay shot glasses adorned with faces of Lacandón gods. Women and men travel to San Cristóbal de Las Casas to sell their goods in the courtyard of Museo Na Bolom and to Mexican cities as distant as Mérida and Mexico City.

The transition of Lacandón Maya from semi-isolation to integrated members of Mexican society brought major changes to their religious system, material culture, and to their transmission of cultural values and knowledge. The metamorphosis of their physical and social environments required a new narrative and new strategies, although elements of the past survive, hidden beneath waves of change. Ancestral beliefs and techniques continue to ripple through Lacandón daily life, providing a link to the past and a lifeline into the future.

Living new lives in an electronic environment, today's Lacandones are nonetheless still tied to the land, still surrounded by rainforest, and still facing forward, determined to protect their homeland. By blending centuries-old practices of resource conservation with new techniques and information, they are molding an Indigenous society adapted to the twenty-first century.

Transitioning Oral History

Several researchers have written that modern Lacandón children do not have the same cultural knowledge their grandparents did "and likely won't acquire it." Based on interviews in Lacandón communities, Norbert Ross concluded that younger Lacandones still know the creation stories evoked by their elders, "but these stories no longer guide their behavior." Yet he acknowledges that "even younger Lacandones are quite expert with respect to the forest" (Ross 2002:135, 137).

While few Lacandón elders (count them on one hand) still practice their traditional religion, underlying spiritual principles nonetheless reverberate in their lives and seep into the lives of their children. Historically, Lacandón Maya regulated their use of natural resources through an oral history infused with practical rules about human relationships with wildlife and rainforest.

Lacandones' continuing reluctance to kill dogs (chapter 2) and their abiding respect for their ancestors' bones (chapter 6) are examples of the persistence of spiritual beliefs and their impact on contemporary behavior. The observation of ethnographer Didier Boremanse still holds true: "These rules are enforced," he wrote, "not by the fear of Kisin's [the devil's] fire but by the fear of evil things happening in this world." For example, "To waste game by killing more than is really needed is very bad," he learned. "The gods would make the animals hide in the forest, and the hunters would not be able to shoot any. To kill for the sake of killing is a sign of great contempt or fear" (Boremanse 1998: 73).

Lacandón oral history still promotes the sustainability of wildlife populations by focusing on fairness in hunting. In the past, hunters were reminded to use arrows with carved, barbed foreshafts when hunting monkeys, because monkeys have hands and, if wounded, must be given the chance to pull out the arrow and escape (chapter 13, "The Lord of the Monkeys"). At the same time, "It is not fair to hunt peccaries with barbed arrows for, unlike monkeys, they have no hands. Peccaries must be shot with normally shafted arrows (**ch'uxte'**), so they still have a chance to get rid of the arrow and escape" (Boremanse 1998: 73). Peccaries wounded with barbless wooden arrows may live to be hunted another day, Lacandones point out. Those wounded with a barbed arrow would bleed out in the forest unseen and unutilized.

Today, Lacandón hunting practices are reinforced by community-established rules that conserve forest and wildlife protection areas. Traditional fables taught hunters to kill only what they intended to eat—a basic principle of subsistence conservation. Today's community forest guards arrest community members or outside intruders who kill wildlife indiscriminately, because these actions are counterproductive to wildlife survival and to the survival of a rainforest society. But these practical regulations are fortified by subtle spiritual beliefs.

Respect for the natural world includes aesthetic sensitivity. Individuals openly demonstrate appreciation for the beauty of plants and rainforest. I've watched Lacandón teenagers pause at a viewpoint overlooking a tropical lake and spend half an hour simply admiring the view. I've seen young Lacandones turn morose on viewing trees illegally felled by encroaching neighbors. I've seen elderly men point to a line of trees at sunset and say,

"Look how the sun lights up the forest." Lacandones remain deeply aware that they are part of the surrounding ecosystem and that they must care for nature if they want to survive.

Traditional Lacandón Maya religion, writes anthropologist Marin Roblero Morales, was "an abstraction of their daily practices, that is: to plant corn, cure sicknesses, hunt deer, fish, be in the forest, pray in the god house, have children, tell stories, or see a bird or a jaguar" (Roblero Morales 2008, citing Dichtl 1987: 47). In modern times, Lacandón religion and oral history have been transformed by outside contact—Jesuklistu became a member of the pantheon of gods during the twentieth century—but the people's connection to the environment endures. Religion and fables have become almost subliminal devices that prompt environmental consciousness. Lacandones may rationally understand that the gods don't eat corn and that animal spirits don't protect the forest (as far as we know), but Lacandón cosmovision, says Roblero Morales, "has not totally changed" (Roblero Morales 2008: 126).

Lacandones still know, for example, that "a jaguar thinks like a person and that tepesquintles [pacas] know how to pray and know when people are going to hunt them and change their path that day" (Roblero Morales 2008: 127). As Chan K'in Juanito López told me in 2019, in total seriousness, "Tepesquintles know the day they are going to die, and they meet in the forest to talk about it among themselves. I saw a group of them doing this just yesterday."

The idea of indiscriminately killing tepesquintles or any other animal is anathema today, as it has been for 100 years. Fables and religious references may not be as commonly voiced in Lacandón communities today, but they still underlie Lacandones' actions to achieve sustainability and forest conservation.

Lacandón children still hear traditional stories at home, recounted by their parents in their native language, and traditional beliefs continue to fortify the families' ecological knowledge. Today, time-honored environmental controls are also magnified by rules and regulations backed by community agreements and federal laws. But the end effect is the same: the conservation of wildlife and rainforest grounded in an ethos of respect and self-preservation. This blended system seems to work in the modern world—and it emerges from the Lacandones' own decisions.

A Natural Economy

The addition of rules and legal agreements to fables and religion accelerated with the creation of the Comunidad Zona Lacandona during the 1970s, when the Lacandón homeland came to be governed by a communal structure that includes thousands of Tzeltal and Ch'ol Maya families as well. The transition was further advanced in Naja' and Mensäbäk by establishment of the Áreas de Protección de Flora y Fauna, which are governed by community-specific agreements (CONANP 2006a, 2006b).

Despite governmental regulations and the erosion of tradition from competing sources (television, radio, missionaries), Lacandones still live in and from the rainforest and are still creating new ways to benefit from their knowledge of forest resources. Today, the ecosystems that have always provided Lacandón families with food and raw materials also provide them with income from handicrafts, ecotourism, and forest protection.

As they experience population growth within a defined geography, change will be the watchword of the future. Not all Lacandones will continue to be farmers forever. They will continue to diversify into conservation-based employment and specialty crops such as shade coffee and xate floral palms. And some will likely continue to earn outside income as consultants to researchers. Adolfo Chan K'in, a Northern Lacandón who lives in Lacanja' Chan Sayab, is already a coauthor of several influential academic papers in which traditional Lacandón knowledge meets Western science (Falkowski et al. 2016, 2019).

The most powerful way Lacandones benefit financially from their traditional knowledge is through community-based, Indigenous tourism.[2] Lacandones have a long history of guiding outsiders such as loggers, archaeologists, and anthropologists through the rainforest (Trench 2002: 246). Adventure tourists are simply the latest in a list of audiences eager to employ Lacandones to take them into the rainforest and bring them back alive. In Lacanja' Chan Sayab, eco-archaeological tourism is a constant presence. The nearby Classic Maya archaeological site of Bonampak, famous for its colorful murals, prompts a constant churn of national and international visitors, bringing income to Lacandón families through guide service, transportation, and the sale of handicrafts. A dozen families have taken advantage of their location on the forested Río Lacanja' to set up ecotourism camps, where they offer rustic lodging, camping, rafting trips, and guided tours to Bonampak and the neighboring archaeological site of Lacanja.'

Lacandón men in white tunics, their long hair pulled back in a ponytail, lead wide-eyed tourists down rainforest trails, past waterfalls and Maya ruins, speaking fluent Spanish, citing bird names in their native language and promoting forest conservation. A few have learned enough English to guide visitors in that language as well. Confident in their traditional clothing and long hair, they pass on ecological information and conservation values while practicing a lucrative (and growing) trade.

Some of the lodges and restaurants in Lacanja' Chan Sayab were built with support from Mexico's Instituto Nacional de Pueblos Indígenas (National Institute of Indigenous Peoples) and Secretaría del Turismo (Department of Tourism), but they are owned and operated by Lacandón Maya (Boremanse 2006: xi).[3] The one individual who attempted a joint venture with a Mexico City businessman was rebuked by other Lacanja' families (Trench 2002: 179). Similarly, adventurous tourists can sign up for kayak and rafting expeditions with companies based in Palenque or Ocosingo, but when the tourists arrive in the rainforest, Lacandón Maya are in charge.

Through agreements with the Mexican federal government, Lacandones control access to the archaeological site of Bonampak and provide transportation to and from the ruins there. Lacandón law enforcement officials also monitor the highway that leads to the site, stopping cars and trucks at Crucero San Javier to prevent contraband, weapons, and drugs from flowing across the Guatemala-Mexico border. Some of the guards are Northerners who live in nearby Bethel, others Southerners who live in Lacanja' Chan Sayab. Dressed in blue uniforms and Kevlar body armor, with M16 rifles and 9 mm pistols, they work together seamlessly, disregarding the decades-old enmity that once separated Northern Lacandones from their Southern Lacandón cousins.

In the northern communities of Mensäbäk and Naja', visitors can pay a small fee for accommodations that range from a hammock strung in an open-sided *palapa* to private cabins with bathrooms, hot water showers, and screened-in porches surrounded by forest. Visitors can prepare their own meals or make arrangements to eat with a family. Lacandones told archaeologist Joel Palka they want to develop tourism because they "believe that their past and current life ways are important for outsiders to learn about and that their forest communities should be shared with the world" (Palka 2020: 866).

An Ecotourism Dilemma

Lacandones' success in capturing the attention of ecotourists has created resentment among some neighboring Tzeltal Maya communities. The Ch'ol Maya seem less envious, because they hold a near monopoly on delivering visitors to the Classic Maya site of Yaxchilán on the Río Usumacinta. Tzeltal Maya whose villages surround the Lacandón settlements view protected areas as a denial of their communities' economic livelihood. Researcher Stephanie Paladino noted that Tzeltales in Nuevo Palestina see the conservation areas and projects and organizations that support them "as a complex that ignores their rights to self-determination over land and livelihood, leverages resources away from them and their futures, and yet provides little in return" (Paladino 2005: 292).

Paladino says, "Palestinos describe finding themselves in a situation where they are being asked to give up land in the [Montes Azules Biosphere] Reserve as a present or future economic option, but are not being offered support for developing alternative economic options" (Paladino 2005: 272).

There is no doubt that Lacandones control some of the best ecotourism spots in the Selva Lacandona, but they have also worked to create and protect those places. Tzeltal communities in the Selva also have rivers, ruins, and blue-green tropical lakes, but they've contravened their opportunities to attract tourism by clearing the rainforest around them to raise beef cattle. Few tourists are eager to dedicate their vacation days to hiking and camping in livestock pastures. When Tzeltal Maya of Nueva Palestina complained that Lacandones were able to capture tourism dollars and they weren't, Paladino acknowledged that Tzeltales lack "the environmental and cultural allure of the Lacandones" (Paladino 2005: 293).

Lacandones are aware of the positive draw of their traditional, "exotic" past. Men who sell bows and arrows at the ruins of Palenque always wear their white cotton tunic and keep their hair long. They likely realize that tourists are paying for the experience of meeting Indigenous Maya as much as they are buying their artifacts. In Mensäbäk, a half dozen Lacandones make extra income by taking visitors on canoe trips to the cliffs around Lake Ts'ibanaj and Lake Mensäbäk, and most of them are careful to maintain the visible aspects of being Lacandón. One young man, whose father has adopted Western clothing, short hair, and a foreign religion, still keeps his long hair and wears his traditional tunic, partly, his relatives imply, to maintain his income from tourism.

The economic potential is indeed attractive. During a month-long stay in Mensäbäk in 2014, I counted ninety-one tourists visiting the community, the majority of them from other regions of Mexico. Only a few were foreign nationals, mostly Canadians and Europeans. The handful of US tourists who showed up admitted that they had been afraid to visit Mexico after hearing of robberies in hotels along the Mexican Riviera of Cozumel, Cancun, and Isla Mujeres.

The 2019 going price for a canoe trip and guided hike to the lookout on top of Chäk Aktun mountain on Lake Ts'ibanaj, was US$25 per canoe. Travelers who wanted to visit the cliffs on adjoining Lake Mensäbäk, another hour's paddling to the north, paid US$50 for the trip there and back with a Lacandón guide.

Additionally, in most years up to 300 Mexican visitors arrive in Mensäbäk during the holiday of Semana Santa, Easter Week, to swim in the lakes, camp on the lakeshore, and hike the rainforest trails. To simply visit the community, outsiders are asked to purchase a CONANP wristband at the community guard house—US$2 for international tourists and US$1 for Mexican nationals. The money remains within the community to help pay for forest protection and cleanup after the visitors leave.

Does this scenario relegate Lacandones to a future as subservient canoe paddlers and trash collectors? Hardly. The lakes and forest are theirs, and families offer guide service and lodging only when they choose to do so. If they don't approve of visitors' behavior, they ask them to leave and watch them drive away.

Lacandones' engagement with adventure tourism also supports their environmental protection efforts. Conservationist Costas Christ points out, "When local communities benefit from tourism, they become partners and allies in saving nature" (Christ 2019). If a family benefits from guiding visitors to 1,000-year-old ruins and teaching them about life in a tropical rainforest, both the family and the visitors are already part of the global constituency for saving biological and cultural diversity (de Lacy and Whitmore 2006). Nature-based tourism is a top foreign-exchange earner in many countries around the world, especially Mexico, and Lacandón Maya stand to benefit from it as self-employed entrepreneurs. Tourism generates 17 percent of Mexico's gross national product—"a larger percentage than in any emerging country other than Thailand" (Sieff 2020: A14).

Of course, not all aspects of ecotourism are positive. As Costas Christ writes, "Businesses, government, and travelers need to work harder to advance sustainable tourism practices that are focused on reducing travel's carbon footprint, saving nature, protecting cultural heritage, and creating jobs" (Christ 2019).

Other Sources of Income

Ecotourism is only one source of income for twenty-first-century Lacandones. An ongoing archaeological project directed by Joel Palka of Arizona State University and Mexico's Instituto Nacional de Antropología e Historia (INAH) is providing jobs, as well as pride in cultural history, to augment income from tourism and agroforestry. The ancient sites that US and Mexican archaeologists are uncovering will bring new interest to the area and its history, drawing national and international adventurers to see rainforest-covered ruins on a lakeshore still occupied by Maya families. Community leaders are coordinating with the archaeological team to revitalize a moribund community museum and cultural center that will showcase their territory's cultural and natural resources.

At a national level, Lacandones—as well as Tzeltal and Ch'ol families of the Comunidad Lacandona—have benefited from millions of dollars in rainforest protection funds granted by the Global Environmental Facility. During 2011 and 2012, families from all three ethnic groups received fifteen monthly payments of US$135 from the United Nations–funded climate change prevention initiative called Reduction of Emissions for Deforestation and Degradation (REDD+) (Trench 2002; Calleros-Rodríguez 2014: 141; Boremanse 2020: 13). These incentives were aimed at remunerating local communities for protecting the Montes Azules Biosphere Reserve and its connected protected areas, demonstrating the link between forest protection and economic well-being.

Adaptations

In the eighteenth century, Lacandones retreated into the rainforest wilderness to avoid contact with outsiders and the violence and disease they brought with them. When missionaries found the families and insisted that the traditional Lacandón gods were devils, the families adopted the names of the missionaries' gods but continued to believe in the old ones. When Tzeltal and Ch'ol colonists surrounded them in the second half of the twentieth century, Lacandón families defended their territory by appealing to the Mexican legal structure. Today, they actively patrol their territory as forest guards and community volunteers. Throughout their existence,

Lacandón Maya have survived because they have been fluid, demonstrating a steady capacity for adaptation and resilience.

This perspective comes in sharp contrast to the academic and popular publications that reference "disappearing Lacandón culture," or Lacandones' "dying culture." Despite these lamentations, Lacandón culture is not disappearing or dying. It is simply changing. It has always been changing. And change—like the future—is not by necessity bad, it's just different. As Palka put it, "Lacandón culture is not a holdover from the past, but a constantly changing social system that adapts to indigenous needs and local concerns" (Palka 2020: 866). Cultures change even as anthropologists are busy writing up their field notes. James Clifford and George Marcus put it succinctly: "Cultures do not hold still for their portraits" (1986: 10).

In a book titled *Reinventing the Lacandón,* Brian Gollnick proposed that the writings of Frans and Trudy Blom "created a new image of the jungle native isolated from modernization and economic development. That image was of the Lacandón Maya as the jungle's spiritual children and guardians" (Gollnick 2018: 76). Spanish researchers Pilar Espeso-Molinero and María José Pastor-Alfonso carried the thought further by stating, "The Lacandón are now perceived, and see themselves, as the guardians of the jungle, a role which has become their principal tourist attraction" (Espeso-Molinero and Pastor-Alfonso 2020:13).

That may be, but there is a "there there." Lacandones continue to display a deep awareness of the ecosystem they live in, and they continue to work for its protection. Anyone who doubts Lacandones' positive impact on the rainforest need only examine a recent satellite image of eastern Chiapas. Where there are Lacandón communities, rainforest covers the land. Where there is no Lacandón influence—including sections of the communally owned lands of the Comunidad Zona Lacandona—rainforest is hard to find.

Are Lacandones Allowed to Change?

Lacandón conservation practices are not a modern myth projected onto contemporary Maya families. The families' environmental ethos began with the practicality of survival supported by folklore and religion. In the twenty-first century, their ethos is producing financial benefits that emanate from traditional ecological knowledge and new information translated into action. If Lacandones can earn money guiding adventurous tourists to visit rainforest and Maya ruins, the world should not complain about culture change, but instead say, "Thank you."

Paul Chaat Smith, curator at the National Museum of the American Indian, writes, "The discourse on Indian art or politics or culture, even among people of goodwill, is consistently frustrated by the distinctive type of racism that confronts Indians today: romanticism. Simply put, romanticism is a highly developed, deeply ideological system of racism toward Indians that encompasses language, culture, and history" (2009: 17). Although Smith is speaking of contemporary North American Indigenous families, his description could easily apply to modern Lacandón Maya.

"The particular kind of racism that faces North American Indians offers rewards for functioning within the romantic constructions, and severe penalties for operating outside them," Smith says. "Indians are okay, as long as they are 'traditional' in a nonthreatening (peaceful) way, as long as they meet non-Indian expectations about Indian religious and political beliefs."

What it really comes down to, Smith maintains, "is that Indians are okay as long as we don't change too much. Yes, we can fly planes and listen to hip-hop, but we must do these things in moderation and always in a true Indian way."

He continues: "It presents the unavoidable question: Are Indian people allowed to change? Are we allowed to invent completely new ways of being Indian that have no connection to previous ways we have lived?"

"The question," he says, "is no longer whether we will survive but how we will live" (Smith 2009: 91, 135).

The true story is simply too messy and complicated. And too threatening. The myth of noble savages, completely unable to cope with modern times, goes down much more easily. "Today," he concludes, "the equation is Indian equals spiritualism and environmentalism. In twenty years it will probably be something else" (Smith 2009: 20).

In the case of the Lacandón Maya, the equation holds true. Lacandón Maya are in fact practicing environmentally positive work, and much of that work is grounded in their spirituality—respect for the real and mythological creatures who live in the forest and reverence for the sacred caves and bones of the ancestors.

Didier Boremanse, who produced the best ethnography yet written on the Lacandón Maya (1998), lamented the changes he saw during a return visit to the communities in 2010: "Women and girls dressed like poor Mexican peasants, whereas a few young men—some with long hair, some with short hair—wore traditional smocks. Others, who were about 18 years old, had short hair and were dressed entirely in a Western fashion, wearing T-shirts and knee breeches" (Boremanse 2020: 13).

Yet he noted, "These young men care for their land and are aware of the necessity to protect the environment. They do their share as forest rangers and cooperate with government agencies that implement reforestation and defense of the fauna and flora." Still, Boremanse did not observe an adherence to the myths and rituals of their ancestors. Instead, he said, "they are young mestizos with a strong leaning toward the global culture. They speak Mayan and maintain a sense of community and identity, but their interests and tastes bring them closer to a multiethnic and open world" (Boremanse 2020: 13).

Still Very Much Alive

Step back a few paces and look at the situation. Societies that adapt and evolve, survive. Those that don't, disappear. Yes, modern Lacandones intermarry with Tzeltal (and mestizo) spouses, and Lacandón children attend school in Spanish and watch television. But they are still Lacandón. Increasing numbers of Lacandones, especially women, are completing secondary school in other communities, in Spanish, but most of them return home on weekends and after they graduate. In addition to their native language, many young Lacandón men and women speak Spanish and Tzeltal perfectly. Yet they remain Lacandón Maya, and on their own terms.

What doubters should take into account is the families' resilience. Lacandones have been adapting and changing since they crossed the Río Usumacinta into Chiapas (and no doubt before that). They continue to change today, sometimes at hyper speed. If the past is any indication, they will continue to adapt to new and constantly changing conditions. If those adaptations bring them closer to a multiethnic and open world, is that not a positive reaction to a modern, globalized reality?

When anthropologist Ella Deloria carried out fieldwork among her own Dakota family and tribe, she came to understand, "To write properly about Indians, you had to stop using the past tense" (King 2019: 242).

"A better method," she realized, "was to give up trying to identify the dying embers of an older civilization and instead get to know the living, right-now culture of the people you were actually surrounded by—women and men who weren't stuck in history, but like Deloria herself, were feeling their way through it" (King 2019: 241).

In the living mélange of tradition and change that characterizes twenty-first-century Lacandón society, a through-line of forest and wildlife conservation continues to thread its way. When asked what message he had for the rising generation of Lacandón children, Chan K'in Antonio Martinez, a Naja' elder, answered without hesitation: "Take care of the forest, like before, like the ancestors did. Take good care of the forest" (Cook 2016: 357). Based on current Lacandón Maya behavior, future generations are poised to follow that admonition.

At the same time, the many elements still at play make predictions difficult. Part of the Lacandones' future depends on how Mexican federal and state officials react to demands from Tzeltal and Ch'ol Maya for more land for corn and cattle. The proposal to divide the remaining forest of the Comunidad Zona Lacandona into three sections separately controlled by Tzeltal, Ch'ol, and Lacandón Maya would be a death sentence for the forest that remains, with Lacandón Maya left in charge only of the core zone of the Montes Azules Biosphere Reserve and the remainder of the forest transformed into pasture and scrub brush.

Beneath that ominous threat is the factor of climate change and its impact on agriculture, water, wildfires, and biological systems. As a nation, Mexico seeks to protect the Montes Azules Biosphere Reserve and its adjoining protected areas to minimize the release of greenhouse gases, to mitigate flooding in the southeastern states, and to maintain the country's status as a megadiversity hotspot for biological diversity (Medellín 1994; Muench 1997). Government officials will hopefully continue to view those actions as wise and healthy investments in the future of Mexico and its people.

Meanwhile, on a global level, Indigenous communities will continue to play a crucial role in tropical rainforest conservation (Dawson et al. 2021; Reid and Lovejoy 2022). A 2020 study by an international team of conservation scientists revealed that 45 percent of the remaining wilderness areas in the Amazon lies within Indigenous territories, and that these areas experience far less forest loss than non-Indigenous lands, despite the major threats impinging on the entire Amazon region. The researchers concluded, "The Amazon is a classic example of how long-term interactions between Indigenous peoples and forests can be linked to positive environmental outcomes. Indigenous peoples, and also other traditional communities, show that it is possible to successfully combine forest conservation, management and agroforestry systems" (University of Helsinki 2020).

As Lacandones increasingly depend on ecotourism for income, as their agricultural traditions expand to include cash crops such as xate palms and shade coffee, and even as they practice their new religions, the families will continue to protect their forest boundaries and conserve their natural resources—as much for economical as for ethical reasons.

The tropical rainforest will survive where there are Lacandones. Visitors may complain that the people look increasingly like mestizos, with short hair and Western clothing, but the families will still be Lacandón Maya, and they will still be protecting their forest.

The fundamental lesson appears to be this: As the legal owners and protectors of the largest tropical rainforest in Mexico, Lacandón Maya are augmenting their centuries-old guardianship of the tropical forest with the economics of twenty-first-century environmental protection. Guided by the subtle wisdom of their ancestors, they are moving purposely and positively into a new Indigenous future of their own making. Their through-line of respect for nature continues, and their rainforest is green and flourishing.

Chronology of Events in the Selva Lacandona

Preclassic Era

1,800 BC–1,000 BC	Early Preclassic
1,000 BC–300 BC	Middle Preclassic
300 BC–AD 200	Late Preclassic

Classic Era

AD 200–500	Early Classic
AD 500–900	Late Classic

Postclassic Era

AD 900–1200	Early Postclassic
AD 1200–1521	Late Postclassic

Colonial Era

1521–1821 European invasion of the Maya world

1559 Spanish military and missionaries invade eastern Chiapas and battle the Ch'olti Maya inhabitants of Lacam Tun in Lake Miramar, Chiapas, giving birth to the term *Lacandón* for all unsubdued rainforest Maya.

1586 Spanish forces again menace the island city of Lacam Tun.

1695–1696 Spanish military subdues the surviving Ch'olti Maya, ending the conquest of the Selva Lacandona and extinguishing the Ch'olti tribe and its language.

1700s   Escaping Spaniards in the Guatemalan Petén, Yucatec-speaking Lacandón Maya begin to cross the Río Usumacinta into the depopulated rainforest of Chiapas.

1786–1793   Spanish missionaries encounter Jach Winik (Yucatec-speaking Lacandón Maya) near Palenque, Chiapas, and establish a temporary settlement called San José de Gracia Real.

1848   Itza Maya lead Modesto Mendez to the "discovery" of the ruins of Tikal, where he finds traces of Lacandón Maya occupation among the ancient buildings (Palka 2005: 148).

1879   Salvador Valenzuela finds seven families of Yucatec Maya and three families of Yucatec-speaking Lacandones living and cultivating milpas among the ruins of the place they call "Tical," giving a formal place name to the archaeological site of Tikal (Palka 2005: 148).

1870s   Logging with oxen begins along the rivers of the Selva Lacandona.

1902–1904   Alfred Tozzer carries out the first ethnographic fieldwork with the Lacandón Maya.

1920s   Timber enterprises collapse in the Selva Lacandona, giving Lacandón Maya a temporary respite from outside invaders.

1940s   Chicle gum harvesters roam the rainforest to tap chicle trees for chewing gum base, interacting with Lacandones in both the Guatemalan Petén and Selva Lacandona.

1948   Phillip and Mary Baer arrive in Chiapas to translate the New Testament into Lacandón and convert the families to the Protestant faith.

1966–1973   Weiss Fricker Mahogany Company—acting as Aserraderos Bonampak—builds a network of roads in the Selva Lacandona to harvest mahogany and tropical cedar, prompting the in-migration of thousands of farm families and cattle ranchers into the Selva Lacandona.

1960s–1970s   A tripartite wave of destruction—logging, colonization, and cattle ranching—devastates the northern half of the Selva Lacandona.

1971   President Luís Echeverría Alvarez nationalizes privately owned lands in the Selva Lacandona.

1972   Federal law establishes the Comunidad Zona Lacandona, declaring 614,321 hectares of tropical rainforest the property of the Lacandón Maya.

1973   Missionary Satuliño Chan moves to Mensäbäk and converts half the community to Seventh-Day Adventism.

1974   Mexican government officials sign logging agreements with the newly mandated Lacandón owners and create parastatal companies to log the forest.

1975   Naja' and Mensäbäk are added to the Comunidad Zona Lacandona, adding 7,215 hectares to the Indigenous reserve.

1976   Mexican federal government concentrates Tzeltal, Tzotzil, and Ch'ol Maya forest communities into new population centers inside the Comunidad Zona Lacandona.

1978   Mexican federal government establishes the 331,200-hectare (1,280–square mile) Montes Azules Biosphere Reserve in the Selva Lacandona.

1979   First dirt roads bulldozed into Mensäbäk and Naja'.

1983   Dirt road completed to Lacanja' Chan Sayab.

1983   Escaped milpa and pasture fires from Tzeltal communities burn 50,000 hectares of old-growth rainforest in the southern Selva Lacandona (Carmelo Chan Bor, Comisariato, personal communication, April 1994).

1980s   A half dozen Christianized Lacandón families from Mensäbäk migrate south and create the community of Bethel, near Lacanja' Chan Sayab.

1991   Electric power lines reach Lacanja' Chan Sayab.

1992   President Carlos Salinas de Gortari establishes the 61,873-hectare Reserva de la Biósfera Lacantún; the 12,184-hectare Refugio de Flora y Fauna Silvestre Chan K'in; the 4,357-hectare Monumento Natural Bonampak; and the 2,621-hectare Monumento Natural Yaxchilán.

1993   Comunidad Zona Lacandona creates the 35,400-hectare Reserva Comunal Sierra la Cojolita as a biological corridor to link Montes Azules, Bonampak, and Yaxchilán

1993   Electric power lines reach Mensäbäk and Naja'.

1993   The Comunidad Zona Lacandona is reduced from 614,000 hectares to 501,106 hectares when the federal government transfers land in Las Cañadas to the Tzeltal Maya organization, ARIC (Carmelo Chan Bor, Comisariato, personal communication, 1994).

1994   North American Free Trade Agreement (NAFTA) goes into effect, facilitating the export of agribusiness-produced corn from the United States to Mexico.

1994   Maya farmers revolt in Chiapas cities and the Selva Lacandona as the Ejército Zapatista de Liberación Nacional, the "Zapatista Army of National Liberation" (EZLN).

1995   First government-sponsored schools open in Mensäbäk and Naja'

1996   Federal government asphalts the road to Lacanja' Chan Sayab and the 422–kilometer Frontier Highway along the Mexico-Guatemala border, making it possible to circumnavigate the Selva Lacandona by vehicle.

1996   Death of Chan K'in Viejo of Naja', the last of the Northern Lacandón spiritual leaders.

1998   Mensäbäk and Naja' declared Áreas de Protección de Flora y Fauna by federal law at the communities' request.

2001   Mexican government provides Naja' and Mensäbäk with satellite phones for external communications.

2019   Cell phones, WhatsApp in widespread use among Lacandón Maya.

Glossary of Terms and Acronyms

Agouti. Dasyprocta puntata and/or *Dasyprocta mexicana,* a 3–4 kilogram, diurnal rainforest rodent prized as bushmeat in the Selva Lacandona.

Artesanía. Handicrafts such as bows and arrows, carved wooden spoons, carved wood animals, and seeds made into bracelets and necklaces.

Balche? A sacred ritual drink made of water, sugarcane juice, and the bark of the cabbage bark tree (*Lonchocarpus longistylus*).

Caribal. A Lacandón Maya forest settlement, from *Caribe,* an early Spanish-language name for Jach Winik, the Lacandón people.

Cenote. A sinkhole in a limestone karst landscape.

COFOLASA. Compañía Industrial Forestal de la Lacandona, a parastatal company created by the Mexican federal government in 1974 to harvest timber in the Comunidad Zona Lacandona.

Comunidad Zona Lacandona. Indigenous land grant and geographical region of eastern Chiapas, established by the Mexican federal government in 1972 to conserve tropical forest and concentrate Lacandón Maya and colonist populations into permanently defined communities; originally 614,321 hectares, it was diminished to 501,106 hectares after several land parcels were ceded to adjoining communities.

CONANP. Consejo Nacional de Áreas Naturales Protegidas (National Council for Protected Natural Areas), Mexico's national protected areas agency.

Copal. The sticky sap of *Protium copal,* tapped from living trees and burned as incense in traditional Lacandón Maya religious ceremonies.

DAAC. Departamento de Asuntos Agrarios y de Colonización (Department of Agrarian Matters and Colonization).

Ejido. A communally held land grant in which community members have usufruct rather than ownership right.

Finca. Rural or agricultural land for crop or cattle production; usually privately owned.

FONAFE. The Fondo Nacional de Fomento Ejidal used funds from timber sales in the Comunidad Zona Lacandona to carry out a series of development projects in Lacandón Maya communities during the 1970s; now called Fideicomiso Fondo Nacional de Fomento Ejidal.

Jach Winik. Indigenous name for "the True People," the Yucatec Maya-speaking Lacandón Maya.

Ladino. Spanish-speaking citizens who dress in Western style.

Latifundista. Wealthy owner of an extensive parcel of privately owned land used for crops or cattle.

Latifundio. An extensive parcel of privately owned land used for crops or cattle.

Liana. Woody vine rooted in soil, which uses a tree for physical support.

Mestizo. Mixed Indigenous-Spanish origin inhabitants of Mexico.

Milpa. Agricultural field cut from tropical forest or forest regrowth, dominated by corn, beans, and squash, but frequently enlivened with other crops and useful trees.

Montane rainforest. Transition forest that blends elements and species of both rainforest and cloud forest.

NAFINSA. Nacional Financiera, S.A., a Mexican federal economic development agency.

Polygyny. A form of polygamy, or multiple marriage, in which one man takes two or more wives.

Regrowth. Alternative name for secondary forest, the vegetation that sprouts naturally after mature forest has been cleared.

SARH. Mexico's Secretaría de Agricultura y Ganadería (Secretary of Agriculture and Ranching)

Secondary growth. "Successional-stage of shrubby and wooded habitats, which differ from mature forest by having smaller trees and lower, more open canopy which lacks emergent trees" (Howell and Webb 2010: 29).

Selva Lacandona. The lowland and montane rainforest of eastern Chiapas, Mexico, named for the Indigenous Lacandón Maya who live there.

SEMARNAT. Mexico's Secretaría del Medio Ambiente y Recursos Naturales, charged with protecting the nation's environment and natural resources.

Tepesquintle. *Agouti paca,* a 6–14 kilogram nocturnal rodent highly prized as bushmeat in the Selva Lacandona. Also known as a paca or gibnut.

Tzeltal Maya. Indigenous families of central and eastern Chiapas who now constitute the majority of rural farmers and ranchers in the Selva Lacandona.

Notes

Preface

1 *After the Fact: Two Countries, Four Decades, One Anthropologist*, by Clifford Geertz, Cambridge, Mass.: Harvard University Press, Copyright © 1995 by the President and Fellows of Harvard College. Used by permission. All rights reserved.

Introduction

1 The Selva Lacandona is a mixture of lowland tropical rainforest, lower montane rainforest, and evergreen seasonal forest characterized by three layers of vegetation and a canopy 35–45 meters tall, with emergent trees reaching up to 60 meters. Annual rainfall fluctuates between 2,300 and 2,800 millimeters, and the temperature averages 25°C (77°F) (Miranda 1952, Muench 1982, Breedlove 1981, Nigh 2008; Durán-Fernández, Aguirre-Rivera, Levy-Tacher, and De-Nova 2018: 221). Originally extending over 1.8 million hectares, the forest has been reduced to just under 500,000 hectares in 2022. The only other Mexican tropical rainforest of approaching size is the Bosque Zoque, which lies in the Isthmus of Tehuantepec, on the border between Oaxaca and Chiapas. The Bosque Zoque originally covered more than 600,000 hectares, including the Chimalapas in Oaxaca, Uxpanapa in Veracruz, and El Ocote Reserve in Chiapas, but only 78 percent of the area is well-conserved, and of this, only 48 percent is tropical rainforest. The rest consists of subtropical forest, pine forest, and savannah. Like the Selva Lacandona of Chiapas, the Bosque Zoque is threatened by deforestation, cattle ranching, wildlife poaching, subsistence agriculture, forest fires, and drug trafficking. The Mexican States of Campeche and Quintana Roo, in the Yucatán Peninsula, include some lowland tropical rainforest, but subtropical moist forest dominates the northern reaches of both states, and up to half the trees lose their leaves during the dry season. Rainfall averages 1,000–1,500 mm per year (Toledo and Ordóñez 1993; Lira-Torres, et al. 2012; Wikipedia Español 2021; Ignacio March, personal communication, April 2021).

2 Estimates of the original extent of the Selva Lacandona range between 1,750,000 hectares and 2,782,180 hectares, depending on the data source. This book uses the territorial size officially accepted by SEMARNAP (2000) of 1,836,611 hectares, a datapoint also adopted by Muench (1997: 95) and de Vos (2011: 46). By this mea-

sure, the Selva Lacandona is the lowland tropical rainforest that once extended east of a line between Palenque and Ocosingo and south to Las Margaritas and Altamirano, all the way to the modern border with Guatemala. The Selva Lacandona is mirrored on the other side of the Río Usumacinta by the larger tropical forest known as the Guatemalan Petén.

3 Aspiring Mexican school teachers are required to perform a year of social service as part of their teaching degree. Among these trainees are the teachers assigned by the government to the Spanish-language elementary schools in the Lacandón Maya communities.

Chapter 1. Sanctuary

1 The name "baglunte'" that de la Cruz recorded was likely "bajlum te'" (in Ch'ol) or **balum te'** (in Lacandón), which, though it does mean "jaguar tree," actually refers to wild cacao (*Theobroma bicolor*), a tree that grows naturally (probably as a feral plant) in the Selva Lacandona.

2 Lacandón structures used for religious ceremonies and storage of sacred objects are called **u yatoch k'uj**, "god houses." Traditionally, each family compound had its own palm and thatch god house.

3 Much as the Lakota Indians of the North American frontier were "neither consulted nor informed" when Napoleon sold their territory to the nascent United States as a sizeable portion of the Louisiana Purchase in 1803 (Hämäläinen 2019: 120).

4 "Because of differences in structure, pronunciation, and vocabulary, a conversation between a Northern Lacandón Maya speaker and someone speaking one of the four other Yucatecan languages [Southern Lacandón, Itzá, Mopan, and Yucatec proper] would be similar to a cockney Englishman talking with a cattle rancher from West Texas—or a Spaniard from Madrid talking with a coastal fisherman from Cuba. In each case, most of the message would get through, but the subtleties and linguistic embellishments would be wasted" (Nations and Valenzuela 2017a; Nations and Valenzuela 2017b: 2).

5 The term *Caribes* for native people in the New World dates from the voyages of Christopher Columbus, who encountered the Calinago or Calino in the Lesser Antilles and corrupted the term to *Caribales*, which also is the origin of the English word *cannibal*. Tzeltal Maya in the Selva Lacandona sometimes refer to the Lacandones as Caribes and to their settlements as caribales, and some older Lacandones use the terms when speaking Spanish (see Bruce 1975: 4).

6 Child sex ratios refer to the ratio of males to females below the age of fifteen years (zero–fourteen years). For detailed analysis of Lacandón Maya sex ratios and their impact on population dynamics, see Nations 1979.

7 Two extended families live outside the legally protected Lacandón settlements: (1) A family of fifteen Northern Lacandones who formerly lived near the Tzeltal community of Ojo de Agua relocated in 2018 to the community of Santo Domingo. The families there maintained an active god house until late 2019, when their religious leader passed away. (2) Another family of seven Northern Lacandones, formerly from Mensäbäk, lives near Flores Magú, a collection of ranches on land originally

called **U Wits E'ele Che'** ("Burned Tree Mountain"), on the road between Chancalá and Bonampak. Census data on Lacanja' Chan Sayab, Bethel, and Crucero San Javier come from the Instituto Mexicano de Seguro Social, 2018, courtesy Carlos Chan Bor of Lacanja'. Figures for Mensäbäk and Naja' are from Mexico's Consejo Nacional de Areas Naturales Protegidas (CONANP) and Lacandón community leaders.

Chapter 2. Lacandones Don't Kill Dogs

1 The most complete versions of the story of the man who married a dog are found in Boremanse 1998: 122 and Boremanse 2006: 237–240. Boremanse writes that the story also points to the historical imbalance between the number of marriageable men and women among Northern Lacandón.

2 Since they began to drive vehicles in the 1980s, Lacandones have accidentally run over a number of dogs while driving through neighboring villages. Minchu Valenzuela says he's killed four. He knows exactly how many and where the events occurred. "The dogs don't think," he said. "They just cross the road all of a sudden. I feel bad about it. **In ch'aik otsi ti,** I take pity on them."

Chapter 3. The Ancient Ones

1 God pots are whitewashed and decorated ceramic bowls with the stylized face of a Lacandón god on one side of the rim.

Chapter 5. The Wooden People

1 *Gynerium sagittatum;* Spanish = *caña carrizo;* Lacandón = **oj.**

2 A longer version of this story appears in Bruce 1974: 276–289.

3 In highland Chiapas, some Tzotzil Maya festivals still include a frightening group of costumed performers known as **hnatikil hol,** "long hairs," a reference to Lacandones, who according to Tzotzil tradition, lived in the forest and ate babies. The performers depict Ch'olti Lacandones who lived in the Selva Lacandona when Spaniards invaded the New World (Laughlin 1975: 459; Chip Morris and Carol Karasik, personal communication, 2019, San Cristóbal de Las Casas, Chiapas).

Chapter 6. The Story of the Stolen Skulls

1 Most, perhaps all, of the individuals whose skeletons rest in the caves today were Ch'ol Maya speakers who died during Colonial times. Lacandón oral history says they died from **nä k'ak',** "mother fire," or **naj k'ak',** "the big fire," their terms for smallpox.

Chapter 7. How to Eat a Rainforest

1 José Camino Viejo's name in Spanish means "José of the Old Road," and José definitely followed the path of tradition. José's half-brother went by José Camino Joven, "José of the Young Road," but the lives of both men were based in the centuries-old traditions of Lacandón life. Both men occasionally used the surname Gavino. For details on Camino's expulsion from Sa'm, see chapter 18.

2 Northern Lacandones traditionally began to clear vegetation for burning and planting when cicadas (*Cicadidae*) started singing in February and March.

3 José Camino Viejo and his farming techniques are highlighted in the video documentaries, *In Good Hands: Culture and Agriculture in the Lacandon Rainforest* (Kibben and Bartz 1996) and *To the Roots,* by Steven Bartz (1998).

4 Respectively, *Sechium edule, Ipomoea batatas, Xanthosoma mafaffa, Manihot esculenta, Carica papaya, Musa* spp.

5 Among scientific and international audiences, the term *maize* is frequently used as the common name for the species, *Zea mays,* because the word *corn* can refer to different plant species in different regions of the world. But in some countries, including the United States, *maize* also denotes "sorghum maize" (*Sorghum bicolor,* also called *milo*), so the confusion continues. In this volume *corn* refers specifically to *Zea mays.*

6 Maya ruins proliferate in Lacandón agricultural fields. In 1977, Ronald Nigh, Ben J. Wallace, and I mapped and measured eleven active milpas in Lacanja' Chan Sayab (Nations and Nigh 1980), eight of which had ruins within their boundaries, indicating that the sites had been cultivated centuries before.

7 The influence of climate and other environmental factors on the timing of biological events is studied in the science of phenology.

8 Mamey sapote (*Pouteria sapota*); sapodilla (*Manilkara zapota*); wild pineapple (*Bromelia pinguin*); wild dogbane (*Ficus* sp.); balsa (*Trema micrantha*); corkwood (*Heliocarpus donnelli-smithii*).

9 No individual "owns" land within Lacandón communities, partly by tradition and partly because their lands are "communal" by Mexican federal law. But Lacandones recognize previous labor on a fallowed plot (**paak che' kol**) and recognize the use rights of the individual who first cleared the plot, even after it has regenerated as forest. When a man dies, his land use rights go to his sons or other close male relatives. Men from outside the Lacandón gene pool are rarely allowed to control land within Lacandón communities.

10 Marona is a large lake between Naja' and Mensäbäk, today part of the Tzeltal Maya community of Agua Dulce Tehuacán. Lake Itsanojk'uj is also known as Guineo or Sival and is today part of the Tzeltal community of Sival. (See chapter 4, "A Memory of Lakes").

11 Lacandón families controlled infestations of cockroaches by allowing marauding columns of army ants (**chäk wayaj**) to invade their house and consume every edible morsel in sight, including live cockroaches. If the ants were unwelcome when they appeared, the families redirected the column by using a feather fan to sweep the lead ants in another direction. The rest of the ants would follow.

12 Weevils are *Sitophilus granarius;* tobacco lice are likely the silverleaf whitefly (*Bemisia tabaci*), which suck juices from tobacco leaves, causing them to wither and drop.

13 Balsa (*Ochroma pyramidale*); shield-leaf pumpwood (*Cecropia peltata*).

14 However, Northern Lacandón folklore holds that eating the meat of the white-nosed coatimundi (*Nasua narica*) enhances sexual prowess.

15 Tobacco cultivation is a major impetus for weeding in the traditional Lacandón agricultural cycle, but it is not crucial. One of the most traditional farmers, Kimboy (1930–199?) of Lacanja' Chan Sayab (although he was born a Northern Lacandón in Sa'm), raised no tobacco, but kept the field around his house absolutely weedless. He planted and harvested the same milpa four to five years in a row. Recent agro-ecological research in Lacanja' Chan Sayab has emphasized the agricultural systems of two of Kimboy's sons, the half-brothers Manuel Castellanos and Adolfo Chan K'in.

16 Armando Valenzuela returned to Mensäbäk in 2015 after earning a forest systems degree from the Maya School of Agricultural Studies in Catazajá, Chiapas. He plants and harvests *Chamaedorea ernesti-augustii* palm (**k'eben**) as an understory crop shaded by natural forest, much the way modern Lacandones also produce shade-grown coffee. He sells the cut fronds to companies in Tenosique, Tabasco, where the leaves are sorted and exported to the Netherlands for use as green background screens for cut flower arrangements.

Chapter 8. Farming with the Ants

1 Reginaldo Chayax, the late Itza Maya leader in San José, Petén, Guatemala, told me in 2017 that if a farmer wants a tree to dry out and lose its leaves, he girdles it during a *luna tierna,* "a new moon."

Chapter 9. Teaching a Canoe to Swim

1 I heard this version of the canoe fable in Mensäbäk (2014); a similar version from Naja' appears in Cook (2019: 394–397). Lacandón Maya continue to carve canoes today. In August 2020, Roberto López worked with Chan K'in Juanito and Enrique Valenzuela in the forest near Mensäbäk to produce and launch a full-size mahogany dugout canoe.

Chapter 10. Fibers, Vines, and Fire in the Night

1 Sa'm was located in a valley south of the Lacandón settlements of Naja' and Mensäbäk. Today, the area forms part of the Tzeltal communities of Ach'lum Monte Líbano and El Censo.

2 **Sits'**, also called **ts'its'** (*Trichospermum mexicanum*, Spanish: *corcho rojo*), is a dye plant with plantain-type leaves, common in fallowed milpa gardens.

3 See Cook (2016: 62–64) for more information on Lacandón use of gourds.

4 Neanderthals living in Europe 40 to 55,000 years ago collected resin from pine trees and used it to haft stone tools to handles made of wood or bone. In at least one known case, they mixed the pine resin with beeswax (University of Colorado at Boulder 2019).

5 Lacandón bow and arrow manufacture is detailed in Nations (1981) and Nations and Clark (1983).

6 During 981 days of wildlife camera placement between October 2006 and December 2008, researchers captured images of twelve of the twenty-five large and medium-sized mammals known in the Área de Protección de Flora y Fauna Men-

säbäk, including jaguar, ocelot, white-lipped peccary, paca, opossum, jaguarundi, agouti, tayra, hooded skunk, and collared peccary (Rodas Trejo et al. 2017).

Chapter 11. Flying Monkeys

1 The story of the Maya Kimin has been published by Roberto Bruce (1976: 131–134), Didier Boremanse (2006: 188–189), and Suzanne Cook (2019: 247–252).

Chapter 12. The Jwan T'ut' K'in

1 Jwan T'ut' K'in literally means "Tinamou Parrot Sun," but the reasoning behind the name is unknown. This version of the story is adapted from the Spanish translation by Boremanse (2006: 170–177). The story appears in English in Cook (2019: 357–376).

2 K'ojo' (*Melipona solani*), k'änik (*Cephalotrigona zexmeniae*), chi' (*Plebeia frontalis*), yuus (*Tetragona mayarum* and *Tetragonisca angustula*), k'än sak (*Scaptotrigona pectoralis*) (Contreras, Vásquez, Aldasora, and Mérida 2020: 211).

Chapter 13. The Lord of the Monkeys

1 This story appears in English in Boremanse 1998: 122–123 and in Spanish in Boremanse 2006: 241–242.

Chapter 14. The Snake in the Lake

1 mäk ulan che' field botanical specimen identified by Juan José Castillo Mont, Profesor Titular y Director del Herbario de la Facultad de Agronomía, AGUAT, Universidad de San Carlos de Guatemala, November 2020. Balick and Arvigo report that *Piper amalago* is similarly used in Belize (2015: 421).

Chapter 15. Creating the World

1 The plumeria tree (*Plumeria rubra*, frangipani).

2 Despite his appearance in the Lacandón origin story, Lacandones report that Äkyanto' emerged after the arrival of Europeans to serve as the God of Foreigners, Metal, and Introduced Diseases. He also created money and Western medicine. Äkyanto' is described as a Ladino who wears pants, a shirt, and a hat, and carries a pistol. He lives in a cave on a high cliff along the Río Usumacinta, near Tenosique, Tabasco, and is said to have a son named Jesuklistu.

3 Mensäbäk is the maker of säbäk, the small speck of matter that lies at the center of each and every raindrop. Technical explanation: In Earth's atmosphere, tiny impurities such as dust and smoke particles are suspended in clouds, where they create cloud condensation nuclei—"seeds"—around which moisture condenses to form raindrops. Lacandones have been talking about the ecological role of Mensäbäk for centuries, which raises the question of when and how they learned the arcane secret about the particle inside every raindrop.

4 *Cestrum nocturnum* (Cook 2016: 103).

Chapter 16. Paying the Gods

1 In 1975, Chan K'in Viejo of Naja' said that Southern Lacandones told him that before they abandoned their traditional beliefs, Southern women also went into the family god house to pray.

2 Corn gruel in this case is **mats** (*atole, pozol*), a refreshing drink made from water and ground corn cooked without calcium hydroxide (*cal*).

3 The quote is from Old Lodge Skins in Arthur Penn's 1970 movie, *Little Big Man*, based on the 1964 novel by Thomas Berger.

4 The phrase, "the old clothes" comes from Charles King's statement about Margaret Mead's understanding of culture change: "Cultural change came about when enough people began to see that the old clothes didn't fit" (King 2019: 274).

Chapter 17. A Special Place in Hell

1 This story was reported by filmmaker and botanist Norman Lippman, who was in Naja' when Chan K'in Viejo said it.

2 *Leviticus* 11.

3 During a public speech in Dallas, Texas, 1973.

4 "This is the way the world ends / Not with a bang, but a whimper." T. S. Eliot, "The Hollow Men," 1925 (Eliot 1952: 56–59).

5 Vine Deloria, Jr. (Standing Rock Sioux) wrote, "While the thrust of Christian missions was to save the individual Indian, its result was to shatter Indian societies and destroy the cohesiveness of the Indian communities" (Deloria 1983: 106).

Chapter 18. What Happened to the Selva Lacandona?

1 Due to high levels of illegal harvesting and the environmental damage that harvesting causes, mahogany is listed in Appendix II of the Convention on International Trade in Endangered Species (CITES), making it illegal to import from anywhere in the new-world tropics. Spanish cedar is listed in Appendix III, outlawing imports from five countries in Latin America, though not from Mexico (U.S. Fish and Wildlife 2020).

2 Two of the colonies relocated into Nueva Palestina were Tzotzil Maya, which would later be associated with and represented by their Tzeltal Maya neighbors. Some Ch'ol men and women who had married into Tzeltal families also relocated into Nueva Palestina (Paladino 2005: 156).

3 Information and quote from Carmelo Chan Bor, field notes of James D. Nations, Lacanja' Chan Sayab, 1994.

4 Information and quote from Minchu Valenzuela, personal communication, Mensäbäk, 2017.

5 Information and quote from Sergio Montes Quintero, Director, Montes Azules Biosphere Reserve, email messages to the author, May and June 2020.

6 Information and quote from Sergio Montes Quintero, Director, Montes Azules Bio-

sphere Reserve, email messages to the author, May and June 2020, used with permission.

7 Interviews with Diego Sánchez, El Tumbo, Chiapas, and Francisco Hernández Luís, Zaragosa, Chiapas, May 2019.

Chapter 19. Saving a Rainforest

1 The drought began to ease in early 2020, and the lakes were 90 percent full by April of that year. In fall 2020, the Selva Lacandona, like much of northern Central America, was hit full force by two hurricanes in sequence, and the lakes overflowed into the logwood forest that grows between the community of Mensäbäk and Lake Ts'ibanaj. The Lacandones adapted to the drastic change in the lakes' levels, tied their canoes to trees near their houses, and likely marveled at the wisdom of the ancestors who knew to build their homes on the highest land around.

2 Roberto Bruce translated the term as "Nuestra Señora del Montículo" (Bruce 1968: 134).

Chapter 20. A Question of How We Will Live

1 Paul Chaat Smith, excerpt from *Everything You Know about Indians Is Wrong* (University of Minnesota Press, 2009) p. 136. Copyright 2009 by Paul Chaat Smith.

2 Lacandón Maya ecotourism meets the accepted definition of Indigenous tourism as "tourism based on the group's land and cultural identity and controlled from within the group" (Swain 1989: 85). Lacandón tourism centers on "small tourism companies owned and managed by Indigenous people, families with ancestral knowledge, and a destination rich in cultural and natural resources offering a variety of possibilities for the design of original tourism products closely linked to the territory" (Espeso-Molinero, Carlisle, and Pastor-Alfonso 2016: 1339).

3 Tim Trench reports that between 1999 and 2002, seven institutions invested the peso equivalent of US$1 million in tourism infrastructure in Lacanja' Chan Sayab (Trench 2002: 168).

References

Aoyama, Kazuo

2021   Warriors and the Transformation of Classic Maya Kingship: A Diachronic Analysis of Lithic Weapons in Copan, Honduras, and in Aguateca and Ceibal, Guatemala. Chapter 5, pp. 64–85, in: Tsubasa Okoshi, Arlen F. Chase, Philippe Nondédéo, and M. Charlotte Arnauld, editors, *Maya Kingship: Rupture and Transformation from Classic to Postclassic Times*. Gainesville: University Press of Florida.

Arnauld, M. Charlotte, Tsubasa Okoshi, Arlen F. Chase, and Philippe Nondédéo

2021   Changes in Maya Rulership at the End of the Classic Period: An Introduction, Chapter 1, pp. 1–17, in: Tsubasa Okoshi, Arlen F. Chase, Philippe Nondédéo, and M. Charlotte Arnauld, editors, *Maya Kingship: Rupture and Transformation from Classic to Postclassic Times*. Gainesville: University Press of Florida.

Arsenault, Chris

2011   Mexican Drug Lords Enjoy Exotic "Narco Zoos." *Aljazeera,* September 22, 2011. https://www.aljazeera.com/features/2011/9/22/mexican-drug-lords-enjoy -exotic-narco-zoos

Baer, Phillip, and Mary Baer

1952   *Materials of Lacandon Culture of the Petha Region.* Manuscript No. 34, Microfilm Collection of Manuscripts on Middle American Cultural Anthropology, Sixth Series. Chicago: University of Chicago Library.

Baer, Phillip, and William R. Merrifield

1971   *Two Studies on the Lacandones of Mexico.* Norman: Summer Institute of Linguistics of the University of Oklahoma.

Balick, Michael J., and Rosita Arvigo

2015   *Messages from the Gods: A Guide to Useful Plants of Belize.* Oxford: Oxford University Press and New York Botanical Garden.

Baragwanath, Kathryn, and Ella Bayi

2020   Collective Property Rights Reduce Deforestation in the Brazilian Amazon. *Proceedings of the National Academy of Sciences,* August 11, 2020. https://www.pnas .org/doi/10.1073/pnas.1917874117. Accessed October 21, 2020.

Bartz, Steve

1996   *To the Roots: A Maya Encounter.* 28 minute video. San Francisco, CA. (English and Spanish versions).

Beckett, Ian F. W.

2001   *Modern Insurgencies and Counter-Insurgencies: Guerrillas and the Opponents since 1750.* London: Routledge.

Berger, Thomas

1964   *Little Big Man.* New York: Bantam Dell.

Blom, Frans

1958   La gran laguna de los Lacandones. *Tlatoani,* 2a época, 4–9. México, D.F.

Blom, Frans, and Gertrude Duby

1955–1957   *La Selva Lacandona.* 2 vols. México, D.F.: Editorial Cultura, T.G., S.A.

Bloomberg News

2021   AMLO Says Mexico to Probe Deforestation in Flagship Program. *Bloomberg.* March 10, 2021. https://www.bloomberg.com/news/articles/2021-03-10/amlo-says-mexico-will-probe-deforestation-in-flagship-program?leadSource=uverify%20wall. Accessed June 1, 2021.

Bogoni, Juliano A., Carlos A. Peres, and Katia M.P.M.B. Ferraz

2020   Extent, Intensity and Drivers of Mammal Defaunation: A Continental-Scale Analysis across the Neotropics. *Scientific Reports* 10(1). https://www.nature.com/articles/s41598-020-72010-w. Accessed September 16, 2020.

Boremanse, Didier

1978   *The Social Organization of the Lacandon Indians of Mexico: A Comparative Study of Two Maya Forest Peoples.* PhD thesis, Social Anthropology, University of Oxford.

1991   Magia y Taxonomía en la Etnomedicina Lacandona. *Revista Española de Antropología Americana* 21: 279–294.

1998   *Hach Winik: The Lacandon Maya of Chiapas, Southern Mexico.* Institute for Mesoamerican Studies Monograph 11. Albany: University at Albany.

2006   *Cuentos y mitología de los lacandones: Contribución al estudio de la tradición oral maya.* Publicación Especial No. 42. Guatemala: Academia de Geografía de Guatemala.

2020   *Ruins, Caves, Gods, and Incense Burners.* Salt Lake City: University of Utah Press.

Breedlove, Dennis E.

1981   *Introduction to the Flora of Chiapas.* San Francisco: California Academy of Sciences.

Brito Foucher, Rodolfo

1931   México Desconocido: las Monterías de Chiapas. *Revista Universidad de México* 1(4): 324–328.

Bruce, Roberto D.

1968   *Gramática del Lacandón.* Departamento de Investigaciones Antropológicas. México, D.F.: Instituto Nacional de Antropología e Historia.

1974   *El Libro de Chan K'in.* Colección Científica, Lingüística 12. México, D.F.: Instituto Nacional de Antropología e Historia.

1975   *Lacandón Dream Symbolism: Dream Symbolism and Interpretation among the*

Lacandón Mayas of Chiapas, Mexico. México, D.F.: Ediciones Euroamericanas Klaus Thiele.

1976   *Textos y Dibujos Lacandones de Naha.* Colección Científica Lingüística No. 45. México, D.F.: Instituto Nacional de Antropología e Historia.

Bruce, Roberto D., Carlos Robles Uribe, and Enriqueta Ramos Chao

1971   *Los Lacandones: Cosmovisión Maya.* Proyecto de Estudios Antropológicas del Sureste. México, D.F.: Instituto Nacional de Antropología e Historia.

Brunhouse, Robert L.

1976   *Frans Blom, Maya Explorer.* Albuquerque: University of New Mexico Press.

Cagnato, Clarissa, and Jocelyne M. Ponce

2017   Ancient Maya Manioc (*Manihot esculenta* Crantz) Consumption: Starch Grain Evidence from Late to Terminal Classic (8th–9th Centuries CE) Occupation at La Corona, Northwestern Peten, Guatemala. *Journal of Archaeological Science Reports* 16: 276. https://doi.org/10.1016/j.jasrep.2017.09.035

Calleros-Rodríguez, Héctor

2014   Land, Conflict, and Political Process: The Case of the Lacandon Community, Chiapas, Mexico (1972–2012). *The Journal of Peasant Studies* 41(1): 127–155. https://doi.org/10.1080/03066150.2013.873891

Campbell, Jonathan A.

1998   *Amphibians and Reptiles of Northern Guatemala, the Yucatán, and Belize.* Norman: University of Oklahoma Press.

Campbell, Jonathan A., and J. Vannini

1988   A New Subspecies of Beaded Lizard, *Heloderma horridum,* from the Motagua Valley of Guatemala. *Journal of Herpetology* 22(4): 457–468.

CARE/Conservation International

1995   *Informe Final: Análisis de los Impactos Ambientales Actuales y Potenciales del Proceso de Reintegración de los Retornados a Guatemala y Recomendaciones para su Mitigación.* Guatemala: CARE Guatemala y Conservación Internacional.

Carpenter, Edmund

1973   *Oh, What a Blow That Phantom Gave Me!* New York: Holt, Rinehart and Winston.

Castellanos-Navarrete, Antonio, and Kees Jansen

2015   Oil Palm Expansion without Enclosure: Smallholders and Environmental Narratives. *Journal of Peasant Studies* 42(3–4): 791–816. http://doi.org/10.1080/03066150.2015.1016920.

CBS News

2018   Alligator vs. Burmese Python. *CBS News,* January 17, 2018, https://www.cbsnews.com/news/viral-photo-alligator-burmese-python-naples-florida-golf-course. Accessed July 18, 2018.

CDC

2018   YellowFeverHistoryTimeline.CentersforDiseaseControlandPrevention.https://www.cdc.gov/travel-raining/local/HistoryEpidemiologyandVaccination/HistoryTimelineTranscript.pdf. Accessed August 31, 2018.

Chase, Arlen F., M. Charlotte Arnauld, Diane Z. Chase, Philippe Nondédéo, and Tsubasa Okoshi

2021　The Rupture and Transformation of Maya Kingship. Chapter 19, pp. 347–356, in: Okoshi, Tsubasa, Arlen F. Chase, Philippe Nondédéo, and M. Charlotte Arnauld, editors, *Maya Kingship: Rupture and Transformation from Classic to Postclassic Times.* Gainesville: University Press of Florida.

Chase, Arlen F., and Diane Z. Chase

2021　Foreword, pp. xv–xvii, in: Okoshi, Tsubasa, Arlen F. Chase, Philippe Nondédéo, and M. Charlotte Arnauld, editors, *Maya Kingship: Rupture and Transformation from Classic to Postclassic Times.* Gainesville: University Press of Florida.

Cheng, Kaity, Stewart A.W. Diemont, and Allan P. Drew

2011　Role of tao (*Belotia mexicana*) in the Traditional Lacandon Maya Shifting Cultivation Ecosystem. *Agroforestry Systems* 82(3): 331–336.

Chiapas Support

2015　Capitalism, War, and Counterinsurgency in Chiapas. https://chiapas-support.org/2015/10/21/capitalism-and-war-and-insurgency-in-chiapas-iii. Accessed January 17, 2018.

Christ, Costas

2019　Is Flying Good for the Planet? *New York Times,* November 20, 2019.

Ciofalo, Andrew J.

2012　*Maya Use and Prevalence of the Atlatl: Projectile Point Classification Function Analysis from Chichén Itzá, Tikal, and Caracol.* MA Thesis, University of Central Florida. http://sciences.ucf.edu/anthropology/wp-content/uploads/sites/19/2013/09content/uploads/sites/19/2013/09/Ciofalo_Andrew.pdf. Accessed October 4, 2018.

Clifford, James, and George E. Marcus, editors

1986　*Writing Culture: The Poetics and Politics of Ethnography.* Berkeley: University of California Press.

Coe, Michael D.

1993　*The Maya.* New York: Thames and Hudson.

Cogolludo, Diego López de

1955　*Historia de Yucatán.* 4th ed., 3 vols. Campeche: Comisión de Historia. Talleres Gráficos del Gobierno Constitucional del Estado.

CONANP

2006a　*Programa de Conservación y Manejo Área de Protección de Flora y Fauna Metzabok.* México, D.F.: Comisión Nacional de Áreas Naturales Protegidas.

2006b　*Programa de Conservación y Manejo Área de Protección de Flora y Fauna Nahá.* México, D.F.: Comisión Nacional de Áreas Naturales Protegidas.

Contreras Cortés, Ulises, and Ramón Mariaca Méndez

2016　*Manejo de los Recursos Naturales entre los Mayas Lacandones de Nahá.* San Cristóbal de Las Casas, Chiapas: El Colegio de la Frontera Sur.

Contreras Cortés, Leonardo Ernesto Ulises, Amparo Vásquez García, Elda Miriam Aldasoro Maya, and Jorge Mérida Rivas
2020   Conocimiento de las Abejas Nativas sin Aguijón y Cambio Generacional entre los Mayas Lacandones de Naja', Chiapas. *Estudios de Cultura Maya* 56: 205–225.
Cook, Suzanne
2016   *The Forest of the Lacandon Maya: An Ethnobotanical Guide.* New York: Springer.
2019   *Xurt'an: The End of the World and Other Myths, Songs, Charms, and Chants by the Northern Lacandones of Naha'.* Lincoln: University of Nebraska Press.
Cucina, Andrea, Vera Tiesler, and Joel Palka
2015   The Identity and Worship of Human Remains in Rockshelter Shrines among the Northern Lacandons of Mensäbäk. *Estudios de Cultura Maya* XLV: 141–169.
Davis, Virginia Dale
1978   *Ritual of the Northern Lacandon Maya.* Unpublished PhD dissertation. New Orleans: Tulane University.
Dawson, Neil M., Brendan Coolsaet, Eleanor J. Sterling, Robin Loveridge, Nicole D. Gross-Camp, Supin Wongbusarakum, Kamaljit K. Sangha, Lea M. Scherl, Hao Phuong Phan, Noelia Zafra-Calvo, Warren G. Lavey, Patrick Byakagaba, C. Julián Idrobo, Aude Chenet, Nathan J. Bennett, Stephanie Mansourian, and Franciso J. Rosado-May
2021   The Role of Indigenous People and Local Communities in Effective and Equitable Conservation. *Ecology and Society* 26(3): 19. https://doi.org/10.5751/ES-12625-260319.
De Jong, Bernardus H. J., Susana Ochoa-Gaona, Miguel Angel Castillo-Santiago, Neptali Ramirez Marcial, and Michael A. Cairns
2009   Carbon Flux and Patterns of Land-Use/Land-Cover in the Selva Lacandona, Mexico. *AMBIO: A Journal of the Human Environment* 29(8): 504–511. https://doi.org/10.1579/0044-7447-29.8.504.
de la Cruz Guillén, Guadalupe
2004   *El Recetario Lacandón.* México, D.F.: CONANP, SEMARNAT, y Espacios Naturales y Desarrollo Sustentable, A.C.
de Lacy, Terry, and Michelle Whitmore
2006   Tourism and Recreation. Chapter 19, pp. 497–527 in: Michael Lockwood, Graeme L. Worboys, and Ashish Kothari, editors, *Managing Protected Areas: A Global Guide.* London: Earthscan.
Deloria, Vine, Jr.
1983   *Custer Died for Your Sins: An Indian Manifesto.* New York: Avon/HarperCollins.
Demarest, Arthur, Bart Victor, Chloe Andrieu, and Paola Torres
2021   The Collapse of the Southern Lowland Classic Maya City-States, Chapter 18, pp. 327–348, in: Tsubasa Okoshi, Arlen F. Chase, Philippe Nondédéo, and M. Charlotte Arnauld, editors, *Maya Kingship: Rupture and Transformation from Classic to Postclassic Times.* Gainesville: University Press of Florida.

Denevan, W.M.

1992   Stone vs. Metal Axes: The Ambiguity of Shifting Cultivation in Prehistoric Amazonia. *Journal of the Steward Anthropological Society* 20: 153–165.

de Vos, Jan

1980   *La Paz de Dios y del Rey: La Conquista de la Selva Lacandona.* México, D.F.: FONAPAS Chiapas.

1988   *Viajes al Desierto de la Soledad: Cuando la Selva Lacandona aún era Selva.* México, D.F.: Programa Cultural de las Fronteras, Secretaría de Educación Pública.

1993   *Las Fronteras de la Frontera Sur: Reseña de los Proyectos de Expansión que Figuraron la Frontera entre México y Centroamérica.* Centro de Investigaciones y Estudios Superiores en Antropología Social. Villahermosa: Universidad Juárez Autónoma de Tabasco.

1996   *Oro Verde: La Conquista de la Selva Lacandona por los Madereros Tabasqueños 1822–1949.* México, D.F.: Instituto de Cultura de Tabasco.

2011   *Una Tierra para Sembrar Sueños: Historia Reciente de la Selva Lacandona, 1950–2000.* México, D.F.: Fondo de Cultura Económica.

Dichtl, Sigrid

1987   *Cae una Estrella: Desarrollo y Destrucción de la Selva Lacandona.* Mexico City: Secretaría de Educación Pública.

Dickenson, J.C., III

1972   Alternatives to Monoculture in the Humid Tropics of Latin America. *The Professional Geographer* 24: 217–222.

Diemont, Stewart A. W., and Jay F. Martin

2009   Lacandon Maya Ecosystem Management: Sustainable Design for Subsistence and Environmental Restoration. *Ecological Applications* 19(1): 254–266.

Diemont, S.A.W., J. F. Martin, S. I. Levy-Tacher, R. B. Nigh, P. Ramirez-Lopez, and J. D. Golicher

2005   Lacandon Maya Forest Management: Restoration of Soil Fertility Using Native Tree Species. *Ecological Engineering* 28(3): 205–212. https://www.sciencedirect.com/science/article/abs/pii/S0925857405002338. Accessed December 28, 2020.

DOF

1972   Resolución sobre reconocimiento y titulación a favor del núcleo de población Zona Lacandona, Municipio de Ocosingo, Chiapas, de una superficie de seiscientas catorce mil trescientas veintiuna hectáreas de terrenos comunales. *Diario Oficial de la Federación,* 6 de marzo, 1972: 10–13.

1975   Decreto por el que se amplía el territorio de la Comunidad Zona Lacandona a 662,000 ha en incorporación de los predios de las comunidades Naja' y Metzabok. *Diario Oficial de la Federación.*

1978   Decreto por al que se declara de interés público el establecimiento de la zona de protección forestal de la Cuenca del Río Tulijá, así como de la Reserva Integral de la Biósfera Montes Azules, en el área comprendida dentro de los límites que se indican. *Diario Oficial de la Federación,* 12 de enero, 1978: 6–8.

1979   Resolución sobre reconocimiento de derechos agrarios comunales en el núcleo de población denominado "Zona Lacandona," Municipio de Ocosingo, Chiapas. *Diario Oficial de la Federación,* 8 de marzo, 1979: 6–8.

Douterlungne, David, Samuel I. Levy-Tacher, Duncan J. Golicher, and Francisco Roman Danobeytia

2010   Applying Indigenous Knowledge to the Restoration of Degraded Tropical Rain Forest Clearings Dominated by Bracken Fern. *Restoration Ecology* 18(3): 322–329.

Durán-Fernandez, Alejandro, Juan Rogelio Aguirre-Rivera, Samuel Israel Levy-Tacher, and José Arturo De-Nova

2018   Estructure de la Selva Alta Perennifolia de Nahá, Chiapas, México. *Botanical Sciences* 96(2): 218–245. https://doi.org/10.17129/botsci.1919.

Eliot, T. S.

1952   *T. S. Eliot: The Complete Poems and Plays 1909–1950.* New York: Harcourt, Brace & World, Inc.

Espeso-Molinero, Pilar, Sheena Carlisle, and María José Pastor-Alfonso

2016   Knowledge Dialogue Through Indigenous Tourism Product Design: A Collaborative Research Process with the Lacandon of Chiapas, Mexico. *Journal of Sustainable Tourism* 4(8–9): 1331–1349.

Espeso-Molinero, Pilar, and María José Pastor-Alfonso

2020   Governance, Community Resilience, and Indigenous Tourism in Naja', Mexico. *Sustainability* 12 (5973): 1–20.

Estrada Monroy, Agustín.

1972   Un Viaje Fascinante al Lacandón del Siglo XIX, de Edwin Rockstroh. *El Imparcial, Diario Independiente.* Guatemala, Guatemala. March 16–18, 20–22, 23–24.

Falkowski, Tomas B., Adolfo Chankin, and Stewart A.W. Diemont

2019   Successional Changes in Vegetation and Litter Structure in Lacandon Maya Agroforests. *Agroecology and Sustainable Food Systems.* https://doi.org/10.1080/21683565.2019.1649784.

Falkowski, Tomasz B., Adolfo Chankin, Stewart A.W. Diemont, and Robert Pedian

2019   More Than Just Corn and Calories: A Comprehensive Assessment of the Yield and Nutritional Content of a Traditional Lacandon Maya Milpa. *Food Security* 11(5). https://doi.org/10.1007/s12571-019-00901-6.

Falkowski, Tomasz B., Stewart A.W. Diemont, Adolfo Chankin, and David Douterlungne

2016   Lacandon Maya Traditional Ecological Knowledge and Rainforest Restoration: Soil Fertility Beneath Six Agroforestry System Trees. *Ecological Engineering* 92: 210–217.

Fisher, Max

2019   How the Amazon Could Self-Destruct. *New York Times,* August 30, 2019: A6.

Fisher, Steve, and Elisabeth Malkin

2019   "Slow-Motion Chernobyl": How Lax Laws Befouled a Mexican River. *New York Times,* December 31, 2019: A4. https://www.nytimes.com/2019/12/30/world/americas/mexico-environment-trade.html

Ford, Anabel

2020   The Maya Forest Domesticated Landscape, Chapter 23 in: Scott Hutson and Traci Ardren, editors, *The Maya World.* Abingdon, Oxford: Taylor and Francis Group, Routledge.

Ford, Anabel, and Ronald Nigh

2016   *The Maya Forest Garden: Eight Millennia of Sustainable Cultivation of the Tropical Woodlands.* New York: Routledge.

Fox, Robin

1975   *Encounter with Anthropology.* New York: Dell Publishing.

Geertz, Clifford

1995   *After the Fact: Two Countries, Four Decades, One Anthropologist.* Cambridge: Harvard University Press.

Gollnick, Brian

2008   *Reinventing the Lacandón: Subaltern Representations in the Rain Forest of Chiapas.* Tucson: University of Arizona Press.

González Pacheco, Cuauhtémoc

1983   *Capital Extranjero en la Selva de Chiapas 1863–1982.* México, D.F.: Instituto de Investigaciones Económicas, Universidad Nacional Autónoma de México.

Greenblatt, Stephen

2017   Why Our Stories Matter. *New York Times,* December 21, 2017.

Grube, Nikolai

2021   Nostalgic Kings: The Rhetoric of Terminal Classic Maya Inscription. Chapter 3, pp. 35–50, in: Tsubasa Okoshi, Arlen F. Chase, Philippe Nondédéo, and M. Charlotte Arnauld, editors, *Maya Kingship: Rupture and Transformation from Classic to Postclassic Times.* Gainesville: University Press of Florida.

Hacienda Chiapas

2020   Programa Regional de Desarrollo: Región XII Selva Lacandona. http://www.haciendachiapas.gob.mx/planeacion/Informacion/Desarrollo-Regional/prog-regionales/SELVA.pdf. Accessed July 1, 2020.

Haldon, John, Arlen F. Chase, Warren Eastwood, Martin Medina-Elizalde, Adam Izdebski, Francis Ludlow, Guy Middleton, Lee Mordechai, Jason Nesbitt, and B.L. Turner II

2020   Demystifying Collapse: Climate, environment, and social agency in premodern societies. *Millennium: Yearbook on the Culture and History of the First Millennium C.E.* 17(1): 1–33.

Hämäläinen, Pekka

2019   *Lakota America: A New History of Indigenous Power.* Ithaca, New Haven: Yale University Press.

Hecht, S. B.

2003   Indigenous Soil Management and the Creation of Amazonian Dark Earths, pp. 355–372, in: J. Lehmann, D. Kern, L. A. German, J. M. McCann, G. C. Martins, and A. Moreira, editors, *Amazonian Dark Earths: Origins, Properties, Management.* Dordrecht, The Netherlands: Kluwer Academic Publishers.

Hernández-Rojas, Dulce A., Faviola López-Barrera, and Martha Bonilla-Moheno

2018   Preliminary Analysis of the Land Use Dynamic Associated with Oil Palm

(*Elaeis guineensis*). *Agrociencia* 52(6). http://www.scielo.org.mx/scielo.php
?script=sci_arttext&pid=S1405-31952018000600875&lng=en&nrm=iso&tlng
=en. Accessed June 14, 2020.

Hofling, Charles Andrew

2014 *Lacandon Maya-Spanish-English Dictionary*. Salt Lake City: University of Utah Press.

Hosler, Dorothy, Sandra Burkett, and Michael Tarkanian

1999 Prehistoric Polymers: Rubber Processing in Ancient Mesoamerica. *Science* 284 (5422): 1988–1991.

Howell, Steve N.G and Sophie Webb

2013 A Guide to the Birds of Mexico and Northern Central America. Oxford: Oxford University Press.

Ibarra, Juan

1956 Los Lacandones de Chiapas Pertenecientes a Nuestra Misión de Tabasco. *Pinceladas Misionales,* Publicación Cuatrimestral de las Misiones de Tabasco y Chiapas, Confiadas a la Provincia Franciscana del Santo Evangelio de México. México, D.F. septiembre–diciembre de 1956: 12–14.

INE-SEMARNAP

2000 *Programa de Manejo Reserva de la Biósfera Montes Azules*. Dirección Ejecutiva de Participación Social, Enlace y Comunicación, Instituto Nacional de Ecología-Secretaría del Medio Ambiente Recursos Naturales y Pesca.

Iñigo-Elías, Eduardo

1996 *Landscape Ecology and Conservation Biology of the Scarlet Macaw (Ara macao) in the Gran Petén Region of Mexico and Guatemala*. PhD dissertation, University of Florida.

Jacobs, Andrew, and Matt Richtel

2017 With NAFTA, Mexico Receives Unexpected Import: Obesity. *New York Times,* December 12, 2017.

Juarez, Santiago, Sebastián Salgado-Flores, and Christopher Hernandez

2019 The Site of Noh K'uk, Chiapas, Mexico: A Late Preclassic Settlement in the Mensäbäk Basin. *Latin American Antiquity* 30(1): 211–217. https://doi.org/10 .1017/laq.2018.81.

Kaplan, Sarah

2021 Colombia Faces a Big Invasive Species—Hippos. *Washington Post,* January 19, 2021: E-1–2.

Kibben, Jamie, and Steve Bartz

1996 *In Good Hands: Agroecology of the Lacandon Maya*. 28 minute video. San Francisco, CA. (Spanish and English versions).

King, Charles

2019 *Gods of the Upper Air: How a Circle of Renegade Anthropologists Reinvented Race, Sex, and Gender in the Twentieth Century*. New York: Doubleday.

Kothari, Ashish

2006a Collaboratively Managed Protected Areas, Chapter 20, pp. 528–548, in: Michael

Lockwood, Graeme L. Worboys, and Ashish Kothari, editors, *Managing Protected Areas: A Global Guide*. London: Earthscan.

2006b   Community Conserved Areas. Chapter 21, pp. 549–573, in: Michael Lockwood, Graeme L. Worboys, and Ashish Kothari, editors, *Managing Protected Areas: A Global Guide*. London: Earthscan.

Laughlin, Robert M.

1975   *The Great Tzotzil Dictionary of San Lorenzo Zinacantán*. Smithsonian Contributions to Anthropology, Number 19. Washington, DC: Smithsonian Institution Press.

Lee, Julian C.

2000   *A Field Guide to the Amphibians and Reptiles of the Maya World*. Ithaca: Cornell University Press.

Legorreta Díaz, Carmen

2015   *Religión, Política y Guerrilla en Las Cañadas de la Selva Lacandona*. México, D.F.: Universidad Nacional Autónoma de México, Centro de Investigaciones Interdisciplinarias en Ciencias y Humanidades. http://computo.ceiich/unam.mx/webceiich/docs/libro/Selva%20Lacandona-web.pdf. Accessed May 26, 2020.

Lennon, Jane

2006   Cultural Heritage Management. Chapter 17, pp. 448–473, in: Michael Lockwood, Graeme L. Worboys, and Ashish Kothari, editors, *Managing Protected Areas: A Global Guide*. London: Earthscan.

Levy-Tacher, Samuel Israel, and John Duncan Golicher

2004   How Predictive is Traditional Ecological Knowledge? The Case of the Lacandon Maya Fallow Enrichment System. *INTERCIENCIA* 29(9): 496–503.

Library of Congress

2020   Oil, Mexico. Country Studies: Mexico. http://countrystudies.us/mexico/78.htm. Accessed: March 27, 2020.

Linares, Olga F.

1976   "Garden Hunting" in the American Tropics. *Human Ecology* 4(4): 331–349.

Lira-Torres, Iván, Carlos Galindo-Leal, and Miguel Briones-Salas

2012   Mamíferos de la Selva Zoque, México: Riqueza, Uso y Conservación. *Revista de Biología Tropical* 60(2). https://www.scielo.sa.cr/scielo.php?script=sci_arttext&pid=S0034-77442012000200022. Accessed May 20, 2021.

Lopez, Jaime

2013   Anaconda on the Loose. *Costa Rica Star,* August 24, 2013. https://news.co.cr/anaconda-on-the-loose-exotic-pet-issues-in-costa-rica/25473/. Accessed July 18, 2018.

Lovell, W. George, and Christopher H. Lutz

1990   The Historical Demography of Colonial Central America. *Yearbook. Conference of Latin Americanist Geographers* 17/18: 127–138. http://www.jstor.org/stable/25765745. Accessed December 5, 2018.

Marion, Marie-Odile

1997   Indigenous Peoples of the Forest, pp. 70–94, in: *The Lacandona Rainforest: A Vanishing Paradise*. Mexico, D.F.: Pulsar/Conservación Internacional México.

Maudslay, Anne, and Alfred P. Maudslay

1899   *A Glimpse at Guatemala, and Some Notes on the Ancient Monuments of Central America.* London: John Murray.

McGee, R. Jon

1990   *Life, Ritual, and Religion among the Lacandón Maya.* Belmont, CA: Wadsworth Modern Anthropology Library.

Medellín, Rodrigo A.

1994   Mammal Diversity and Conservation in the Selva Lacandona, Chiapas, Mexico. *Conservation Biology* 8(3): 780–799.

México Desconocido

2020   Viaje al Río Tulijá, Corazon Tzeltal en Chiapas. *México Desconocido,* No. 366. https://www.mexicodesconocido.com.mx/viaje-al-rio-tulija-corazon-tzeltal-en -chiapas.html. Accessed September 4, 2020.

Miranda, F.

1952   *La Vegetación de Chiapas.* Tuxtla Gutiérrez: Gobierno del Estado de Chiapas.

Mongabay Latam

2020   La Invasión de la Palma Africana en la Selva Lacandona. *Biodiversidad LA,* 20 febrero. http://www.biodiversidadla.org/Documentos/La-invasion-de-la -palma-africana-en-la-Selva-Lacandona. Accessed February 27, 2020.

Montañez, Pablo

1972   *La Agonía de la Selva.* México, D.F.: Talleres de B. Costa-Amic Editor.

Moretti-Sánchez, J. Carlos, and Celsa Cosío-Ruiz

2016   Panorama de los Ejidos y Comunidades Agrarias en México. *Agricultura, Sociedad, y Desarrollo.* http://redalyc.org/journal/3605/360550545007/html. Accessed April 4, 2022.

Morgan, Melissa A.

2015   Exotic Addiction. *Duke Law Journal* 65. http://dlj.law.duke.edu/2015/08/exotic -addiction/. Accessed June 4, 2018.

Muench, Pablo

1982   Las Regiones Agrícolas de Chiapas. *Geografía Agrícola (Mexico)* 2: 33–44.

1997   Transformation of the Natural Environment, pp. 95–125, in: Pulsar, *The Lacandona Rainforest: A Vanishing Paradise.* México, D.F.: Pulsar.

Nations, James D.

1979   *Population Ecology of the Lacandon Maya, Chiapas, Mexico.* PhD dissertation, Department of Anthropology, Southern Methodist University.

1981   The Lacandón Maya Bow and Arrow: An Ethnoarchaeological Example of Post-Classic, Lowland Maya Weapon Manufacture, in: *Proceedings of the Simposio La Obsidiana en Mesoamérica.* México, D.F.: Instituto Nacional de Antropología e Historia, Secretaría de Educación Pública.

1984   The Lacandones, Gertrude Blom, and the Selva Lacandona, Chapter 2, pp. 27–41, in: Alex Harris and Margaret Sartor, editors, *Gertrude Blom: Bearing Witness.* Chapel Hill: Center for Documentary Photography, Duke University, by the University of North Carolina Press.

1994   The Ecology of the Zapatista Revolt. *Cultural Survival Quarterly* 18(1): 31–33.

2001a Biosphere Reserves, pp. 1231–1235, in: N. J. Smelser and Paul B. Bates, editors, *International Encyclopedia of the Social and Behavioral Sciences,* Oxford: Pergamon.

2001b Indigenous Peoples and Conservation: Misguided Myths in the Maya Tropical Forest, Chapter 28, pp. 462–471, in: Luisa Maffi, editor, *On Biocultural Diversity: Linking Language, Knowledge, and the Environment.* Washington, DC: Smithsonian Institution Press.

2006 *The Maya Tropical Forest: People, Parks, and Ancient Cities.* Austin: University of Texas Press.

Nations, James D., and Chan K'in José Valenzuela

2017a *Maya Lacandón: El Idioma y el Medio Ambiente.* Columbia, SC: KindleDirect .com.

2017b *Lacandón Maya: The Language and Environment.* Columbia, SC: KindleDirect .com.

Nations, James D., and John E. Clark

1983 The Bows and Arrows of the Lacandón Maya. *Archaeology* 36(1): 36–43.

Nations, James D., and Daniel I. Komer

1983a Rainforests and the Hamburger Society. *Environment* 25(3): 12–20.

1983b Central America's Tropical Rainforests: Positive Steps for Survival. *AMBIO: A Journal of the Human Environment* 12(5): 233–238.

Nations, James D. and Ronald B. Nigh

1980 The Evolutionary Potential of Lacandon Maya Sustained-Yield Tropical Forest Agriculture. *Journal of Anthropological Research* 36: 1–30.

Newton, Peter, Andrew T. Kinzer, Daniel C. Miller, Johan A. Oldekop, and Arun Agrawal.

2020 The Number and Spatial Distribution of Forest-Proximate People Globally. *One Earth* 3(3): 363. https://doi.org/10.1016/j.oneear.2020.08.016.

Newton, Peter, Daniel C. Miller, Mugabi Augustine, Ateenyi Byenkya, and Arun Agrawal

2016 Who Are Forest-Dependent People? A Taxonomy to Aid Livelihood and Land Use Decision-Making in Forested Regions. *Land Use Policy* 57: 388–395. https://www.sciencedirect.com/science/article/pii/S0264837716300497?via%3Dihub. Accessed September 24, 2020.

Nigh, Ronald B.

2008 Trees, Fire and Farmers: Making Woods and Soil in the Maya Forest. *Journal of Ethnobiology* 28(2): 231–243.

Nuestro-México

2020a Jol Tulijá-Chiapas. http://www.nuestro-mexico.com/Chiapas/Ocosingo/Jol -Tulija. Accessed September 10, 2020.

2020b Puerto Bello Metzabok-Chiapas. http://www.nuestro-mexico.com/Chiapas/ Ocosingo/Areas-de-menos-de-100-habitantes/Puerto-Bello-Metzabok. Accessed September 9, 2020.

Nuwer, Rachel

2014 Like Columbus, It Floated Here. *New York Times,* February 25, 2014: D3.

O'Brien, Karen L.
1998   *Sacrificing the Forest: Environmental and Social Struggles in Chiapas.* Boulder, CO: Westview Press.

Okoshi, Tsubasa, Arlen F. Chase, Philippe Nondédéo, and M. Charlotte Arnauld, editors
2021   *Maya Kingship: Rupture and Transformation from Classic to Postclassic Times.* Gainesville: University Press of Florida.

Orozco y Jiménez, Ilmo, y Rmo. Sr. Doctor Don Francisco
1911   *Colección de Documentos Inéditos Relativos a la Iglesia de Chiapas.* 2 vols. San Cristóbal de Las Casas, México: Imprenta de la Sociedad Católica.

O'Shea, Mark
2011   *Boas and Pythons of the World.* Princeton, NJ: Princeton University Press.

Palacio Peralta, Manuel Gustavo, and Reyna M. C. Moguel Viveros
2008   La Disputa por los Recursos Naturales en la Selva Lacandona a Partir de la Reforma al Artículo 27 Constitucional. *Revista de la Procuraduría Agraria.* http://www.pa.gob.mx/publica/rev_37/Manuel%20Gustavo%20Palacio%20Peralta.pdf. Accessed April 8, 2020.

Paladino, Stephanie R.
2005   *We Are the Guardians of the Selva: Conservation, Indigenous Communities, and Common Property in the Selva Lacandona, Mexico.* PhD dissertation, Anthropology, University of Georgia. https://getd.libs.uga.edu/pdfs/paladino_stephanie_r_200512_phd.pdf. Accessed March 26, 2019.

Palka, Joel W.
2005   *Unconquered Lacandon Maya: Ethnohistory and Archaeology of Indigenous Culture Change.* Gainesville: University Press of Florida.
2014   *Maya Pilgrimage to Ritual Landscapes.* Albuquerque: University of New Mexico Press.
2020   Lacandon Maya Culture: Continuity and Change. Chapter 44, in: Scott Hutson and Traci Ardren, editors, *The Maya World.* Abingdon, Oxford: Taylor and Francis Group, Routledge.

Palka, Joel W., and A. Fabiola Sánchez Balderas
2012   Sitios Sagrados de los Maya Posclásicos e Históricos en Mensabak, Selva Lacandona, Chiapas, México, in: Lynneth S. Lowe and Mary E Pye, editors, *Arqueología Reciente en Chiapas.* Papers of the New World Archaeological Foundation, 72. Provo, UT: Brigham Young University.

Palka, Joel W., Fabiola Sánchez Balderas, Ian Hollingshead, Rebecca Deeb, and Nam Kim
2008   Recorrido Arqueológico en Mensabak, Chiapas y los Mayas Postclásicos e Históricos en las Tierras Bajas, pp.808–835, in: J.P. Laporte, B. Arroyo and H. Mejíam, editors, *XXI Simposio de Investigaciones Arqueológicas en Guatemala, 2007.* Museo Nacional de Arqueología y Etnología, Guatemala (versión digital). Accessed October 5, 2018.

Pant, Anupum

2014   Stone Age Technology Still Makes the Best Blades. http://awesci.com/stone-age
        -technology-best-blades/. Accessed July 30, 2021.

Peel, Daniel S.

2005   The Mexican Cattle and Beef Industry: Demand, Production, and Trade. *Western Economic Forum*. Spring. https://core.ac.uk/download/pdf/6995827.pdf.
        Accessed April 23, 2021.

Perera, Victor, and Robert D. Bruce

1982   *The Last Lords of Palenque: The Lacandon Mayas of the Mexican Rain Forest.*
        Boston: Little, Brown and Company.

Procuraduría Agraria

2019   Comunidad Lacandona Solicita Asesoría de la Procuraduría Agraria para Resolver Añejos Conflictos por la Tenencia de la Tierra. Procuraduría Agraria,
        Prensa, 11 de agosto de 2019. https://www.gob.mx/pa/prensa/comunidad
        -lacandona-solicita-asesoria-de-la-procuraduria-agraria-para-resolver-anejos
        -conflictos-por-la-tenencia-de-la-tierra-212802. Accessed April 24, 2020.

Ramos Ortiz, Arturo

2019   Planean Dejar a la Lacandona Sólo un Tercio de Su Territorio. http://www
        .biodiversidadla.org/Noticias/Planean-dejar-a-la-Lacandona-solo-un-tercio-de
        -su-territorio. Accessed April 10, 2020.

Reid, John W., and Thomas E. Lovejoy

2022   *Ever Green: Saving Big Forests to Save the Planet.* New York: W.W. Norton and
        Co.

Remesal, Fray Antonio de

1619/1966   *Historia General de las Indias Occidentales y Particular de las Gobernación
        de Chiapas y Guatemala.* 3rd ed., 4 vols. Guatemala: Departamento Editorial
        y de Producción de Material Didáctico "José de Piñeda Ibarra," Ministerio de
        Educación.

Ríos Flores, Jesús Armando, and Miriam Liliana Castillo Arce

2014   Competitiveness of Fresh Mexican Beef in the U.S. Market. *Estudios Fronterizos*
        16: 32.

Rivero Torres, Sonia E.

1992   *Laguna Miramar, Chiapas, México: Una Aproximación Histórica-arqueológica
        de los Lacandones desde el Clásico Temprano.* Tuxtla Gutiérrez, Chiapas: Consejo Estatal de Fomento a la Investigación y Difusión de la Cultura, Instituto
        Nacional de Antropología e Historia, Gobierno del Estado de Chiapas.

Roblero Morales, Marin

2008   La Relación Hombre-Naturaleza Entre los Lacandones de Nahá, Ocosingo, Chiapas. *Revista LiminaR: Estudios Sociales y Humanísticos* 6(1): 125–140.

Rodas Trejo, Jenner, Alejandro Estrada, Jaime Rau Acuña, Manuela Morales Hernández, and Herman Mandujano Camacho

2017   Riqueza y Abundancia de Mamíferos Medianos y Grandes en Metzabok, Chiapas, México, Chapter 6, in: Orantes Alborez, S. Jordán, and Christian F. Camacho Méndez, editors, *Lekil Kuxlejal: Cultura, Educación y Sustenabilidad.* Chiapas: Historia Herencia Mexicana Editorial.

Ross, Norbert

2002   Cognitive Aspects of Intergenerational Change: Mental Models, Cultural Change, and Environmental Behavior among the Lacandon Maya of Southern Mexico. *Human Organization* 61(2): 125–138. https://sfaajournals.net/doi/pdf/10.17730/humo.61.2.9bhqghxvpfh2qebc. Accessed May 20, 2020.

Roys, Ralph

1968   *The Book of Chilam Balam of Chumayel.* Carnegie Institution of Washington, Publication No. 438. Norman: University of Oklahoma.

Russell, Jordan

2018   Keeping the Green Anaconda. *Reptiles.* http://www.reptilesmagazine.com/Keeping-the-Green-Anaconda/. Accessed July 18, 2018.

Sánchez Balderas, Adriana Fabiola, and Joel Palka

2007   Proyecto Arqueológico en el Lago Mensabak, Chiapas. Manuscript, courtesy Dr. Joel Palka, University of Illinois-Chicago.

Sandrea, Rafael

2019   Understanding the Challenges to Mexico's Oil & Gas Future. The Energy Policy Research Foundation, Inc. (EPRINC). https://eprinc.org/wp-content/uploads/2019/07/Sandrea-Mexico-Paper-July-2019-FINAL-1.pdf. Accessed May 28, 2020.

Sauer, Carl Ortwin

1969   *The Early Spanish Main.* Berkeley: University of California Press.

Scholes, F.V., and R.L. Roys

1968   *The Maya Chontal Indians of Acalan-Tixchel: A Contribution to the History and Ethnography of the Yucatan Peninsula.* Carnegie Institution of Washington, Publication 560. Norman: University of Oklahoma Press.

Schumann, Debra Ann

1982   *Fertility and Economic Strategy in a Southern Mexican Ejido.* PhD dissertation, Department of Anthropology, Dallas, Texas: Southern Methodist University.

Science News

1999   Juice Put the Bounce in Ancient Rubber. *Science News* 156: 31.

SEMARNAP

2000   *Programa de Manejo, Reserva de la Biósfera Montes Azules, Mexico.* Secretaría de Medio Ambiente, Recursos Naturales y Pesca. México, D.F.: Instituto Nacional de Ecología.

Shapiro, Milt

2000   The Origins of the Zapatista National Liberation Army (EZLN). Washington, DC: Committee of Indigenous Solidarity (CIS-DC). http://www.londonmexicosolidarity.org/sites/default/files/cis_ezln_roots_1.pdf. Accessed January 17, 2018.

Sharer, Robert J.

1996   *Daily Life in Maya Civilization.* Westport, CT: Greenwood Press.

Shono, K., and L. Snook
2006   Growth of Big-Leaf Mahogany (*Swietenia macrophylla*) in Natural Forests in Belize. *Journal of Tropical Forest Science* 18(1): 66–73.

Sieff, Kevin
2020   Mexico's Economy Gets Hit in Sectors Where It Hurts Most. *Washington Post*, April 25, 2020: A14.

Smith, Paul Chaat
2009   *Everything You Know About Indians Is Wrong*. Minneapolis: University of Minnesota Press.

Soberanes, Rodrigo
2018   Illegal Cattle Ranching Deforests Mexico's Massive Lacandon Jungle. *Mongabay*. https://news.mongabay.com/2018/03/illegal-cattle-ranching-deforests-mexicos-massive-lacandon-jungle. Accessed May 19, 2020.

Swain, M. B.
1989   Gender Roles in Indigenous Tourism: Kuna Mola, Kuna Yola, and Cultural Survival, pp. 83–104, in: V.L. Smith, editor, *Host and Guest: The Anthropology of Tourism*. Philadelphia: University of Pennsylvania Press.

Toledo, Victor Manuel, and María de Jesús Ordóñez
1993   The Biodiversity Scenario of Mexico: A Review of Terrestrial Habitats. Chapter 26, pp. 757–777, in: T. P. Ramamoorthy, Robert Bye, Antonio Lot, and John Fa, *Biological Diversity of Mexico: Origins and Distribution*. New York: Oxford University Press.

Tozzer, Alfred M.
1902–1903   Report of the Fellow in American Archaeology. *American Journal of Archaeology* 7, Supplement: Annual Reports 1902–1903.
1903–1904   Report of the Fellow in American Archaeology. *American Journal of Archaeology* 8, Supplement: Annual Reports 1903–1904.
1907   *A Comparative Study of the Mayas and the Lacandones*. New York: MacMillan.

Tranquilin Marco Vinícius, Ricardo Coelho Lehmkuhl, Angela Maron, Lineu Roberto da Silva, Liuane Ziliotto, Meire Christina Seki, Gabriela Ronchi Salomon, and Adriano de Oliveira Torres Carrasco
2013   First Report of Yellow Fever Virus in Non-human Primates in the State of Paraná, Brazil. *Revista da Sociedade Brasileira de Medicina Tropical* 46(4). http://www.scielo.br/scielo.php?script=sci_arttext&pid=S0037-86822013000400522. Accessed September 17, 2018.

Trench, Tim
2002   *Conservation, Tourism and Heritage: Continuing Interventions in Lacanja' Chansayab, Chiapas, Mexico*. Unpublished PhD thesis, Department of Social Anthropology, University of Manchester.

UNESCO
2020   *Man and the Biosphere (MAB) Programme*. United Nations Educational, Scientific, and Cultural Organization. https://en.unesco.org/mab. Accessed April 24, 2020.

US Fish and Wildlife Service

2020   Convention on International Trade in Endangered Species. https://www.fws
        .gov/international/plants/current-cites-listings-of-tree-species.html. Accessed
        January 14, 2020.

University of Colorado at Boulder

2019   Neanderthals Used Resin "Glue" to Craft Their Stone Tools. *Science Daily.*
        http://www.sciencedaily.com/releases/2019/06/190626133802.htm

University of Helsinki

2020   Amazonian Indigenous Territories Are Crucial for Conservation. *Science Daily,*
        July 29, 2020. http://www.sciencedaily.com/releases/2020/07/200729114743
        .htm. Accessed August 1, 2020.

van Gils, H.A.J.A., and C. Vanderwoude

2012   Leafcutter Ant (*Atta sexdens*) (*Hymenoptera: Formicidae*) Nest Distribution
        Responds to Canopy Removal and Changes in Micro-climate in the Southern
        Colombian Amazon. *Florida Entomologist* 95(4): 914–921.

Vidal, John

2018   Mexico's Zapatista Rebels, 24 Years on and Defiant in Mountain Strong-
        holds. *Guardian,* February 17, 2018. https://www.theguardian.com/global
        -development/2018/feb/17/mexico-zapatistas-rebels-24-years-mountain
        -strongholds. Accessed April 2, 2020.

Villa Rojas, Alfonso

1967   Los Lacandones: Su Origen, Costumbres y Problemas Vitales. *América Indígena*
        27(1): 25–53.

Wikipedia Español

2021   Selva de los Chimalapas. https://es.wikipedia.org/wiki/Selva_de_los
        _Chimalapas. Accessed May 20, 2021.

Womack, John, Jr.

1999   *Rebellion in Chiapas: An Historical Reader.* New York: The New Press.

World Bank

1994   Interviews with World Bank personnel, Washington, DC.

Ximénez, Fray Francisco

1901/1973   *Historia de la Provincia de San Vicente de Chiapa y Guatemala de la Or-
        den de Predicator's.* Guatemala: Sociedad de Geografía e Historia de Guatemala,
        bk. 5, chapt. 57.

Zinsser, Hans

1971   *Rats, Lice, and History.* New York: Bantam Books.

Index

Xate: burials, 29; cultivation, 241, 250, 263n16;
divination, 155; poaching, 219, 222, 224;
sales, 74–75, 241
Xkalejox, 148

Yajaw Petja', 41, 45; and Tozzer, 14
Yaxchilán: Lacandón name, 218; Monumento
Natural, 200; tourism, 243
Yum K'ax, 147

Zapatistas: 1994 rebellion, 49; Selva Lacandona, 206–210
Zea mays: definition, 262n5; planting, 57

James D. Nations has spent four decades working to protect national parks, wildlife reserves, and Indigenous territories in Latin America and the United States. He is the author of *The Maya Tropical Forest: People, Parks, and Ancient Cities,* and co-author, with Chan K'in José Valenzuela, of Spanish and English versions of *Lacandón Maya: The Language and Environment.*